the **gluten-free** cookbook

the **gluten-free** cookbook

LONDON, NEW YORK, MUNICH, MELBOURNE, DELHI

Senior editor Alastair Laing
Project art editor Katherine Raj
Managing editor Dawn Henderson
Managing art editor Christine Keilty
Art director Peter Luff
Senior jackets creative Nicola Powling
Production editor Raymond Williams
Production controller Claire Pearson
Creative technical support Sonia Charbonnier

DK INDIA
Senior editor Chitra Subramanyam
Editors Divya Chandhok, Ligi John
Assistant editor Tina Jindal
Art editors Prashant Kumar, Anamica Roy
Managing editor Glenda Fernandes
Managing art editor Navidita Thapa
DTP/CTS manager Sunil Sharma
DTP designer Anurag Trivedi

Recipe photography William Shaw

Important Every effort has been made to ensure that the information contained in this book is complete and accurate. However, neither the publisher nor the authors are engaged in rendering professional advice or services to the individual reader. Professional medical advice should be obtained on personal health matters. Neither the publisher nor the authors accept any legal responsibility for any personal injury or other damage or loss arising from the use or misuse of the information and advice in this book.

First published in Great Britain in 2012
by Dorling Kindersley Limited
80 Strand, London WC2R 0RL
Penguin Group (UK)

A CIP catalogue record for this book is available from the British Library

ISBN 978-1-4053-9431-4

Colour reproduction by Media Development & Printing Ltd
Printed and bound in China

Discover more at **www.dk.com**

CONTENTS

INTRODUCTION

Changing to a gluten-free diet is a great opportunity to eat well and take control of your health.

This introduction will explain why going gluten free may be the right choice for you, and will guide you through all the stages required to eliminate gluten from your food and plan healthy, balanced gluten-free meals: at home, on the go, and dining out.

You will also find all the information you need to start cooking with gluten-free ingredients. A gallery of gluten-free grains and flours explains each one's particular qualities and how best to use them in dishes, while recipes with step-by-step photographs demonstrate how to bake delicious bread and cakes, and make perfect pastry and pasta using gluten-free flour.

EATING WELL ON A GLUTEN-FREE DIET

Finding out you have a gluten intolerance can prompt mixed feelings. Relief that finally you're taking control of your health, but probably also concern that adopting a gluten-free diet might mean cutting out many of your favourite foods and accepting a less enjoyable, less flavourful diet. Yet nothing can be further from the truth and this book is here to prove you can eat fantastically well on a gluten-free diet.

DISCOVERING NEW FLAVOURS

Far from being a life sentence of disappointing food, cutting out gluten is a wonderful opportunity to explore new dishes made with grains and flours you may never have heard of before. Going gluten free is also the perfect excuse to release the home baker in you. A new generation of pre-blended flours, combined with the magic of xanthan gum, has transformed gluten-free baking, so that with our step-by-step instruction and specially created recipes you will still be able to enjoy all your favourite bakes.

Spiced lamb and hummus wraps (page 188)

Ricotta and squash ravioli with sage butter (page 138)

EATING FOR HEALTH

Going gluten free is also about recovery. When first diagnosed, you are likely to be suffering the effects of poor nutrient absorption, which could include fatigue, joint pains, and various conditions related to vitamin and mineral deficiencies. By simply cutting out gluten your body will begin to recover, but it is also crucial to assess your diet to ensure it is properly balanced and that you're getting enough of the full range of nutrients. In the following pages, we outline the principles of a healthy, balanced diet and identify nutrients you should be eating more of. In the recipes, we have employed a nutrient boost icon to highlight particular health benefits, and each recipe features calorie and nutrient analysis so that you can plan a balanced, calorie-controlled diet.

We have selected a broad range of recipes to provide all the meal inspirations for healthy eating, but it should be emphasized that this is not a "diet" book of calorie-restricted recipes. Pies, cakes, pastries, and desserts are the dishes that people who give up gluten can miss the most, yet they tend to be high in calories. In creating gluten-free versions we have been guided by taste, not calorie counts, but just because they're gluten free doesn't mean you should be eating pies and cakes all the time! You'll find plenty of healthy recipes to choose for every day, and the guidelines will show you which dishes to enjoy as a rare treat.

GUIDELINES PER SERVING

●●○ CALORIES

●○○ SATURATED FAT

●●○ SALT

Red velvet cupcakes (page 314)

Chocolate cheesecake (page 296)

FOUR STEPS TO GLUTEN FREE

GET AN APPOINTMENT

1 If you suspect you may have a problem with gluten but have not yet been diagnosed, read pages 12–15 to learn more about symptoms and conditions, and make an appointment to see your doctor to discuss your concerns. Meanwhile, you must keep eating gluten foods for the medical examination to be effective. If you are diagnosed, ask your doctor to make an appointment for you to see a registered dietitian, who will give you detailed advice about changing to a gluten-free diet and how to ensure it is healthy and balanced. They can also tell you about any vitamin and mineral supplements you might need to take, and will provide you with a list of gluten-free products available on prescription.

GET ORGANIZED

2 Once diagnosed, it's a good idea to join an organization for people with coeliac disease and other gluten issues. They will be able to provide you with up-to-the-minute medical advice, contacts to local support groups, a list of products containing gluten, and details of restaurants that offer gluten-free meals. Next, spend some time examining what you normally eat, identifying where gluten needs to be cut out, and making a menu plan for the week ahead (see page 24). When you're tired at the end of a busy day you are much more likely to make mistakes with your diet. Planning in advance gives you time to think about what you are going to eat and check that everything is gluten free.

If you think you may benefit from cutting gluten out of your diet, these four steps and the pages that follow will take you from initial diagnosis to your first gluten-free meal.

GET SHOPPING SAVVY

3 Contact the supermarket you regularly shop at and ask for a list of gluten-free products, or look online. Some supermarkets even offer a guided tour around the store with a dietitian. If there is a particular product you'd like to see stocked, don't be embarrassed to ask the manager: "free from" is an increasingly lucrative market and it makes business sense for supermarkets to build up their range. You should also get to know your local health food shops and the specialist websites out there selling some of the more difficult-to-find gluten-free flours, grains, and other products. International food shops, particularly south and east Asian and Mexican, will also sell a whole host of gluten-free foods.

GET IN THE KITCHEN

4 You've planned what you're going to eat and sourced all the ingredients, but before you start cooking you need to turn your kitchen into a gluten-free zone, or at least an environment where the risk of gluten contamination is minimized (see pages 30–31). With the kitchen properly organized, you are ready to cook and will find that the recipes in this book, as well as being utterly delicious, have been designed to be easy to follow. Extra help can be found on pages 38–47 where step-by-step recipes demonstrate how to make gluten-free bread, cakes, pasta, and pastry. If you're new to cooking, though, you may find it useful to enrol in cookery classes: look out for gluten-free courses.

WHY GO GLUTEN FREE?

COELIAC DISEASE

The most common reason to follow a gluten-free diet is in order to treat coeliac disease (CD). Often referred to as an allergy or intolerance, coeliac disease is, in fact, an auto-immune disease that occurs when the body's immune system reacts abnormally to gluten and produces antibodies that attack its own tissues. CD affects 1 in 100 adults in the UK, although some experts believe that only 1 in 8 people with the condition are clinically diagnosed, which means around 500,000 people in the UK may have the disease without knowing it. The number of people suffering from coeliac disease has quadrupled in the last few decades. This can be partly attributed to greater awareness and better diagnostic techniques, but this does not fully explain the rise.

SYMPTOMS OF COELIAC DISEASE

The symptoms of coeliac disease can vary from one person to another and can range from mild to severe. Symptoms include:

- diarrhoea
- excessive wind and/or constipation
- nausea
- vomiting
- stomach pain
- cramping
- bloating
- tiredness
- headache
- mouth ulcers
- alopecia (hair loss)
- skin rash
- unexplained weight loss

Left untreated, coeliac disease can increase the risk of other conditions, including infertility, repeated miscarriages, osteoporosis, and depression. Although weight loss is a common symptom of coeliac disease, it is not always the case and many people are of normal weight or even overweight when they are diagnosed.

DON'T STOP EATING GLUTEN... YET!
If you suspect you or a family member may have coeliac disease do not immediately start cutting gluten from your diet. It is essential to keep eating foods that contain gluten for 6 weeks before being tested for coeliac disease, otherwise you could get a false negative result.

DIAGNOSIS AND TREATMENT

Coeliac disease can occur at any age: symptoms may first appear when a baby is weaned onto wheat-containing cereals (see page 25), but they can also occur later in life. The disease runs in families and studies show that if a family member has the condition, there is a 1 in 10 chance that a close relative will develop the disease. There is no cure or medication for CD and the only treatment is a strict gluten-free diet. Even a tiny amount of gluten, from particles of flour contaminating a work surface for instance, is enough to cause problems.

The first thing your doctor will want to do is take a simple blood test to check for antibodies to gluten. Next step is a referral to a hospital to see a gastroenterologist who will perform a procedure called a biopsy, which allows the doctor to take a small sample from your gut lining for detailed examination. If you are diagnosed with coeliac disease your consultant should then refer you to a registered dietitian who will be able to advise you on a gluten-free diet. Some people start to feel better soon after they start on a gluten-free diet, for others it can take several months: everyone is different.

COELIAC DISEASE EXPLAINED

The wall of the small intestine is lined with fleshy projections called "villi", responsible for absorbing nutrients into the body from food. Coeliac disease leads to a blunting of the villi that seriously diminishes their ability to absorb nutrients.

DAMAGE TO SMALL INTESTINE

Healthy gut

Gut showing coeliac damage

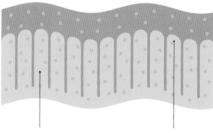

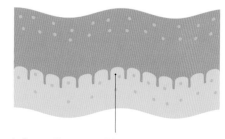

Nutrients passing through the gut are absorbed through the villi walls into blood vessels

Tongue-like shape of the villi maximizes surface area for absorption

Inflammation causes blunted villi that are unable to absorb nutrients so effectively

DERMATITIS HERPETIFORMIS

Dermatitis herpetiformis (DH) is a skin condition characterized by intensely itchy blisters on the buttocks, back of the neck, scalp, elbows, knees, and back. It affects about 1 in 10,000 people in the UK, is more common in men than women, and typically appears between the ages of 15 and 40 years. Like coeliac disease it is caused by gluten and treated with a strict gluten-free diet.

OTHER MEDICAL CONDITIONS THAT MAY BENEFIT FROM A GLUTEN-FREE DIET

The use of gluten-free diets for other conditions remains controversial, but many people with conditions listed here feel that experimenting with a gluten-free diet for a trial period may be worth trying. However, no one should embark on a gluten-free diet without first consulting a doctor.

OTHER CONDITIONS WITH A POSSIBLE LINK TO GLUTEN	
AUTISM	Although scientific evidence is limited, some children with autistic spectrum disorder (ASD) may benefit from a gluten- and casein-free diet. Much more research is, however, required.
MULTIPLE SCLEROSIS (MS)	Multiple sclerosis is an auto-immune disease and people with MS have a greater risk of suffering from coeliac disease, although the use of a gluten-free diet for people with MS remains controversial.
ME/CHRONIC FATIGUE SYNDROME	There is anecdotal evidence that some people with ME or chronic fatigue syndrome find their symptoms improve by adopting a gluten-free diet. It certainly doesn't work for everyone but may be worth a try.
IRRITABLE BOWEL SYNDROME (IBS)	The symptoms of coeliac disease and irritable bowel syndrome are very similar, and a recent survey carried out by Coeliac UK revealed that nearly 60% of people with coeliac disease had previously been wrongly diagnosed with IBS.
LUPUS	Lupus is another auto-immune disease where the body's immune system becomes hyperactive and attacks healthy tissue. As coeliac disease is also auto-immune, lupus sufferers may be at greater risk of developing it.
MISCARRIAGE AND INFERTILITY	Evidence suggests undiagnosed coeliac disease could be one cause of infertility and repeated miscarriages. The proportion of women attending fertility clinics found to have undiagnosed CD is greater than in the general population.

STILL UNSURE? – A QUICK Q&A

There are a lot of uncertainties and myths about choosing a gluten-free diet, especially if you feel it's unlikely you are a coeliac sufferer or have no symptoms. This Q&A aims to answer some of the most common questions.

SHOULD I CHANGE TO A GLUTEN-FREE DIET TO LOSE WEIGHT?

I OFTEN FEEL TIRED AND BLOATED AFTER EATING: WILL I BENEFIT FROM A GLUTEN-FREE DIET?

Some weight-loss diets advocate avoiding carbohydrates, but there is no scientific evidence to suggest that cutting out gluten helps people lose weight. Weight loss is a common symptom of coeliac disease (CD), and when people who have lost weight as a result of undiagnosed CD switch to a gluten-free diet, they often regain the weight they lost.

Bloating and lethargy are common symptoms associated with coeliac disease, but they are also symptoms of other medical conditions and can be caused by lifestyle factors, such as eating too fast. A gluten-free diet is not necessarily the answer. Keeping a food diary may help you to identify other factors. If symptoms persist, discuss with your doctor.

IS IT POSSIBLE TO BE SUFFERING FROM COELIAC DISEASE YET NOT HAVE ANY SYMPTOMS?

IS IT BENEFICIAL TO REDUCE WHEAT IN MY DIET EVEN IF I HAVE NO RELATED MEDICAL CONDITION?

Although uncommon it is possible. Some experts now talk about a "coeliac spectrum": at one end of the spectrum are people who have all the classic symptoms of the condition, while at the other end people may not be aware of any physical symptoms but may still have damage to the lining of the small intestine. The best advice is to consult a doctor.

Many people eat wheat at breakfast in the form of cereal, again at lunch as a sandwich, and yet again in the evening, for instance as pasta. Some alternative practitioners believe this over-reliance on a single food is a bad idea and can lead to an intolerance or allergy to that food. For this reason it might be a good idea not to rely too heavily on wheat.

DON'T D-I-Y DIAGNOSE
Home testing kits and allergy tests available in some health food stores or by mail order are not reliable ways to diagnose coeliac disease. If you suspect you have the condition, the first thing you should do is make an appointment with your doctor.

ELIMINATING GLUTEN

WHAT IS GLUTEN?

Gluten is a protein found in wheat, rye, and barley and in foods made from these grains, such as cakes, pastry, bread, and pasta. Gluten has qualities useful for cooking and baking, including elasticity, an ability to hold water, and a tendency to hold shape and harden in high heat.

WHAT DOES GLUTEN DO?

It is the gluten in flour that gives bread and baked goods, such as cakes and muffins, their characteristic texture and structure. When flour is mixed with water the gluten becomes elastic, turning the mixture into a soft, stretchy dough that can be kneaded and shaped. Carbon dioxide produced by yeast or baking powder is trapped within the dough and held there by the gluten, enabling breads and cakes to rise and giving them their "airy" texture. Thanks to a miraculous little ingredient called xanthan gum, however, it's possible to mimic the action of gluten in doughs made with gluten-free flours. And by carefully mixing the different gluten-free flours available, and adding additional flavours and glazes, it is possible to recreate the taste, texture, and appearance of all your favourite bakes in gluten-free form. See pages 38–47 for flour blends and illustrated techniques.

Gluten-containing grains

Cultivated grains containing gluten are limited to wheat, spelt (an ancient form of wheat), barley, and rye. Triticale, a hybrid of wheat and rye, also contains gluten and can be found in some health food shops, but is mainly used as an animal feed.

MAIN GLUTEN-CONTAINING PRODUCTS

- All biscuits, breads, cakes, chapattis, crackers, muffins, pastries, pizza bases, rolls, and scones made from wheat, rye, or barley flour
- Wheat noodles and pasta
- Wheat-based breakfast cereals
- Meat and poultry cooked in batter or breadcrumbs, e.g. breaded ham, faggots, haggis, rissoles, Scotch eggs
- Fish or shellfish coated in batter or breadcrumbs, e.g. fish cakes, fish fingers
- Fromage frais and yogurt containing muesli or cereals
- Vegetables and fruit in batter, breadcrumbs, or dusted with flour
- Potatoes in batter, breadcrumbs, or dusted with flour, e.g. potato croquettes
- Soy sauce
- Ice cream cones and wafers, puddings made using semolina or wheat flour
- Stuffing made from breadcrumbs

CAN I EAT OATS ON A GLUTEN-FREE DIET?

Oats contain a protein similar to gluten but it doesn't seem to cause the same adverse reaction. Coeliacs wishing to introduce oats into their diet should start by adding small amounts, but children and severe sufferers should consult their dietitian first. Oats are often contaminated with gluten during processing, so buy gluten-free brands.

**WHEAT »
Triticum spp.**

Wheat varieties often have different names: Emmer, Kamut, Einkorn, Faro, Farrina, and Dinkel are all types of wheat. Bulgur wheat (pictured), couscous, and semolina are also made from wheat.

**« BARLEY
Hordeum vulgare**

Pearl barley can be added to stews and barley flakes are sometimes added to muesli. Beer, barley waters or squash, and malted milk drinks all contain barley.

**RYE »
Secale cereale**

Rye bread and pumpernickel are popular in Germany and eastern Europe. Rye is also used to make crisp breads and crackers.

**« SPELT
Triticum spelta**

An ancient form of wheat that has seen a resurgence in popularity in recent years as a health food. Used in baked goods and beer.

Finding hidden gluten

Eliminating gluten from your diet is not as simple as cutting out obvious sources of gluten, such as bread and pasta. Wheat and other gluten-containing grains are often used as ingredients in other foods, and in some cases foods that are naturally gluten free can become contaminated with gluten during processing or storage. For this reason it's important to check the label on certain products and choose brands certified gluten free where contamination is a risk, such as with oats and polenta.

PRODUCTS THAT MAY CONTAIN HIDDEN GLUTEN

Check closely the packaging of food products listed here for the presence of hidden gluten.

GRAINS AND FLOURS
Sometimes naturally gluten-free grains are milled with wheat, barley, or rye and are thereby contaminated with gluten. These include: buckwheat, chestnut, chickpea, gram, millet, mustard, oats, polenta, potato, quinoa, rice, sorghum, soya, tapioca, teff, and urad

BREAKFAST CEREALS
Buckwheat, corn, millet, and rice-based breakfast cereals and those that contain barley malt extract or oats

PRESERVES AND SPREADS
Lemon curd, mincemeat, peanut and other nut butters

FRUITS AND VEGETABLES
Fruit pie fillings and processed vegetable dishes made with sauces, such as cauliflower cheese

SOUPS AND SAUCES
Canned or packet soups, sauces in jars and packets

Blended seasonings, gravy granules, stock cubes, curry powder, curry paste

Mustard products such as English mustard

Chutneys and pickles

Dressings, salad cream, and mayonnaise

DRINKS
Cloudy fizzy drinks, drinking chocolate, malted milk

DAIRY AND FATS
Coffee and tea whiteners

Fruit and flavoured yogurts or fromage frais desserts

Soya desserts, rice milk, soya milk

Some soft, spreadable cheeses

BAKING INGREDIENTS
Cake decorations, marzipan, ready-to-use icing

Baking powder, bicarbonate of soda

Suet, vegetarian suet

The names of some additives used by the food industry can hide the fact they are derived from gluten grains and may not be safe. Look out for the following:

✘ **Rusk** made from wheat flour is often used as a carrier for flavours and colours.

✘ **Cereal fillers** made from breadcrumbs, or wheat flour are often added to foods like sausages.

✘ **Cereal or vegetable proteins** are flavour enhancers that can be derived from wheat.

✘ **Starch**, whether "modified", "food" or "edible" can be made from wheat or rye. Often used as thickeners.

✘ **Malt extract or flavouring** is used in baking and brewing and derives from malted barley.

INGREDIENTS TO AVOID: ...Cereal filler...Starch...Modified starch...Food starch...Edible starch...Cereal protein...Vegetable protein...Rusk...Bran...Malt extract...Malt flavouring...

SAFE WHEAT-DERIVED INGREDIENTS: ...Glucose...Dextrose... Glucose powder...Glucose syrup...Maltodextrin...Codex wheat starch...Monosodium glutamate (MSG)...

✔ See page 20 for information on **Codex wheat starch** and **MSG**.

✔ **Dextrose and glucose**, including powder and syrup, are flavour and texture enhancers that can be made from the starch of wheat and barley. They are safe for coeliacs because they contain so little protein.

✔ **Maltodextrin** is an additive used in soft drinks and sweets that can be derived from wheat. Most of the protein is first removed, making it safe for coeliacs.

NUTS AND SAVOURY SNACKS
Dry roasted nuts, popcorn (not home-made), potato and vegetable crisps, pretzels

Baked beans and other beans in sauce

POTATO PRODUCTS
Frozen chips and potato wedges, instant mash, potato waffles, ready-to-roast potatoes

MEAT AND FISH
Any meat or poultry marinated or in a sauce, burgers, meat pastes, pâtés, sausages

Fish pastes, fish pâtés, taramasalata, and fish in sauce

MEATLESS ALTERNATIVES
Marinated tofu, soya mince, falafel, vegetable burgers and bean burgers

CAKES AND BISCUITS
Shop-bought meringues, macaroons, and flapjacks are likely to have come into contact with gluten-containing cakes

CONFECTIONERY AND DESSERTS
Chocolates, ice cream, mousses, and all kinds of sweets, especially liquorice sweets

TO EAT OR NOT TO EAT? – A QUICK Q&A

You should now have a good sense of which foods to avoid completely and which to check first, but there will inevitably be many more questions as you examine your diet. Here we try to answer the most common ones. For a comprehensive list of safe products it is a good idea to buy Coeliac UK's annual Food and Drink Directory.

IS IT SAFE TO EAT FOODS COOKED IN THE SAME OIL USED TO FRY FOODS COATED IN GLUTEN BATTERS OR CRUMB COATINGS?

No. The oil can be contaminated with gluten from batter used to coat fish and other foods. Look out for gluten-free evenings, however, which are becoming popular with local fast food outlets, when they use gluten-free batter and clean oil to prevent cross contamination.

ARE PRODUCTS LABELLED AS WHEAT-FREE SUITABLE FOR SOMEONE ON A GLUTEN-FREE DIET?

Not necessarily. Wheat is not the only gluten-containing grain and the product may still have rye- or barley-based ingredients, or oats contaminated with gluten.

WHAT IS CODEX WHEAT STARCH?

Codex wheat starch is added to processed foods to improve their taste and texture. Though made from wheat, it has been processed to contain less than 20 parts per million (ppm) of gluten. Research shows this tiny amount of gluten is not toxic to coeliacs.

IS MONOSODIUM GLUTAMATE (MSG) GLUTEN FREE?

MSG is a flavour enhancer used in many ready meals, stock cubes, and savoury snacks and can be made from wheat. However, during processing the gluten protein is completely broken down, so MSG is safe for people with coeliac disease.

CAN I USE MALT VINEGAR?

Although malt vinegar is made from barley, the end product only contains a trace amount of gluten, well below the level that is safe for most people with coeliac disease, and is fine to use. Balsamic, cider, sherry, white wine, and red wine vinegars are all safe.

DO SOME MEDICINES AND SUPPLEMENTS CONTAIN GLUTEN?

Most medicines and drugs prescribed in the UK are gluten free. Although they can sometimes contain wheat starch as a filler, it is highly processed and safe for anyone on a gluten-free diet. If you are buying non-prescription medicines and supplements, however, you should check with a pharmacist.

Naturally gluten-free foods

The idea of cutting gluten out of your diet can seem slightly daunting, but all the foods listed here are naturally gluten-free and can still be enjoyed.

MEAT, POULTRY, AND FISH »

- All fresh meats and poultry
- Cured pure meats, plain cooked meats, smoked meats
- All fresh, dried, kippered, and smoked fish, fish canned in brine, oil or water, and shellfish

« FRUIT, VEGETABLES, NUTS, AND SEEDS

- All fresh, frozen, canned, dried, and juiced pure fruits and vegetables
- Vegetables pickled in vinegar
- All plain potatoes, baked, steamed, boiled, or mashed
- Plain nuts and seeds, all pulses (peas, beans, lentils)

DAIRY, EGGS, AND FATS »

- All milk (liquid and dried), all cream (single, double, whipping, clotted, soured, and crème fraîche), buttermilk, plain fromage frais, plain yogurt
- Butter, cooking oils, ghee, lard, margarine, reduced and low-fat spreads
- Cheese, eggs

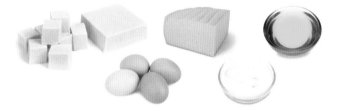

ʌ RICE, QUINOA, & OTHER GLUTEN-FREE GRAINS AND FLOURS

All grains, flours, and flour mixes labelled "gluten-free", including: amaranth, buckwheat, cassava, chestnut flour, chickpea flour, corn (maize), corn starch, gram flour, millet, mustard flour, polenta (cornmeal), potato flour, potato starch, oats (see page 17), quinoa, rice, rice bran, rice flour, sago, sorghum, soya flour, tapioca, tapioca starch, teff, and urad flour – see pages 32-7 for more information

GOODBYE TO PASTA, BREAD, CAKES, PASTRY, AND BISCUITS?

As more people follow a gluten-free diet, the food industry has responded to their needs by developing an expanding range of gluten-free products, including cakes, biscuits, pasta, ready-made pastry, and bread. Of course, there's no need to rely on ready-made products: you can use commercial gluten-free flour blends – or blend your own (see page 38) – to bake at home, adapt favourite recipes, and try new ones. Some shop-bought bakes are better than others, but none can match the taste of home-made.

A BALANCED GLUTEN-FREE DIET

Choosing a balanced diet is important for everyone and a gluten-free diet can be very healthy due to the emphasis placed on fresh and unprocessed foods. A balanced gluten-free diet should include plenty of fruit and vegetables, moderate amounts of lean protein, healthy unsaturated fats, wholegrain and unrefined gluten-free carbohydrates, and minimal amounts of saturated fats, salt, and sugar.

TACKLING NUTRIENT DEFICIENCY

Untreated coeliac disease can lead to nutritional deficiency in iron, calcium, magnesium, and zinc. When you start on a gluten-free diet make sure it contains foods rich in these nutrients. Standard breakfast cereals and bread are often fortified with these nutrients, as well as B-group vitamins and fibre, but gluten-free versions are rarely fortified and alternative sources should be sought.

IRON
Needed for the manufacture of red blood cells.
Good GF sources of iron include lean red meat, eggs, quinoa, dried fruit, lentils and chickpeas, baked beans, dark green leafy vegetables.

CALCIUM
Needed for strong bones, especially important for children, teenagers, and young adults.
Good GF sources include yogurt, milk, cheese, canned fish eaten with their bones (e.g. sardines), almonds, sesame seeds, tofu.

MAGNESIUM
Helps maintain muscle and nerve function, a healthy immune system, and strong bones.
Good GF sources include nuts and seeds, beans and pulses, brown rice, dark green leafy vegetables.

ZINC
Essential for growth and development, a healthy immune system, and wound healing.
Good GF sources include lean red meat, poultry, eggs, shellfish, beans, and nuts, especially Brazil nuts.

FOLATE
Involved in the production of red blood cells. Found in oranges, green vegetables, chickpeas, pulses.

IRON
Found in red meat, beans, and pulses. The body can more easily absorb iron from non-meat sources if eaten in conjunction with foods rich in vitamin C.

DIETARY FIBRE
Helps to keep the intestine healthy and prevent constipation. Sources include lentils, beans, pulses, quinoa, buckwheat, brown rice, fruit, and veg.

B VITAMINS
Have many vital functions. Sources include potatoes, broccoli, and bananas.

VITAMIN B12
B12 is important for a healthy nervous system and is found in fish, lean red meat, and eggs.

CALCIUM
Found in milk, yogurt, cheese, canned sardines. Choose low- and reduced-fat dairy products when possible.

Planning your diet

Planning a menu for the week ahead enables you to check that everything is gluten free. Aim to eat a wide variety of foods to supply all your nutritional needs, opt for healthy dishes with the occasional treat, and try to prepare fresh meals if possible. Here's a sample 7-day menu plan for guidance and inspiration.

	BREAKFAST	LUNCH	EVENING MEAL
DAY 1	• Glass of fruit juice • Gluten-free porridge with fresh or dried fruit and nuts (page 53)	• Masala dosa and a green salad (page 234) • Fruit yogurt	• Lemon and asparagus pasta (page 136) • Lemon sorbet and fresh berries
DAY 2	• Glass of fruit juice • Breakfast blueberry muffins (page 74)	• Gluten-free toast with hummus • Fresh fruit salad	• Creamy chicken crumble (page 180) • Rice pudding
DAY 3	• Glass of fruit juice • Granola with apple crisps (page 54)	• Quinoa, broad bean, and dill salad (page 124) • Fresh fruit	• Haddock and turmeric rice (page 161) • Gluten-free fruit crumble (page 291)
DAY 4	• Glass of fruit juice • Gluten-free bread with jam or honey (pages 38 and 216)	• Gluten-free minestrone soup with a gluten-free roll (pages 107 and 218–19) • Fruit yogurt	• Chicken and parsley pot pies (page 260) • Fresh fruit salad
DAY 5	• Glass of fruit juice • Gluten-free muesli with fresh fruit (page 52)	• Beetroot and ginger soup (page 110) • Caraway seed bread spread with low-fat soft cheese (page 228)	• Sweet and sour chicken with green beans (page 177) • Gluten-free ice cream with fresh fruit (page 299)
DAY 6	• Glass of fruit juice • Breakfast berry bars (page 76)	• Gluten-free baked beans (page 70) on gluten-free toast • Yogurt with fruit	• Mee goreng (page 150) • Banana and gluten-free custard (page 286)
DAY 7	• Glass of fruit juice • Scrambled eggs on gluten-free toast	• Soba noodle and prawn salad (page 128) • Fresh fruit	• Salmon en croûte (page 166) • Gluten-free apple and blackberry pie (page 280)

DO I NEED TO TAKE VITAMIN SUPPLEMENTS?

The intestinal damage caused by untreated coeliac disease frequently leads to nutritional deficiencies. When you are first diagnosed, your dietitian will probably recommend taking a vitamin and mineral supplement. In serious cases it may even be necessary to have vitamins injected. Check with your dietitian before taking supplements and ensure the supplements are gluten free.

GLUTEN-FREE DIETS FOR CHILDREN

Cooking for children on a gluten-free diet requires special planning to ensure they get all the nutrients they require, and you will need to meet with carers or school staff to ensure they stay gluten free away from home. When your child is diagnosed, try to explain the condition in terms they understand and involve them in planning their new diet. Encouraging your child to help with the preparation of meals is another good way for them to learn about and enjoy eating gluten free. Children can get upset if they are singled out as being different and it is important to keep their diet as "normal" as possible, while still excluding gluten. A coeliac child doesn't have to miss out on all the fun: you will find plenty of recipes in this book perfect for parties, whether you are hosting or sending your child along with their own gluten-free treats to share. And we have highlighted easily adaptable, kid-friendly recipes for every day, which all the family can enjoy. As soon as they are old enough, it's important to give children the independence to manage their own diet.

INTRODUCING GLUTEN INTO A BABY'S DIET

Cereals containing gluten should not be introduced into a baby's diet before they are 6 months old, but there is no reason to delay the introduction any later than 6 months. Once a baby is weaned onto solids, gluten should be included regularly, since coeliac disease can only be diagnosed once gluten is established in the diet, and if your child does suffer from coeliac disease it's better to discover sooner rather than later.

Gluten-free diet and lactose intolerance

Lactose intolerance is a common consequence of untreated coeliac disease (CD) because the enzyme lactase, which is needed for the digestion of lactose (a sugar found in milk), is made in the area of the intestine that is damaged by gluten. Without lactase, lactose passes unchanged into the large intestine where the bacteria that naturally live there metabolize it, and in the process produce large amounts of gas. Symptoms of lactose intolerance include bloating, stomach cramps, diarrhoea, and flatulence and usually occur 30 minutes to 2 hours after eating or drinking milk products. Lactose intolerance associated with CD is usually temporary because, once established on a gluten-free diet, the gut starts to heal. However, it can take up to 2 years for lactase production to return to normal. Lactose intolerance is treated by avoiding or restricting lactose in the diet. Lactose can occur in unexpected sources, such as crisps, biscuits, and some medicines, which you wouldn't think contained milk, so always check labels carefully. Dairy products provide a lot of calcium in the diet and you will need to replace them with plenty of non-lactose sources. You should also discuss the need for supplements with your doctor.

NON-LACTOSE SOURCES OF CALCIUM

⌃ **NUTS AND SEEDS**
Almonds, hazelnuts, Brazil nuts, and walnuts are all particularly high in calcium, as are sunflower seeds and sesame seeds.

⌃ **DRIED FRUITS**
Dried fruits tend to contain more calcium than most fresh fruit. Figs are a particularly rich source, but apricots, dates, and prunes also provide good amounts.

⌃ **HARD CHEESE**
Traditionally made, aged hard cheeses, such as Parmesan, contain only small amounts of lactose and may be more easily tolerated.

⌃ **DARK GREEN LEAFY VEG**
Leafy greens such as broccoli, cabbage, kale, and chard are calcium-rich, but avoid spinach, which contains a chemical that interferes with the absorption of calcium.

Gluten-free diet and diabetes

Coeliac disease and dermatitis herpetiformis are both more common in people with type 1 diabetes. This is probably due to a shared genetic risk for both conditions. Coeliac disease associated with diabetes is often the latent type that exhibits no symptoms and is often only discovered during screening. Unexplained hypoglycaemia (low blood sugar) and poor blood sugar control, particularly in young children, can be a symptom of undiagnosed coeliac disease. If you have both type 1 diabetes and coeliac disease, it is even more important that you see a registered dietitian regularly, and one who specializes in both conditions, as each requires ongoing review and management. When first diagnosed with coeliac disease, a person with diabetes will need to monitor their blood sugar levels more closely, as once the intestine starts to heal it will begin to absorb more carbohydrate, and insulin levels often need to be adjusted to reflect this. The principles of a healthy diabetic diet are the same for people who also have a gluten intolerance, the only difference being that unrefined carbohydrates must obviously be non-gluten (see opposite).

Diabetes UK (diabetes.org.uk) and Diabetes Australia (www.diabetesaustralia.com.au) have a range of useful literature designed for people with both diabetes and coeliac disease.

PRINCIPLES OF A HEALTHY DIABETIC DIET

« GET YOUR 5-A-DAY
Aim to eat a minimum of 5 portions of fruit and vegetables each day.

EAT MORE HEALTHY FATS »
Replace saturated with unsaturated fats, found in foods including nuts, seeds, avocados, and olive oil.

REDUCE SALT INTAKE »
Use strongly flavoured ingredients such as chillies to replace salt in cooking.

« REDUCE SUGAR INTAKE
Wean yourself off sugar or replace it with lower-GI alternatives such as fructose.

⚹ EAT MORE UNREFINED CARBS
Choose low-GI gluten-free carbs like brown rice.

GLUTEN FREE ON THE GO

EATING AT A RESTAURANT

Eating out may seem a little daunting when you first start on a gluten-free diet. Follow a few simple ground rules, however, and there is absolutely no reason why you can't enjoy dining out at restaurants just as much as before.

6 TIPS FOR DINING OUT

1 **Ask around** If you have joined a coeliac group, ask local members if they can recommend restaurants in your area that cater for gluten-free diets.

2 **Look online** Many online review sites now list gluten-free restaurants. You will also often find menus published online to check ahead.

3 **Get in touch** Contact the restaurant at least 24 hours before you intend to visit, to check whether they are properly set up for gluten-free cooking.

4 **Don't be shy** Emphasize to the restaurant just how important it is for you to remain gluten free. Try to talk to the chef to confirm what's in each dish.

5 **Check their set-up** Explain that even a tiny amount of gluten flour is harmful and ask if they have kitchen systems to guard against cross contamination.

6 **BYO** If you want to bring your own gluten-free bread to eat at the start of the meal, do ask ahead and confirm again with the waiter when you arrive.

WHAT ABOUT TAKEAWAYS?

At chip shops and burger outlets you need to be certain everything you ask for is cooked in fresh oil. Prepared meats are usually not suitable and if they use frozen chips these are often coated in flour. Many dishes from Indian takeaways will be fine to eat, provided they use fresh ingredients and whole spices. Watch out for soy sauce in Chinese takeaways.

HOW DO I STAY GLUTEN FREE TRAVELLING ABROAD?

If you have joined a coeliac organization, it should be able to provide you with country-specific leaflets about gluten-free eating abroad, including language translations with useful phrases to help when you are dining out. It's always worth packing emergency gluten-free snacks, however, and items such as pasta, bread, and toaster bags in your suitcase.

GLUTEN-FREE PACKED LUNCH

A growing number of cafés are beginning to offer gluten-free choices, but they are few and far between and you may pay extra for the privilege. Packing your own lunch and snacks is often the best option, and providing your child with a packed lunch will help reassure you that they are eating well and staying gluten free away from home.

NUTS
A handful of nuts provide healthy fats and protein. Avoid roasted nuts, which can contain flour.

DRIED FRUIT
Ready-to-eat dried fruit, such as apricots, are a good source of dietary fibre, but do contain concentrated sugars, so go easy.

FRESH FRUIT
An apple or other piece of fresh fruit is the perfect gluten-free and healthy choice for snacking.

HOME-MADE SWEET TREATS
Treat yourself to a home-made biscuit or slice of cake a couple of times a week: teabreads are a healthier, low-fat option (see pages 328–9 and 332–9).

BREAKFAST BARS
Granola-type bars made with oats and crispy rice are great for breakfast on the go or a mid-morning snack (see pages 75–6).

SANDWICH
Baking your own bread for sandwiches will make eating them a treat, not a chore. Bake a few loaves at a time and freeze them for several weeks' supply (see pages 38–9 and 216–19).

6 SNACKING TIPS FOR KIDS

1 Send them prepared Make sure you always send your kids off with plenty of gluten-free snacks in case there is nothing else suitable to eat.

2 Offer variety Children can quickly get bored of eating the same snacks, so try to provide them with a changing menu across the week.

3 Go natural If your child is concerned about feeling different, include naturally gluten-free snacks like cheese portions, sesame bars, popcorn, and smoothies.

4 Make at home Cakes and biscuits are easy and fun for children to bake at home, and they will be excited to eat a snack they've made themselves.

5 Don't spoil the party Secretly bring some gluten-free snacks and treats when you drop off your child at a party, so they don't miss out on a party bag.

6 Teach independence Make sure older children know what to look for on the ingredients list, so they can choose suitable snacks for themselves.

SETTING UP
A GLUTEN-FREE KITCHEN

One of the most important things you learn when you are first diagnosed with coeliac disease is that even tiny traces of gluten can be enough to cause problems. This means that if you are preparing both gluten-free and ordinary meals, you will need to set up a "dual use" kitchen and adopt some simple cleaning and food preparation habits to prevent food becoming contaminated with gluten.

KITCHEN TIPS

- If you share a kitchen with non-coeliacs, make sure everyone understands the rules.
- If you're preparing two meals, prepare the gluten-free version first to avoid any possibility of cross contamination.
- Gluten is invisible to the naked eye, so always wipe down surfaces before you start cooking.
- For the same reason, it's advisable to wash pans and other equipment with detergent and hot water before using, or keep separate sets.
- Gluten remains in oil after frying, so always fry gluten-free first or, better still, use fresh oil.
- To avoid contamination from oven racks, baking sheets, and grill pans, cover first with a fresh piece of aluminium foil.

« DEEP CLEAN
When first going gluten free, empty out all cupboards and clear surfaces, then give the kitchen a thorough scrub from top to bottom, to get rid of any gluten flours and crumbs that might be lurking in unseen places. Repeat the process regularly throughout the year.

⌃ KEEP IT SEPARATE
Use a separate board for cutting gluten-free bread and other bakes. Plastic boards are easier to clean than wooden ones, which have tiny pores where crumbs will remain.

⚹ PACK IT AWAY

Store both gluten and gluten-free dry goods, like flour and pasta, in separate airtight containers and, if possible, keep in separate cupboards. Make sure everything is clearly labelled as gluten free or not, and if you need to retain cooking instructions you can tape the relevant part of the label to the container. Always keep a store of extra plastic containers for fresh items like biscuits, cakes, and leftovers. Chilled and frozen items with a contamination risk should also be placed in separate containers or labelled plastic bags.

« COLOUR CODE

It can be difficult to wash away all traces of gluten from equipment like colanders, serving tongs, and serving spoons, and you may find it helpful to keep a set exclusively for gluten-free cooking. Buy colour-coded sets so it's absolutely clear which is gluten free.

DON'T DOUBLE DIP! »

Always use separate, clean knives and spoons when, for example, spreading butter and jam onto toast. Don't return the same cutlery to the jar or spread or you will contaminate it with gluten-containing crumbs.

BREAD MAKERS

If you intend to make your own gluten-free bread, a bread maker can be a convenient way of ensuring a steady supply. Look for models with a special setting for gluten-free breads and cakes. You will need to keep the machine exclusively for gluten-free baking.

⚹ BAG YOUR TOAST

Ideally, you should keep separate toasters for gluten-free and ordinary bread, but if space is an issue you can use toaster bags to prevent cross contamination.

GLUTEN-FREE GRAINS

A trip to a good health food shop or a large, well-stocked supermarket will reveal a huge range of gluten-free grains that are nutritious, tasty, and extremely versatile. Exploring the many non-gluten grains can transform going gluten free into an opportunity to discover a new world of tastes and textures.

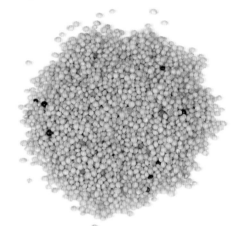

« AMARANTH
Amaranthus spp.

A seed rather than true grain, amaranth is rich in protein and provides useful amounts of calcium, iron, and magnesium, with more fibre than other gluten-free grains. Amaranth has a slightly peppery, nutty flavour and sticky texture. It can be cooked as a cereal, ground into flour, popped like popcorn, sprouted, or toasted. The seeds can be added to stir-fries, soups, and stews as a thickening agent.

QUINOA »
Chenopodium quinoa

Sacred to the Incas, quinoa has been cultivated in South America since 3,000 BC. It is extremely high in protein and provides useful amounts of phosphorus, calcium, iron, vitamin E, and B vitamins, as well as fibre. With a delicious nutty flavour and pleasant texture, quinoa can be boiled and used instead of rice for salads or pilafs, to make stuffings, as an accompaniment to stews, or added to breakfast cereals. It is also available as flour.

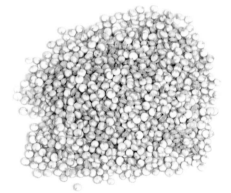

« BUCKWHEAT
Fagopyrum esculentum

Despite the name, buckwheat is not related to wheat and does not contain gluten: it is a seed from a plant that is a relative of rhubarb. Buckwheat groats are buckwheat kernels stripped of their inedible outer coating and then crushed into smaller pieces. Unprocessed groats are slightly bitter, so before you cook them it's a good idea to toast them in oil for a few minutes; this removes the bitterness and brings out a pleasant, nutty flavour. Buckwheat groats can be used as an alternative to couscous.

⌃ OATS
Avena sativa

Compared to other cereals, oats contain higher levels of both protein and fat. They also provide useful amounts of B vitamins and the minerals calcium, magnesium, iron, and zinc. Oats are rich in beta glucan, a type of soluble fibre that can help to reduce high blood cholesterol levels. Whole oats or oat groats take 1¼ hours to cook, retaining their shape but turning creamy. They make a delicious addition to meat or vegetable stews, and precooked oats can be baked into coarse-grain bread doughs.

SAGO »
Metroxylon sagu

Extracted from the spongy centre of tropical palm stems grown in Papua New Guinea and Southeast Asia, sago is virtually pure carbohydrate and offers very little protein, vitamins, minerals, or fibre. Sago pearls are small grains similar to tapioca and can be used to make desserts. Sago can also be ground into flour, which can be used to make pancakes, baked goods, noodles, or for thickening stews or gravies.

⋏ KASHA
Fagopyrum esculentum

Kasha, not to be confused with kamut, a variety of wheat, is the Russian name for a wholegrain cereal made from roasted whole buckwheat groats. Toasting the groats helps to remove buckwheat's natural bitterness and to bring out a sweeter, nuttier flavour. They come whole or crushed into a coarse, medium, or fine grain.

« MILLET
Pennisetum glaucum

Millet is a small, round, yellow grain containing useful amounts of protein, vitamins, minerals, and fibre. A staple food in many parts of Africa and Asia, where it is eaten as a porridge or used to make bread, it has a rather mild flavour and can be used in breakfast cereals or for dishes such as pilaf. It can be ground and made into flour for Indian-style breads like rotis.

⌄ WILD RICE
Zizania spp.

Wild rice is not actually rice but the seeds of freshwater grass. It contains twice as much protein as rice, and higher levels of B vitamins, zinc, iron, and fibre. The long, thin black seeds have a distinctive nutty, slightly woody flavour, and a chewy texture. It can be cooked and served in the same way as ordinary rice, although it takes about 10 minutes longer to cook. Try mixing half and half with basmati rice.

⋏ RICE
Oryza sativa

There are many different varieties of rice including basmati, sticky, red, brown, and risotto, all of which are gluten free. As well as served plain as an accompaniment, rice can be used to make sweet and savoury dishes such as pilaf, risotto, and rice pudding. It can also be made into rice flour, noodles, pancakes, spring roll wrappers, and rice cakes. Brown rice is a wholegrain cereal and contains more vitamins, minerals, and fibre than refined white rice, from which the germ and bran are removed.

GLUTEN-FREE FLOURS

Wheat is not the only flour. Around the world, and often for thousands of years, people have been producing and using flours from an array of non-wheat grains, seeds, nuts, beans, and vegetables. Learn how to cook with them, get to know their distinctive qualities, and create your favourite blends for baking.

« CORNMEAL FLOUR

Cornmeal flour is made from sweetcorn kernels that have been dried, soaked in lime water, washed, and ground into a coarse flour. Stoneground cornmeal retains some of the bran and germ of the dried kernels that standard milling removes, and thus tends to have a better flavour and nutrient value. Cornmeal flour is a good ingredient to use as a crumb coating for fried foods and in addition can be used to make corn tortillas (try to source the authentic Mexican variety *masa harina*), pancakes, muffins, and corn bread. Popcorn is made from a special hard variety of corn kernel and is a good gluten-free snack.

CORNFLOUR »

Not to be confused with cornmeal, cornflour is the pure starch extracted from corn kernels. Almost tasteless and easily blended with liquids without the need for additional fat, the fine white powder is commonly used as a thickener for sauces but can be mixed with other flours for baking.

⌃ CORNMEAL (COARSE)

Coarsely ground cornmeal, also known as polenta, can be cooked as a savoury accompaniment, either boiled to give a "porridge" (wet polenta) or left to set then cut into slabs and fried or grilled. Coarse cornmeal can also be used in conjunction with other flours in baked goods, but instant or quick-cook varieties have a grittier, crunchy texture that is less appealing in cakes.

« BUCKWHEAT FLOUR

Buckwheat is higher in protein than other gluten-free flours and has a strong, slightly sweet taste and speckled appearance. Japanese soba noodles are traditionally made with buckwheat flour and it is also good for making pancakes, blinis, and pasta.

TEFF FLOUR »

High in protein and fibre, and with a slightly sweet, nutty flavour, teff flour is made from the seeds of a grass native to Ethiopia. The flour can be used in combination with other gluten-free flours in baking. The whole seeds can be used to make porridge, added to soups or stews, or served as an accompaniment instead of rice, millet, or bulgur wheat. Teff also provides useful amounts of iron, calcium, magnesium, and zinc.

⚡ OATMEAL

Oatmeal is produced by milling the hulled whole oats. The grains are milled to different levels of fineness: coarse oatmeal can be used for stuffings, thickening soups and stews, and sprinkling in place of breadcrumbs over dishes to be gratinéed; medium oatmeal is the most versatile for baking and gives an even coating to fried fish; fine oatmeal can be worked to a smooth texture suitable for pancakes, pastry, and gravies. Always choose oatmeals marked gluten-free as they can be contaminated in the milling process.

« TAPIOCA FLOUR

Low in protein and other nutrients, tapioca flour is almost pure starch and largely flavourless. It can be used by itself to make puddings and to thicken soups or sauces, or blended with other gluten-free flours for baking. Tapioca also makes a crisp, golden crust when used as a batter or "bread" coating for fried food.

⚡ CHESTNUT FLOUR

Made from the ground whole nuts, chestnut flour is high in fibre, healthy fats, and protein, and contributes additional texture, moisture, and a slightly sweet flavour to cakes and biscuits. Chestnut flour is also good for making pancakes.

⚡ ALMOND FLOUR

Made by grinding blanched almonds, almond flour is high in fibre, healthy fats, and protein, and provides good amounts of calcium. Use it in gluten-free baking to add extra flavour, moisture, and texture, and for improving nutritional value.

« SOY FLOUR

Soy flour is made from ground soybeans and comes in defatted, low fat, and full-fat varieties. An excellent source of protein and B vitamins, it has a strong "beany" flavour and is best used in combination with other flours.

⚹ WHITE RICE FLOUR

White rice flour has a mild flavour and can be used as a sauce thickener in the same way as cornflour: simply mix first with cold water before adding to the sauce and cooking until thickened. It is also used, particularly in Asian cooking, to make dumplings, pancakes, cakes, and sweets. "Ground rice" is also made from white rice and has a slightly grittier texture that helps give a crispy finish to pastries and biscuits.

POTATO FLOUR »

Also called potato starch or farina, potato flour helps retain moisture and gives a fine, light texture to baked goods. It also makes an excellent thickening agent. Like cornflour and tapioca, potato flour is high in refined carbohydrates and low in fibre and nutrients.

⚹ SORGHUM FLOUR

Milled from grains of sorghum, a cereal crop, sorghum flour is a high-protein flour with a smooth texture and bland taste. It is best mixed in small proportions with other gluten-free flours to provide extra protein.

⚹ BROWN RICE FLOUR

Brown rice flour can be used in the same way as white rice flour but it has a more grainy texture and stronger, nutty flavour that helps to provide a "wholemeal" taste and texture when used in flour blends for baking.

URAD DAL FLOUR

Milled from urad beans, urad dal flour is a protein-rich staple of South Indian cooking where it is used to make dosas, uttapams, idli, and papadums. The flour can also be used in conjunction with other flours in flatbreads, as a thickener, and added to soups and purées for additional protein.

CHICKPEA FLOUR

Also known as gram or besan flour, chickpea flour is high in protein and fibre, and has a distinctive "beany" flavour. It is widely used in Indian cuisine to make the batter for bhajis and pakoras, and in papadums and breads. Chickpea flour is also useful for thickening soups and sauces, but should be mixed with other flours for general baking.

Other useful ingredients

Going gluten free is a great opportunity for many people to bake at home for the first time. As well as raising agents common to all baking, a gluten-free baker needs extra ingredients to help replace the elastic quality of gluten-containing flours.

GLUTEN-FREE BAKING POWDER

Used in cake baking, once activated by the liquid in a cake mix, baking powder undergoes a chemical reaction that produces carbon dioxide gas to help the cake rise.

GLUTEN-FREE BICARBONATE OF SODA

Bicarbonate of soda is similar to baking powder but requires the addition of the natural acid in ingredients such as buttermilk or yogurt to produce the same chemical reaction.

YEAST

Yeast is a living micro-organism, which, when added to dough, creates the carbon dioxide that causes bread to rise. Available fresh or dried, fast-action dried yeast is probably the most useful for novice bakers.

XANTHAN GUM

Xanthan gum helps gluten-free doughs to bind together and adds some elasticity, making bread less crumbly and pastry easier to roll and handle. Buy it online, in health food shops, or large supermarkets. Guar gum has similar properties but can be more difficult to source.

ARROWROOT

A white starch made from the root of a tropical herb, arrowroot helps to bind ingredients together, adding body and texture to baked goods. It is also useful as a clear thickener for soups and sauces.

BAKING BREAD

Home-made gluten-free bread is far superior to shop-bought. The right blend of flours is key, as is the inclusion of xanthan gum, which enables the dough to rise. Suggested flour blends for white and brown bread are included below, but you can experiment with your own mix, or buy pre-blended. If blending your own, scale up as required and store in an airtight container; keep only until the earliest use-by date of the flours.

MAKES 1 LOAF
PREP 20 MINS
PLUS RISING
COOK 45 MINS
FREEZE 3 MONTHS

oil for greasing
450g (1lb) gluten-free
  white bread flour
  blend (see below), plus
  extra for dusting
2 tsp fast-action
  dried yeast
1 tsp salt
1 tbsp caster sugar
1 egg
2 tbsp vegetable oil
1 tsp vinegar
1 egg, beaten, for brushing

SPECIAL EQUIPMENT
450g (1lb) loaf tin

> **BREAD FLOUR BLENDS**
> Makes 700g (1lb 8½oz)
> White bread flour
> 450g (1lb) white
>   rice flour
> 115g (4oz) potato flour
> 60g (2oz) tapioca flour
> 60g (2oz) cornflour
> 4 tsp xanthan gum
>
> Brown bread flour
> 450g (1lb) brown
>   rice flour
> 115g (4oz) potato flour
> 60g (2oz) tapioca flour
> 60g (2oz) cornflour
> 4 tsp xanthan gum

CLASSIC WHITE LOAF

This moist, springy loaf slices brilliantly for sandwiches and makes great toast too. The bread will keep for 2–3 days wrapped in a plastic bag. Turn any leftovers into breadcrumbs and store in the freezer to use in stuffings, coatings for fried food, and so on. If you like, double the quantities and bake two loaves at the same time, then freeze one.

1 Lightly oil the tin. Sift together the flour, yeast, and salt into a large bowl, then stir in the sugar. Measure 300ml (10fl oz) lukewarm water into a jug, add the egg, oil, and vinegar and lightly whisk together with a fork.

2 Make a well in the centre of the dry ingredients and add the wet ingredients. Draw the flour into the liquid with a wooden spoon, mix well, and then bring together with your hands to form a dough.

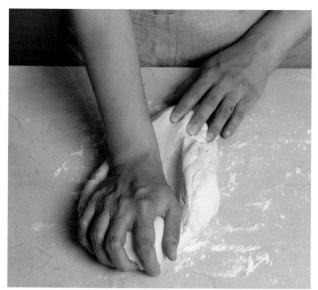

3 Turn the dough out onto a lightly floured surface and knead for about 5 minutes, or until smooth. To knead, hold the dough with one hand and stretch it with the palm of the other hand, then bring it back together, turn, and repeat.

4 Shape the dough into a rectangle roughly the size and shape of the tin and place it in the tin. Make 3 or 4 slashes on the top with a sharp knife. Cover loosely with oiled cling film and leave in a warm place to rise for 1 hour or until doubled.

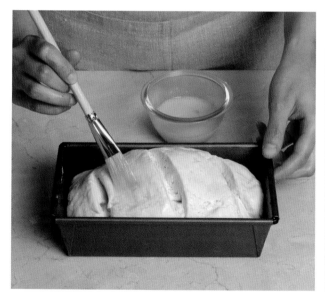

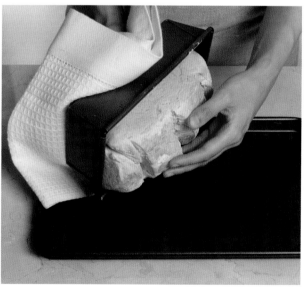

5 Preheat the oven to 220°C (425°F/Gas 7). Brush the top of the loaf with egg – this will help to colour it as gluten-free bread tends to bake to a paler colour than standard bread – and sprinkle with a little flour.

6 Bake for 35 minutes or until the loaf is risen and golden brown on top. Remove from the tin, transfer to a baking tray, and bake for a further 10 minutes to crisp the crust. Remove from the oven and leave to cool on a wire rack.

BAKING CAKES

Excellent new commercial blends of gluten-free self-raising flour have made baking gluten-free cakes far easier, helping to provide good lift and a light texture. As with traditional baking, however, it is crucial to whisk thoroughly to incorporate air into the mix. To blend your own self-raising flour, add 3–4 teaspoons xanthan gum and 11 teaspoons baking powder for every 700g (1lb 8½oz) total weight of flour.

SERVES 8
PREP 15 MINS
COOK 25–30 MINS
FREEZE 3 MONTHS
SPONGES ONLY

175g (6oz) unsalted butter, softened, plus extra for greasing
175g (6oz) caster sugar
3 eggs
175g (6oz) gluten-free self-raising flour
3 tbsp milk
1 tsp vanilla extract
5 tbsp strawberry jam
icing sugar, for dusting

SPECIAL EQUIPMENT
2 x 20cm (8in) round cake tins

VARIATIONS
Orange
Omit the vanilla extract and milk, and instead add the finely grated zest and juice of 1 orange at the same time as the flour. Sandwich together with quality marmalade.

Chocolate
Replace 60g (2oz) of the flour with cocoa powder and bake and cool as described. Sandwich together with gluten-free chocolate spread or fresh whipped cream.

VICTORIA SPONGE

This buttery, vanilla-scented sponge has a light, fluffy texture and (if it's not eaten in a single session!) can be stored in an airtight container for 3–4 days. Strawberry jam is a classic filling, but you can use whatever jam you have in the cupboard. You could also fill with whipped cream and fresh fruit, but eat this version on the same day.

1 Preheat the oven to 180°C (350°F/Gas 4). Lightly grease the tins and line the bases with baking parchment. Cream together the butter and sugar with an electric whisk until the mixture is pale, light, and fluffy.

2 Add the eggs one at a time, beating well between additions, until the mixture is well combined and fluffy. If required, add 1–2 tablespoons flour with the last egg to stop the mixture from curdling.

3 Add the remaining flour, milk, and vanilla extract to the bowl. Mix in with an electric whisk for 1 minute until thoroughly incorporated and no trace of flour remains.

4 Take the prepared tins and divide the mixture equally between them. Spread the mixture out to the edges of the tins and use the spoon or a spatula to even the tops.

5 Bake in the preheated oven for 25–30 minutes. When ready, the sponges should look golden and spring back when lightly touched in the centre; alternatively, a metal skewer inserted into the centre of the cake should come out clean. Leave to cool in the tins for 5 minutes.

6 Carefully remove the sponges from the tins, peel away the lining paper, and cool completely on a wire rack. To finish, transfer one of the sponges to a serving plate, spread the jam over the top, and sandwich with the second sponge. Dust with icing sugar to serve.

MAKING PASTA

Making your own pasta is time-consuming but hugely rewarding, and the results are a world apart from the dried gluten-free pasta available to buy. If pasta is your passion, then, it is well worth investing in a pasta machine (or dusting off the one you've never used!). Set aside time to make a large batch and freeze in individual portions; fresh pasta freezes well and can be cooked straight from frozen.

MAKES 350G (12OZ)
PREP 40 MINS
COOK 3-4 MINS

85g (3oz) tapioca flour
85g (3oz) cornflour
3 tbsp potato flour
3 tsp xanthan gum
½ tsp salt
3 eggs
2 tbsp olive oil
gluten-free plain flour,
  for dusting

SPECIAL EQUIPMENT
pasta machine with
  tagliatelle attachment

FRESH EGG PASTA

Here the pasta dough is formed into tagliatelle. Other standard cutter attachments include spaghetti and fettuccine, but the rolled pasta can be formed into any shape or left flat for lasagne sheets and ravioli. If not using immediately, place the pasta on trays dusted with cornmeal, cover with cling film or a tea towel, and leave for up to 4 hours.

1 Sift the flours, xanthan, and salt into a large bowl. In another bowl, beat together the eggs and oil. Make a well in the centre of the flours, then pour in the egg and oil mix.

2 Use a palette knife or round-bladed table knife to draw the flour into the liquid. Mix until it starts to bind, then finally bring it together with your hands to form a dough.

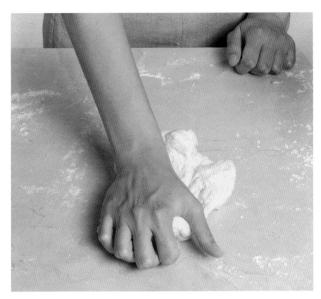

3 Transfer the dough to a lightly floured surface and knead gently until it becomes smooth. Wrap tightly in cling film and leave to rest for 10 minutes. Unwrap the dough and divide it into 4 equal pieces.

4 Take one of the pieces of dough and, using a rolling pin, roll it out to a long strip, about 12cm (5in) wide and 5mm (¼in) thick. Set aside and cover with a damp, clean tea towel, as you repeat the process with the remaining dough.

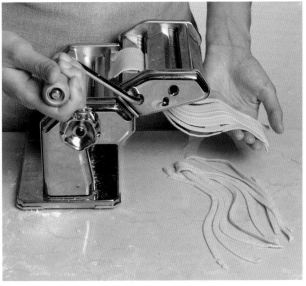

5 Dusting well with more flour, pass each strip of dough through a pasta machine 4 times. Adjust the dial by a stop each time until the pasta is really thin; don't worry if a few holes appear. Dust and set aside each sheet.

6 Attach the cutter and pass the flour-dusted strips through the machine to form the tagliatelle. To cook, bring a large pan of water to a rolling boil, add the pasta, and cook for 3–4 minutes; the pasta should still have some "bite".

MAKING PASTRY

Though a little more delicate to handle than traditional pastry, with practice you will soon master the art of gluten-free pastry and the results are well worth the effort. The addition of egg and xanthan gum helps the dough to bind, making it easier to roll out and giving the cooked pastry a crisp, flaky consistency that is almost indistinguishable from pastry made with wheat flour.

MAKES 400G (14OZ)
ENOUGH FOR A
MEDIUM TART CASE
PREP 20 MINS
COOK 20 MINS
PLUS CHILLING

225g (8oz) gluten-free
plain flour, plus extra
for dusting
1 tsp xanthan gum
pinch of salt
100g (3½oz) cold butter,
cubed
1 egg, beaten

SPECIAL EQUIPMENT
23cm (9in) round tart tin,
ceramic baking beans
(optional, see step 5)

VARIATION
Sweet shortcrust pastry
Add 2 tbsp icing sugar
with the flour before
blending into crumbs.
After blind baking, brush
the pastry case with egg
wash from 1 egg, beaten,
and bake for a further
5 minutes to crisp up.

SHORTCRUST PASTRY

The pastry dough is here used to "blind" bake a case for tarts and quiches, but it is also perfect for making single and double crust pies and tartes Tatin. If you get a few cracks and holes as you lift the pastry and line the tin, simply patch them up with excess pastry and "glue" together with a little water to seal.

1 Preheat the oven to 200°C (400°F/Gas 6). Sift the flour, xanthan, and salt into a bowl and mix. Add the butter and rub it in with your fingertips until the mixture forms crumbs. Alternatively, you can do this by pulsing the mixture in a food processor.

2 Add the egg and mix it in with a palette knife or round-bladed table knife. Gradually add 1–2 tablespoons cold water, a few drops at a time, mixing after each addition. Keep adding water and mixing until it just comes together to form a dough.

3 Transfer the dough to a floured surface and briefly and lightly knead until smooth. Wrap in cling film and chill in the fridge for 10 minutes. Roll out the pastry on a lightly floured surface until it is about 5mm (¼in) thick and large enough to fill the tin.

4 Carefully wrap the pastry around the rolling pin, lift over the tin, and unroll the pastry. To line the tin, gently press the pastry into the base and sides, pressing it into the flutes if you are using a fluted tin. Trim the edges, repair any holes, and prick the base with a fork.

5 Line the pastry with baking parchment and weigh down the parchment with ceramic baking beans (or you can use ordinary dried beans, such as haricots). Place on a baking sheet and bake in the preheated oven for 15 minutes.

6 Remove the tart from the oven and carefully lift out the parchment and beans. Return to the oven for another 5 minutes to crisp up, then add the filling of your choice and bake as per recipe instructions.

ROUGH PUFF PASTRY

115g (4oz) butter, wrapped
  in foil and frozen for
  1 hour until hard
175g (6oz) gluten-free plain
  flour, plus extra for dusting
large pinch of salt
1 tsp xanthan gum

1 Sift the flour, xanthan, and salt into a large bowl. Unwrap the butter and, still holding it in the foil (this stops the heat of your hand melting it), coarsely grate it into the flour.

2 Stir the butter and flour until well mixed. Gradually add 120ml (4fl oz) ice-cold water, stirring with a palette knife or round-bladed table knife until it forms a dough.

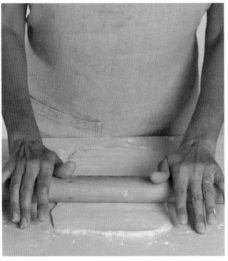

3 On a lighty floured surface, briefly knead the dough into a ball, then wrap in cling film and chill in the fridge for 10 minutes. Roll out the pastry to a rectangle 20 x 35cm (8 x 14in).

4 Mentally divide the pastry into thirds, or you could lightly score it with the back of a knife. Fold the bottom third of the pastry up over the middle third.

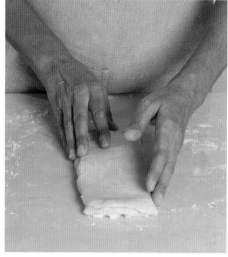

5 Now take the top third of the pastry and fold it down over the bottom third. Lightly press together the edges to seal the "parcel".

6 Give the dough a quarter turn. Roll out again and fold as before, wrap in cling film, and chill in the fridge for at least 20 minutes.

HOT WATER CRUST

MAKES 500G (1LB 2OZ)
PREP 20 MINS

350g (12oz) gluten-free plain
  flour, plus extra for dusting
2 tsp xanthan gum
1 tsp salt
3 tbsp milk
100g (3½oz) lard or white
  vegetable fat
1 egg

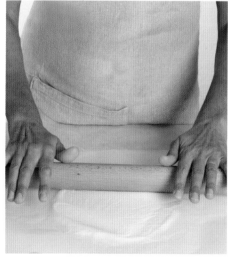

1 Sift the flour, xanthan, and salt into a large bowl. Gently heat 250ml (8fl oz) water with the milk and lard until just boiling. Pour the hot liquid into the flour and quickly beat with a wooden spoon until it forms a dough.

2 Turn the dough out onto a lightly floured surface and knead gently until smooth. This pastry can be sticky and difficult to handle, and when rolling out you may find it easier to roll between sheets of baking parchment.

RECIPES

The recipes in this book have been selected, devised, and tested to provide delicious gluten-free replacements to many favourite dishes normally made with gluten-containing grains, or where the shop-bought variety often include added gluten. We have also sought to offer a wide range of options for dishes that use ingredients from non-gluten grains, and some gluten-free versions of takeaway favourites.

A "Guidelines per serving" chart is provided for each recipe, weighted according to the type of meal and the proportion of daily intake you should be getting from that meal. This tells you at a glance whether the recipe is high (3 dots), medium (2 dots), or low (1 dot) in calories, saturated fat, and salt – three key areas to watch for a healthy diet. If you choose a recipe that is high in any of these areas, aim to choose dishes that are medium or low in those areas for the rest of the day. Each recipe also has a "Statistics per serving" breakdown of the number of calories and amount of protein, fat, carbohydrate, sugar, fibre, and salt in the dish. So if you really need to crunch the numbers, you can ensure you're getting the exact balance.

Flours and other ingredients made from non-gluten grains, such as rice noodles and cornmeal, are assumed to be gluten free in the ingredients lists, but always check the label as there can be a risk of contamination with gluten grains at the milling stage.

BREAKFAST AND SNACKS

● ● ● CALORIES

● ● ● SATURATED FAT

● ○ ○ SALT

MUESLI WITH TOASTED COCONUT

SERVES 6   **PREP** 15 MINS   **COOK** 5 MINS

The sticky dates add a toffee-flavoured sweetness to this super-healthy mix of flakes, seeds, fruits, and nuts.

75g (2½oz) rice flakes
75g (2½oz) buckwheat flakes
75g (2½oz) milled linseed
175g (6oz) soft pitted dates, chopped
75g (2½oz) dried sour cherries
125g (4½oz) Brazil nuts,
  roughly chopped

50g (1¾oz) sunflower seeds
100g (3½oz) desiccated coconut
milk, Greek yogurt, and fresh seasonal
  fruit of your choice, to serve

1 Place the flakes, linseed, dates, cherries, Brazil nuts, and sunflower seeds in a large bowl and mix.

2 Place the desiccated coconut in a frying pan and dry fry gently for a few minutes until golden, stirring it around the pan so it doesn't burn.

3 Divide the muesli between 6 individual serving bowls, then sprinkle with the coconut. Pour over enough milk for serving and top with Greek yogurt and fresh fruit, if desired.

COOK'S TIP
The quantities can easily be scaled up and the muesli stored in an airtight container for up to 3 weeks. If storing, allow the coconut to cool before stirring it into the mix.

STATISTICS PER SERVING

Energy 557kcals/2322kJ

Protein 12g

Fat 34g
Saturated fat 14g

Carbohydrate 49g
Sugar 29g

Fibre 10g

Salt trace

« Dried sour cherries
These have a marvellously tart, yet fruity flavour. As well as in muesli, try them on their own as a snack or use in baking. Store in an airtight container for up to 6 months.

PORRIDGE WITH FRUIT COMPOTE

SERVES 6   **PREP** 10 MINS   **COOK** 20 MINS

Classic porridge, served with aniseed-infused fruits, is
a real treat for breakfast. For a less indulgent porridge,
replace the cream with more milk.

GUIDELINES PER SERVING

●●● CALORIES

●●● SATURATED FAT

●○○ SALT

200g (7oz) rolled oats
750ml (1¼ pints) milk, plus extra
  if needed
250ml (9fl oz) single cream

For the compote
200g (7oz) soft pitted prunes
75g (2½oz) sour cherries
300ml (10fl oz) fresh orange juice
1 star anise

GREAT FOR KiDS

1 First prepare the compote. Place the prunes and cherries in a pan and
pour over the orange juice, add the star anise, bring to the boil, then reduce
the heat and simmer gently for 15 minutes. Set aside to steep.

2 Meanwhile, place the oats in a pan. Add two-thirds of the milk and stir
well so it is all incorporated. Bring slowly to the boil, stirring continuously,
until the milk has been absorbed by the oats. Gradually stir in the remaining
milk and the cream, bring back to the boil, and simmer gently, stirring, for
10–15 minutes or until thick and creamy. Add more milk, if needed.

3 Drain the dried fruit, reserving the liquid, and remove the star anise.
Ladle the porridge into deep bowls and top with the drained fruit and
a little of the reserved juice.

NUTRIENT BOOST
Prunes are rich in fibre,
good for digestion and
controlling blood
cholesterol.

VARIATIONS
Try flavouring the porridge with some warming cinnamon spice: add 1 cinnamon
stick and 2 teaspoons ground cinnamon to the oats along with the milk. When it's
ready, remove the stick and serve with a sprinkle of cinnamon and a swirl of cream.
The spice gives the porridge a sweet flavour, so there is no need to add sugar. You
can also swap the fruits with dried apricots and sultanas, or figs and cranberries.

COOK'S TIP
You can store the fruit compote in an airtight container in the fridge for up to 1 week.

STATISTICS PER SERVING

Energy	403kcals/1692kJ
Protein	11g
Fat	16g
Saturated fat	8g
Carbohydrate	54g
Sugar	31g
Fibre	7g
Salt	0.3g

GRANOLA WITH APPLE CRISPS

SERVES 8　　**PREP** 20 MINS　　**COOK** 1½–2 HOURS

This granola is on the right side of sweetness and will give you bags of energy at the start of the day.

4–6 dessert apples, cored
　and very thinly sliced into rings
juice of 1 lemon
1 tsp demerara sugar
3 tsp ground cinnamon
200g (7oz) buckwheat flakes
200g (7oz) rice flakes

drizzle of clear honey or maple syrup
3 tbsp sunflower oil
200g (7oz) blanched almonds
300g (10oz) dried apricots,
　roughly chopped
100g (3½oz) dried cranberries
milk and natural yogurt, to serve

1　For the apple crisps, preheat the oven to 150°C (300°F/Gas 2). Toss the apples in lemon juice and arrange them in a single layer on baking sheets lined with baking parchment. Sprinkle with the sugar and 1 teaspoon of the cinnamon and put in the oven. Leave for about 1–1½ hours, keeping an eye on them and turning them halfway through. Turn the oven down to 140°C (275°F/Gas 1) if they begin to colour too much. Remove and spread on clean parchment to dry out. If you have time, leave them in the oven overnight, after switching off the heat, to crisp up some more.

2　Set the oven temperature to 180°C (350°F/Gas 4). Place the buckwheat flakes, rice flakes, and the remaining cinnamon in a large bowl (you can substitute other gluten-free grains, such as quinoa flakes or puffs, millet flakes, or soya flakes). Mix the honey or maple syrup with the oil, pour it over the grain mixture, and toss until all the flakes are well coated. Tip out onto a baking tray and bake for 10 minutes or until golden. Stir well, add the almonds, and cook for a further 20 minutes or until the nuts are lightly toasted. Remove from the oven, stir in the dried fruit, and leave to cool. Serve with the apple crisps, milk, and a dollop of natural yogurt.

STATISTICS PER SERVING

Energy 446kcals/1868kJ

Protein 8.5g

Fat 12.4g
Saturated fat 1.1g

Carbohydrate 64.2g
Sugar 27g

Fibre 7.4g

Salt trace

COOK'S TIP
You can also double up the quantities for the granola and apple crisps and store them in separate airtight containers for up to 3 weeks.

SAVOURY GRITS

SERVES 4   **PREP** 10 MINS   **COOK** 10 MINS

An authentic Southern-style breakfast dish, made from ground corn kernels, that is both hearty and filling.

110g (3¾oz) instant grits
  (see Cook's tip)
125g (4½oz) mature Cheddar cheese,
  grated
50g (1¾oz) butter
1 tbsp sunflower oil

4 rashers smoked streaky bacon
freshly ground black pepper
splash of Tabasco sauce (optional)
handful of freshly grated Parmesan
  cheese
3-4 spring onions, finely sliced

1 Add 450ml (15fl oz) water to a large pan and bring to the boil. Tip in the grits and stir, then cover and cook on a low heat for 5–8 minutes, stirring occasionally, until they begin to thicken; or cook as per pack instructions.

2 Stir in the Cheddar and butter until melted, then simmer the mixture for another 2–3 minutes until creamy. Remove from the heat.

3 While that is cooking, heat the oil in a non-stick frying pan, add the bacon, and cook on a medium-high heat for 5–8 minutes until crispy. Remove and transfer to kitchen paper.

4 Season the grits with lots of black pepper and add a dash of Tabasco sauce, if you like. Spoon the mixture out into shallow bowls or plates. To serve, crumble the bacon over the grits along with the Parmesan and finally top with spring onions.

STATISTICS PER SERVING

Energy 452kcals/1873kJ

Protein 17g

Fat 33g

Saturated fat 17g

Carbohydrate 19.5g

Sugar 0.8g

Fibre 1g

Salt 1.7g

COOK'S TIP

Grits can be found in health food stores or online. If unavailable, polenta is a good substitute: use the same weight of polenta mixed with the same volume of water.

VARIATIONS

You can also serve the grits with sautéed garlic prawns or shrimps, topped with chillies or tomatoes, or alongside gluten-free sausages.

AMERICAN-STYLE PANCAKES

SERVES 5   **PREP** 10-15 MINS   **COOK** 15 MINS

These light and fluffy pancakes are great for a weekend brunch. Serve with crispy grilled bacon and maple syrup.

GUIDELINES PER SERVING

● ○ ○ CALORIES

● ● ○ SATURATED FAT

● ● ○ SALT

125g (4½oz) gluten-free plain flour
1 tsp gluten-free baking powder
½ tsp xanthan gum
½ tsp salt
2 tbsp caster sugar
150ml (5fl oz) milk

2 eggs
15g (½oz) butter, melted
vegetable oil, for frying
grilled bacon and maple syrup,
  to serve

1 Sift the flour, baking powder, xanthan, and salt into a large bowl, and stir in the sugar. In a jug, beat together the milk and eggs, then add to the dry ingredients along with the butter. Beat the mixture until it's smooth and lump-free; it should have a soft, dropping consistency.

2 Heat a non-stick frying pan, add a few drops of oil, and swirl it around. Use a dessertspoon to carefully drop 2–3 rounds of batter in the hot pan; they should spread to about 9cm (3½in) in diameter. Reduce the heat to low.

3 After 2 minutes, flip the pancakes and cook the other side until golden brown and risen to 1cm (½in) thick.

4 Wrap the pancakes in a clean tea towel to keep them warm while you cook the remaining pancakes. Serve with grilled bacon and maple syrup.

VARIATION

Blueberry pancakes Add a large handful of fresh blueberries to the batter before cooking and serve with maple syrup and natural yogurt or soured cream.

STATISTICS PER SERVING

Energy 226kcals/944kJ

Protein 6g

Fat 11g
Saturated fat 3.6g

Carbohydrate 26g
Sugar 8g

Fibre 0g

Salt 1g

⬤⬤◯ CALORIES

⬤◯◯ SATURATED FAT

⬤◯◯ SALT

CRUMPETS

SERVES 4   **PREP** 15 MINS   **COOK** 20-25 MINS   **FREEZE** 6 MONTHS
PLUS RISING

Warm, toasted crumpets spread with butter and honey or jam make a quintessentially British breakfast treat.

GREAT FOR KIDS

225g (8oz) gluten-free white bread
  flour mix (see page 38)
1 tsp xanthan gum
1 tbsp caster sugar
1 tsp fast-action dried yeast
½ tsp salt

250ml (9fl oz) milk
vegetable oil, for greasing and frying

SPECIAL EQUIPMENT
4 x 8cm (3¼in) metal crumpet rings

1 Sift together the flour, xanthan, sugar, yeast, and salt. In a pan, heat the milk with 250ml (9fl oz) water until lukewarm and stir into the flour. Beat well with a balloon whisk, then cover with lightly oiled cling film and leave to rise for 1 hour.

2 Heat a heavy frying pan and add a little oil. Lightly oil the crumpet rings and place them in the pan to heat up. Gently stir the batter and ladle enough into each ring to fill halfway. Cook over a low heat for 15–20 minutes; holes will appear on the surface and the batter will dry out.

3 Carefully remove the rings and turn the crumpets over to cook for a further 5–10 minutes on the other side. Transfer to a wire rack to cool and repeat until the batter is used up. Serve lightly toasted.

STATISTICS PER SERVING

Energy 300kcals/1264kJ

Protein 8g

Fat 8g
Saturated fat 2g

Carbohydrate 48g
Sugar 8g

Fibre 2g

Salt 0.6g

CORNMEAL DROP SCONES

SERVES 4   **PREP** 10 MINS   **COOK** 20 MINS   **FREEZE** 1 MONTH
PLUS RESTING

Cornmeal gives these drop scones a savoury, nutty flavour and texture. Let the batter sit for 30 minutes or overnight so that the flour can fully absorb the liquid.

250g (9oz) fine cornmeal or polenta
250g (9oz) gluten-free plain flour
2 tbsp sugar
pinch of salt
2 tsp gluten-free baking powder

½ tsp gluten-free bicarbonate of soda
500ml (16fl oz) buttermilk
1 egg
50g (1¾oz) butter, melted
sunflower oil, for frying

1 Place the cornmeal, flour, sugar, salt, baking powder, and soda into a bowl and mix. Make a well in the centre. Mix the buttermilk, egg, and melted butter in a jug until well combined. Gradually pour this into the flour mixture and stir, spooning a little flour from the edge of the bowl as you go. Add and stir until incorporated, but don't overwork the batter or you will end up with dense pancakes. Leave to rest for a minimum of 30 minutes.

2 Heat a little oil in a large, non-stick frying pan over a high heat until hot, swirl it around the pan to coat, then tip out any excess into a jug (to reuse). Reduce the heat to low-medium and add 3–4 separate ladlefuls of batter to the pan to form individual drop scones. Cook for 2 minutes until the edges start to cook and the underside turns golden, then flip using a spatula and cook the other side. Repeat until the batter is used up. Serve with a sweet or savoury accompaniment (see below).

CHOOSE YOUR ACCOMPANIMENT

Sweet Try one or more of the following: orange juice, sugar, sliced banana, honey, yogurt, or blueberries.
Savoury Best with crispy bacon and scrambled eggs.

COOK'S TIP

To freeze, layer the cooled drop scones between greaseproof paper and seal in a freezer bag. To reheat, defrost and heat through in a frying pan or microwave.

STATISTICS PER SERVING

Energy 686kcals/2865kJ

Protein 15g

Fat 21g
Saturated fat 8g

Carbohydrate 104g

Sugar 14g

Fibre 2g

Salt 2g

● ● ○ CALORIES

● ○ ○ SATURATED FAT

● ○ ○ SALT

GREAT FOR KIDS

BUTTERMILK PANCAKES

SERVES 4　**PREP** 5 MINS　**COOK** 10 MINS　**FREEZE** 6 MONTHS

A stack of pancakes served with maple syrup and fresh fruit is hard to beat for a special family breakfast. Heat the pancakes slowly so that they cook in the middle.

85g (3oz) rice flour
1 tsp xanthan gum
1 tbsp caster sugar
1½ tsp gluten-free baking powder
pinch of salt
150ml (5fl oz) buttermilk

4 tbsp milk
2 large eggs, separated
a few drops of vanilla extract
vegetable oil, for frying
maple syrup and fresh berries,
  to serve

1 Sift the flour, xanthan, sugar, baking powder, and salt together into a bowl. Add the buttermilk, milk, egg yolks, and vanilla, and beat well.

2 In a clean bowl, whisk the egg whites with an electric whisk until they are stiff. Stir a good spoonful of egg white into the batter mix to loosen it, then gently fold in the remainder.

3 Heat a large, heavy frying pan over a medium-high heat, add a few drops of oil, and wipe it around the pan with a piece of kitchen paper. Drop 4 separate heaped dessertspoons of batter into the hot pan to make 4 pancakes, leaving plenty of space between them; they should spread to be about 8cm (3¼in) wide. Cook them over a low heat for about 2–3 minutes until the base is golden, then flip them over and cook for a further 2 minutes.

4 Once cooked, wrap the pancakes in a clean tea towel to keep them warm. Repeat to make 8 pancakes in total. Serve warm, drizzled with maple syrup and with a handful of fresh berries scattered on top.

STATISTICS PER SERVING

Energy 218kcals/912kJ

Protein 8g

Fat 10g
Saturated fat 2g

Carbohydrate 22g
Sugar 6g

Fibre 0.6g

Salt 1g

CHESTNUT PANCAKES WITH CHOCOLATE AND PRUNES

SERVES 4   **PREP** 20 MINS   **COOK** 20 MINS   **FREEZE** 1 MONTH
PLUS RESTING

Chestnut flour is available from Italian delis or online and is well worth seeking out to make these rich, nutty pancakes.

75g (2½oz) chestnut flour
75g (2½oz) gluten-free plain flour
pinch of salt
1 tsp sugar
1 tsp gluten-free bicarbonate of soda
300ml (10fl oz) milk, plus extra
 if needed

1 egg
sunflower oil, for frying

For the filling
250g (9oz) soft pitted prunes
100g (3½oz) chocolate (70% cocoa
 solids), broken into even-sized pieces

1 For the batter, place the flours in a large bowl with the salt, sugar, and soda and mix. In a jug, gently whisk together the milk and egg, then slowly pour into the flour, whisking continuously until well incorporated. If the batter is too thick, add a little more milk. For best results, allow the batter to sit for 30 minutes or overnight in the fridge.

2 For the filling, place the prunes in a small pan and just cover with water. Simmer gently for about 10 minutes to soften the prunes, then remove with a slotted spoon and chop each prune in half. Set aside.

3 Place the chocolate in a heatproof bowl over a pan of barely simmering water, stir occasionally until it melts, remove the bowl, and set aside.

4 Heat a non-stick frying pan or crêpe pan over a high heat until hot. Add a drizzle of oil, swirl it around the pan, and tip out into a jug (to reuse). Reduce the heat to low-medium, add a ladleful of batter, and tip the pan so it spreads. Cook for 2 minutes until it starts to come away from the sides. Flip over with a spatula and cook the other side until it begins to crisp. Turn out on to a plate; top with a few prunes and a drizzle of melted chocolate, then fold or roll. Drizzle with more chocolate and serve. Repeat using up all the batter and filling.

STATISTICS PER SERVING

Energy 422kcals/1766kJ

Protein 9g

Fat 18g
Saturated fat 7.2g

Carbohydrate 68g
Sugar 44g

Fibre 8g

Salt 1.4g

BUCKWHEAT PANCAKES WITH ORANGE

SERVES 4   **PREP** 15 MINS   **COOK** 30 MINS   **FREEZE** 1 MONTH
PLUS RESTING

The slightly nutty flavour of buckwheat flour combines well with oranges. The secret is to treat the batter gently.

100g (3½oz) buckwheat flour
25g (scant 1oz) rice flour
salt
1 tsp sugar
1 egg, beaten
200ml (7fl oz) milk

3 oranges, peeled and thinly sliced, any juice reserved
1½ tbsp maple syrup, plus extra
sunflower oil, for frying

SPECIAL EQUIPMENT griddle pan

1 To make the batter, place the flours in a bowl along with a pinch of salt and the sugar and mix. Make a well in the middle and add the egg. Stir well. Mix the milk and 150ml (5fl oz) water in a jug and gradually pour it into the flour, whisking with a balloon whisk until the batter is smooth and no longer lumpy. Set aside for 30 minutes to rest or overnight in the fridge.

2 For the oranges, heat a griddle pan over a high heat until hot. Mix any reserved orange juice with the maple syrup and brush over the orange slices to coat both sides. Place a few slices at a time on the griddle pan and cook each side for 2 minutes until they take on a little colour. Set aside.

3 Stir the batter. Heat 1 tablespoon oil in a non-stick frying pan or a crêpe pan over a high heat until hot. Swirl it around the pan so it just coats, and tip most of it out into a jug (to reuse). Reduce the heat to low-medium and add a ladleful of batter. Tilt the pan so it spreads; the mixture will be thick so it won't cover the pan completely. Cook for 2 minutes or until the underside is pale golden, then flip it and cook for 2 more minutes. To serve, top with orange slices and a drizzle of maple syrup. Repeat to use up all the batter.

COOK'S TIP
If freezing, layer the pancakes between greaseproof paper and seal in a freezer bag. To serve, defrost overnight and reheat in a frying pan or microwave.

NUTRIENT BOOST
This dish is rich in vitamin C.

STATISTICS PER SERVING

Energy 258kcals/1078kJ

Protein 6g

Fat 8g
Saturated fat 2g

Carbohydrate 40g
Sugar 16g

Fibre 3.4g

Salt trace

● ○ ○ CALORIES

● ● ○ SATURATED FAT

● ○ ○ SALT

GREAT FOR KiDS

FRENCH-STYLE CRÊPES

SERVES 6   **PREP** 10-15 MINS   **COOK** 10-15 MINS

These classic French pancakes should be cooked as thin as you dare! Choose a filling (see below) and roll up to serve.

60g (2oz) gluten-free plain flour
½ tsp xanthan gum
pinch of salt
250ml (9fl oz) milk

2 eggs
15g (½oz) butter, melted
vegetable oil, for frying

1 Sift the flour, xanthan, and salt into a large bowl. In a jug, beat the milk and eggs together, then add to the dry ingredients with the butter. Beat the mixture until smooth and lump-free; it should have the consistency of single cream to spread thinly in the pan. The batter will thicken as it stands, so add a little water, if necessary, to retain a free-flowing consistency.

2 Heat a non-stick frying pan over a high heat until hot, add a few drops of oil, and swirl around. Use a ladle to add enough batter to thinly coat the base of the pan, tilting the pan so that the batter spreads evenly.

3 When the surface appears to be dry, flip the pancake over and cook on the other side until golden brown. Transfer the pancake to a plate and cover with foil to keep warm. Repeat to make 5 more crêpes in the same way. Serve with your choice of filling (see below).

STATISTICS PER PLAIN CRÊPE

Energy 126kcals/525kJ

Protein 5g

Fat 8g
Saturated fat 3g

Carbohydrate 9g
Sugar 2g

Fibre 0.4g

Salt 0.4g

CHOOSE YOUR FILLING

Classic Add a good squeeze of lemon juice and a sprinkling of caster sugar.
Banana and chocolate Spread a dessertspoon of chocolate hazelnut spread over the crêpe, top with sliced bananas, and roll up.
Brie and ham Thinly slice ripe Brie (about 30g/1oz per person) and scatter over the crêpe, top with a thin slice of ham, and roll up to enclose the filling.
Mushroom and blue cheese Sauté 30g (1oz) mushrooms per person in a little butter, then add a heaped dessertspoon of crème fraîche and 15g (½oz) crumbled blue cheese. Bubble until slightly reduced. Spoon into the crêpe and fold.

BUTTERMILK BISCUITS

GUIDELINES PER SERVING

●●● CALORIES

●●● SATURATED FAT

●●● SALT

SERVES 4   **PREP** 10 MINS   **COOK** 12–15 MINS   **FREEZE** 6 MONTHS

These American-style "biscuits" from the Deep South are a cross between pastry and scones, traditionally served with sausage gravy, but equally good spread with butter or jam.

vegetable oil, for greasing
225g (8oz) gluten-free plain flour,
  plus extra for dusting
2 tsp xanthan gum
1 tbsp gluten-free baking powder
½ tsp gluten-free bicarbonate of soda
salt
115g (4oz) white vegetable fat
  or butter, cubed

200ml (7fl oz) buttermilk,
  plus extra for brushing
ground cayenne pepper,
  for sprinkling (optional)

SPECIAL EQUIPMENT
6cm (2½in) round metal cutter

1 Preheat the oven to 200°C (400°F/Gas 6). Lightly oil a baking sheet. Place the flour, xanthan, baking powder, soda, and ½ teaspoon salt in a food processor. Whizz to mix well. Add the vegetable fat and pulse until well blended. Alternatively, sift the dry ingredients into a bowl and rub in the fat with your fingertips until the mixture resembles breadcrumbs.

2 Tip the mixture into a bowl, add the buttermilk, and mix until a soft dough forms. Tip the dough onto a lightly floured surface and knead briefly, then roll out to a thickness of 2cm (¾in). Dip the cutter in flour, then use to press out circles of dough.

3 Place the biscuits on the prepared baking sheet, a little apart. Brush the tops with buttermilk, and sprinkle with a little salt and cayenne pepper, if using. Bake for 12–15 minutes or until risen and lightly golden brown. Serve still warm from the oven.

STATISTICS PER SERVING

Energy 444kcals/1856kJ

Protein 8g

Fat 26g
Saturated fat 16g

Carbohydrate 46g
Sugar 4g

Fibre 1.8g

Salt 2.2g

● ○ ○   CALORIES

● ○ ○   SATURATED FAT

● ● ○   SALT

SWEET POTATO CAKES WITH ONION SEEDS

SERVES 6   **PREP** 30 MINS   **COOK** 20–30 MINS   **FREEZE** 1 MONTH

Onion seeds add a subtle spice to the mixture and cut through the richness of sweet potato. These make a lower-carb option to regular potato pancakes.

2 medium sweet potatoes, skin on
2 eggs, lightly beaten
175g (6oz) rice flour
3 tsp gluten-free baking powder
½ tsp freshly grated nutmeg

1 tbsp black onion (nigella) seeds
salt and freshly ground black pepper
knob of butter, for frying
bacon and fried tomatoes, to serve

1 Cook the whole potatoes in a pan of salted water for about 15–20 minutes or until soft, then drain. When cool enough to handle, peel and mash until smooth. Add the eggs and mix until well incorporated. Set aside.

2 Sift the flour and baking powder into a bowl, add the nutmeg, and mix. Add to the sweet potato and stir gently to mix well. Don't overwork the mixture or it will become sloppy. Stir in the onion seeds and season.

3 In a non-stick frying pan, heat a little butter over a medium heat until it is foaming, then add 1 heaped tablespoon of the potato mixture and flatten slightly with a palette knife. Cook for 4–5 minutes until the underside becomes golden, then flip, and cook the other side for the same time or until browned. Repeat to use up the batter. Serve with bacon and fried tomatoes.

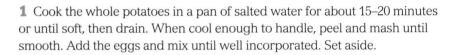

NUTRIENT BOOST

Sweet potatoes are rich in the antioxidant betacarotene.

STATISTICS PER SERVING

Energy 210kcals/880kJ

Protein 6g

Fat 5g
Saturated fat 1.6g

Carbohydrate 36g
Sugar 4g

Fibre 2g

Salt 0.8g

VARIATION
Add 1 finely chopped green chilli or, for a sweeter version, omit the onion seeds and seasoning, add 1 teaspoon ground cinnamon, and serve with maple syrup.

COOK'S TIP
To reheat from frozen, defrost in the fridge overnight and reheat in a non-stick frying pan or microwave on a medium heat for 2 minutes, or in the oven at 180°C (350°F/Gas 4) for 10–15 minutes.

POTATO FARLS

GREAT FOR KIDS

GUIDELINES PER SERVING

●●● CALORIES

●●● SATURATED FAT

●○○ SALT

SERVES 4   **PREP** 15 MINS   **COOK** 40 MINS   **FREEZE** 1 MONTH

These Irish potato cakes can be fried or griddled – they are wonderfully creamy on the inside and crisp on the outside.

675g (1½lb) floury potatoes, such as Maris Piper or Estima, skin on
salt and freshly ground black pepper
50g (1¾oz) butter
150g (5½oz) gluten-free plain flour, plus extra for dusting

3 tbsp olive oil or a knob of butter, for cooking
crispy bacon and eggs, to serve

SPECIAL EQUIPMENT griddle pan (optional)

1 Cook the potatoes in a large pan of boiling salted water for 20–25 minutes or until tender when poked with a sharp knife. Drain and, when cool enough to handle, peel and mash. Add the butter and mash until smooth.

2 Sift the flour into the mash, season well, and mix with a spoon. With your hands, bring the dough together. Turn it out onto a lightly floured surface and either roll or use the back of your hand to flatten it, so it is about 5mm (¼in) thick. Cut the dough out to make 4 x 6cm (1½ x 2½in) rectangles, then slice these into triangles.

3 To fry, heat a large, non-stick frying pan over a medium heat with half the oil or half the butter. Add half the potato cakes and fry for 2 minutes on each side until golden. Sit them on kitchen paper to drain. Repeat for the remaining farls and drain. To griddle, brush the griddle pan with a little oil, heat it to hot, add the farls a few at a time, and griddle for 2–3 minutes. Turn and cook the other side. Sit them on kitchen paper to drain. Repeat to cook the remaining farls. Serve for breakfast with crispy bacon and eggs.

COOK'S TIPS
Cooking the potatoes with their skin on helps keep them dry. You can also use leftover mashed potato, but warm it slightly first. To reheat the farls from frozen, defrost overnight and reheat in a frying pan or microwave on a medium heat for 2 minutes, or in the oven at 180°C (350°F/Gas 4) for 10-15 minutes.

STATISTICS PER SERVING

Energy 422kcals/1765kJ

Protein 7g

Fat 19g
Saturated fat 8g

Carbohydrate 55g
Sugar 1.5g

Fibre 4.5g

Salt 0.2g

EGGS BENEDICT

SERVES 4   **PREP** 20 MINS   **COOK** 35 MINS   **FREEZE** 3 MONTHS
PLUS RISING

If you prefer white muffins, use the gluten-free white bread flour blend on page 38 and add two tablespoons caster sugar.

450g (1lb) gluten-free brown bread
  flour blend (see page 38), plus extra
  for dusting
2 tsp fast-action dried yeast
1 tsp xanthan gum
salt and freshly ground black pepper
300ml (10fl oz) milk

90g (3oz) unsalted butter, plus extra
2 tbsp black treacle
5 eggs, plus 2 egg yolks
3 tbsp white wine vinegar

SPECIAL EQUIPMENT 7.5cm (3in) round
  metal cutter, griddle pan

1 Sift the flour, yeast, xanthan, and a pinch of salt into a large bowl and stir to combine. Warm the milk to lukewarm, add 15g (½oz) butter, the treacle, and 1 egg, and whisk with a fork. Make a well in the centre of the dry ingredients, add the wet ingredients, and mix. Turn onto a lightly floured surface and knead for 5 minutes until smooth. Roll out the dough 2cm (¾in) thick and cut out 8 rounds. Transfer to a floured baking sheet, cover with oiled cling film, and leave somewhere warm for 1 hour until doubled.

2 Heat a large, heavy frying pan or flat griddle. Add the muffins, making sure they don't touch each other, and cook over a medium heat for 6–7 minutes or until the bases are golden. Turn over, place a baking sheet on top of the pan to intensify the heat, and cook for 7–8 minutes until golden.

3 To poach the eggs, place a frying pan over a low heat and add boiling water to a depth of 2.5cm (1in). Carefully break 4 eggs, one at a time, into the water and let them barely simmer, for 1 minute. Remove the pan from the heat and set aside for 10 minutes to finish poaching.

4 For the hollandaise sauce, simmer the vinegar in a small pan until reduced by half. Pour into a heatproof bowl with the egg yolks and place over a pan of gently simmering water. Melt 75g (2½oz) butter, gradually add it to the bowl, and whisk continuously with a balloon whisk until a smooth, thick sauce forms. Remove from the heat and season. Split and butter the muffins, top each half with an egg, and pour over the sauce.

STATISTICS PER SERVING

Energy 753kcals/3167kJ

Protein 28g

Fat 38g

Saturated fat 19g

Carbohydrate 75g

Sugar 11g

Fibre 13.5g

Salt 0.8g

BAKED BEANS

SERVES 4 **PREP** 10 MINS **COOK** 40 MINS **FREEZE** 3 MONTHS

Commercial baked beans often contain gluten, but making your own is surprisingly easy.

1 tbsp olive oil
1 onion, finely chopped
salt and freshly ground black pepper
2 garlic cloves, finely chopped
1 tsp ground allspice
1 tsp paprika
1 tbsp tomato purée
1 tsp Dijon mustard

1 tbsp black treacle
600ml (1 pint) passata
2 x 400g cans haricot beans,
   drained and rinsed
gluten-free toast (see pages 38
   or 216) or grilled streaky bacon,
   to serve

1 Heat the oil in a large pan, add the onion, season with salt and pepper, and cook gently for about 2–3 minutes until translucent; do not allow to brown. Stir through the garlic, allspice, paprika, tomato purée, and mustard and cook for a few seconds.

2 Now add the treacle and 2 tablespoons passata, stir well, cook for a few minutes, then add the remaining passata and bring to the boil. Reduce to a low heat and simmer for about 20–30 minutes.

3 Tip in the beans, stir, and cook for a further 15 minutes or until thickened. Taste and season some more if required. Serve with gluten-free toast or grilled streaky bacon.

The soluble fibre in beans balances blood sugar and controls cholesterol.

COOK'S TIP
You can also use cannellini beans or butter beans as an alternative.

STATISTICS PER SERVING

Energy 210kcals/889kJ

Protein 10.5g

Fat 4g
Saturated fat 0.7g

Carbohydrate 34g
Sugar 5.3g

Fibre 12g

Salt 0.2g

HASH BROWNS

GREAT FOR KiDS

SERVES 4   **PREP** 20 MINS   **COOK** 45 MINS   **FREEZE** 3 MONTHS

These crispy, golden shredded potato cakes certainly shouldn't be reserved just for breakfast.

GUIDELINES PER SERVING

● ● ○ CALORIES

● ○ ○ SATURATED FAT

● ○ ○ SALT

900g (2lb) waxy potatoes,
  such as Maris Peer or Charlotte
1 egg, lightly beaten
salt and freshly ground black pepper

1-2 tbsp rice flour
vegetable oil, for frying
eggs, bacon, and baked beans
  (see opposite), to serve

1 Peel the potatoes, pat them dry, and coarsely grate into a large bowl. Transfer to a clean tea towel and squeeze to remove as much moisture as possible. Dry the bowl and return the grated potato to it.

2 Trickle in the egg, just enough to bind the mixture; you may not need it all. Stir well and season with salt and pepper. Sprinkle over the rice flour and turn with a spoon so it coats the potato.

3 Take a scoop of the mixture, form it into a ball, then flatten into a patty. Make 2–3 patties at a time; you should get about 12 in total. Heat 1 tablespoon oil in a large non-stick frying pan over a medium heat until hot and add 2–3 patties at a time, giving them plenty of room. Cook for 4–5 minutes, undisturbed, so the underside gets really crispy and golden. Turn with a spatula and cook the other side for the same amount of time or until golden and cooked right through. Remove, drain on kitchen paper, and cover with foil to keep warm. Cook the remaining patties a few at a time. Serve as part of a breakfast with eggs, bacon, and some home-made baked beans.

COOK'S TIP
The potatoes must be as dry as possible before adding the egg, for the hash browns to properly crisp up. To reheat the hash browns from frozen, defrost in the fridge overnight, then reheat in a frying pan, or in the microwave on a medium heat for 2 minutes, or in the oven at 180°C (350°F/Gas 4) for 10-15 minutes.

STATISTICS PER SERVING

Energy 303kcals/1270kJ

Protein 7g

Fat 13g
Saturated fat 1.7g

Carbohydrate 39g
Sugar 1.3g

Fibre 4g

Salt trace

PORK PATTIES

SERVES 4   **PREP** 20 MINS   **COOK** 20–25 MINS   **FREEZE** 3 MONTHS

Shop-bought sausages often contain gluten in the form of rusk. Here's how to make your own gluten-free patties using lean pork, which makes them much more healthy.

350g (12oz) pork tenderloin,
  roughly chopped
3 sage leaves
4 sprigs of thyme, leaves only
½ tsp freshly grated nutmeg
½ tsp ground allspice

1 tsp paprika
salt and freshly ground black pepper
rice flour, for dusting
sunflower oil, for frying
eggs or oven-roasted tomatoes,
  to serve

1 Place the pork, sage, and thyme leaves in a food processor, pulse a few times until the meat is minced, and transfer to a large bowl.

2 Add the nutmeg, allspice, paprika, and seasoning and thoroughly mix together with your hands. Lightly flour your hands and divide the mixture into 12 equal-sized portions. Form each portion into a ball, then flatten to form a patty; use more flour if needed.

3 Place the patties on baking parchment on a baking sheet and put in the fridge to firm up for 30 minutes, if you have time.

4 Heat a little oil in a large, non-stick frying pan and cook the patties on a medium-high heat in 2 batches, for about 5–6 minutes on each side or until golden and cooked through. Serve as part of a breakfast with eggs or oven-roasted tomatoes.

COOK'S TIPS

If you don't have a food processor, use lean pork mince instead and chop the herbs before adding. To freeze, layer the uncooked patties between greaseproof paper and seal in a freezer bag.

STATISTICS PER SERVING

Energy 166kcals/696kJ

Protein 19g

Fat 9g
Saturated fat 2g

Carbohydrate 2g
Sugar trace

Fibre trace

Salt 0.15g

HAM AND CHEESE BREAKFAST MUFFINS

SERVES 6   **PREP** 15 MINS   **COOK** 25-30 MINS   **FREEZE** 6 MONTHS

These savoury muffins are a great treat for a weekend breakfast or just as good for a packed lunch or picnic.

175g (6oz) gluten-free plain flour
60g (2oz) rolled oats
1 tsp xanthan gum
1½ tsp gluten-free baking powder
½ tsp gluten-free bicarbonate of soda
2 tsp mustard powder
salt and freshly ground black pepper
100g (3½oz) mature Cheddar
  cheese, grated

60g (2oz) gluten-free smoked sliced
  ham, finely chopped
100ml (3½fl oz) vegetable oil
100ml (3½fl oz) milk
3 eggs

SPECIAL EQUIPMENT deep 12-hole
  muffin tray lined with paper cases

1 Preheat the oven to 180°C (350°F/Gas 4). Mix together the flour, oats, xanthan, baking powder, soda, and mustard powder in a large bowl. Season with a good pinch of salt and plenty of pepper.

2 Stir in three-quarters of the cheese and all the ham. Mix together the oil, milk, and eggs. Add to the dry ingredients and mix together briefly.

3 Spoon the mixture into the paper cases and sprinkle over the remaining cheese. Bake for 25–30 minutes or until risen and golden brown on top. Cool in the tin for 5 minutes before transferring to a wire rack. The muffins are best served slightly warm.

COOK'S TIP

For a vegetarian version, omit the smoked ham and add 60g (2oz) chopped sun-dried tomatoes instead.

STATISTICS PER SERVING

Energy 784kcals/3272kJ

Protein 48.8g

Fat 54g
Saturated fat 14g

Carbohydrate 30g
Sugar 1.2g

Fibre 2g

Salt 2.2g

● ● ○ CALORIES

● ● ○ SATURATED FAT

● ○ ○ SALT

NUTRIENT BOOST
Blueberries are rich in antioxidants, linked to heart health and fighting cancer.

GREAT FOR KiDS

BLUEBERRY BREAKFAST MUFFINS

SERVES 6　　**PREP** 10 MINS　　**COOK** 25–30 MINS　　**FREEZE** 6 MONTHS

Start the day with a boost of fresh blueberries packed into muffins. Serve with a glass of milk, American style!

175g (6oz) gluten-free plain flour
60g (2oz) polenta or fine cornmeal
115g (4oz) caster sugar
1 tsp xanthan gum
1½ tsp gluten-free baking powder
½ tsp gluten-free bicarbonate of soda
pinch of salt
140g (5oz) blueberries

zest of 1 lemon
100ml (3½fl oz) vegetable oil
100ml (3½fl oz) milk
3 eggs

SPECIAL EQUIPMENT deep 12-hole
　muffin tray lined with paper cases

1 Preheat the oven to 180°C (350°F/Gas 4). Mix together the flour, polenta, sugar, xanthan, baking powder, soda, and salt in a large bowl.

2 Stir in the blueberries and lemon zest. Mix together the oil, milk, and eggs, add to the dry ingredients, and mix briefly.

3 Spoon the mixture into the paper cases. Bake for 25–30 minutes or until risen and golden brown on top. Cool in the tin for 5 minutes before transferring to a wire rack. Best served slightly warm.

STATISTICS PER SERVING

Energy　390kcals/1640kJ

Protein　8g

Fat　17g
Saturated fat　3g

Carbohydrate　48g
Sugar　22g

Fibre　2g

Salt　0.6g

« Blueberries
Blueberries have a mild flavour that is markedly enhanced by cooking, one reason why they are such a popular fruit for baking. Raspberries or chopped strawberries would also work in this recipe.

FRUIT AND NUT BREAKFAST BARS

SERVES 8   **PREP** 15 MINS   **COOK** 30-35 MINS

These energy-packed oat bars are perfect for breakfast on the go and equally good as a mid-morning snack.

vegetable oil, for greasing
115g (4oz) ready-to-eat dried apricots
85g (3oz) blanched hazelnuts
85g (3oz) unskinned almonds
85g (3oz) raisins or sultanas
85g (3oz) dried cranberries
397g can sweetened condensed milk

200g (7oz) rolled oats
85g (3oz) crispy rice
  or puffed rice

SPECIAL EQUIPMENT
23 x 33cm (9 x 13in) baking tray

GREAT FOR KiDS

1 Preheat the oven to 160°C (325°F/Gas 3). Lightly oil the tray and line with baking parchment.

2 Use scissors to snip the apricots into small pieces and place in a bowl. Roughly chop the hazelnuts and almonds, keeping them fairly chunky. Add the nuts to the bowl with the raisins or sultanas and cranberries.

3 Pour the condensed milk into a large, heavy pan and slowly bring to the boil over a low heat. Stir constantly as it can catch at the bottom and burn. Remove once it is boiling, add the fruit, nuts, oats, and rice, and mix well with a wooden spoon. Tip into the prepared tray and level the surface with the back of a wetted spoon. Bake for 30–35 minutes or until pale golden.

4 Remove from the oven, cool in the tray for 5 minutes, then tip out onto a chopping board. Cut into 16 bars and leave to cool completely. They will store in an airtight container for up to 1 week.

VARIATION

Chocolate fruit and nut bars Stir 2 tablespoons cocoa powder into the condensed milk before mixing in the remaining ingredients and add 60g (2oz) roughly chopped dark chocolate (70% cocoa solids).

NUTRiENT BOOST
Almonds are a source of calcium, also rich in vitamin E and heart-friendly fats.

STATISTICS PER SERVING

Energy 534kcals/2244kJ

Protein 12g

Fat 20g
Saturated fat 4g

Carbohydrate 66g
Sugar 40g

Fibre 6g

Salt 0.4g

BREAKFAST BERRY BARS

SERVES 8   **PREP** 10 MINS   **COOK** 30–35 MIN

So easy to make, these fruit-packed bars are ready
to grab for a breakfast on the go!

GREAT
FOR KIDS

oil, for greasing
397g can sweetened condensed milk
300g (10oz) mixed dried berries,
  such as cranberries, blueberries,
  and sour cherries
250g (9oz) rolled oats

50g (1¾oz) crispy rice
30g (1oz) sunflower seeds
30g (1oz) pumpkin seeds

SPECIAL EQUIPMENT 23 x 33cm
  (9 x 13in) rectangular baking tin

1 Preheat the oven to 160°C (325°F/Gas 3). Lightly oil the baking tray.

2 Gently heat the condensed milk in a large, heavy pan and slowly bring
to the boil. Remove it from the heat, then tip in the fruit, oats, crispy rice,
and seeds. Mix well with a wooden spoon.

3 Tip into the prepared tin, then level the surface with the back of a wetted
spoon. Bake for 30–35 minutes or until pale golden.

4 Remove from the oven, cool in the tin for 5 minutes, and cut into 16 bars.
Transfer the bars to a wire rack to cool completely. Store in an airtight
container for up to 1 week.

NUTRIENT
BOOST
Oats provide
low-GI carbohydrate
energy.

COOK'S TIP

Tailor these to suit your personal taste: chopped dried apricots, sultanas, or raisins
can be used instead of the berries, just keep the quantity the same; and try using
the same quantity of chopped hazelnuts in place of the seeds.

STATISTICS PER SERVING

Energy 476kcals/2000kJ

Protein 11g

Fat 12g
Saturated fat 4g

Carbohydrate 80g
Sugar 44g

Fibre 7g

Salt 0.3g

STARTERS, PARTY FOOD, AND DIPS

● ● ○ CALORIES

● ● ● SATURATED FAT

● ● ○ SALT

BREADSTICKS WITH PEPPER DIP

MAKES 18 **PREP** 15 MINS **COOK** 45–50 MINS
PLUS RISING

These party nibbles come in three different flavours,
but if preferred, simply dust with polenta.

350g (12oz) gluten-free white bread
  flour blend (see page 38), plus extra
  for dusting
2 tsp fast-action dried yeast
2 tsp xanthan gum
2 tsp caster sugar
1 tsp salt
2 eggs
2 tbsp olive oil
vegetable oil, for brushing
4 tbsp poppy seeds
4 tbsp sesame seeds
6 tbsp finely grated Parmesan cheese

For the roasted pepper dip
2 large red peppers
4 garlic cloves, unpeeled
3 tbsp olive oil
1 tsp smoked paprika
½ tsp caster sugar
½ tsp ground cumin
½ tsp salt
dash of Tabasco sauce

1 Preheat the oven to 220°C (425°F/Gas 7). Sift the flour, yeast, xanthan,
sugar, and salt into a large bowl. Lightly beat 1 egg with the olive oil and
250ml (9fl oz) lukewarm water, add to the dry ingredients, and mix to form
a dough. Transfer to a lightly floured surface and knead for 5 minutes.
Return to the bowl, cover with oiled cling film, and leave to rise in a warm
place for about 1 hour until doubled in size.

2 Meanwhile, roast the peppers on a baking tray for 15–20 minutes until
lightly charred. Add the garlic and cook for a further 10 minutes. Transfer
the peppers and garlic to a plastic bag and leave to cool. Core and deseed
the peppers and peel off the skin. Pop the garlic from their skins. Combine
with the remaining ingredients in a food processor and blitz to a coarse dip.

3 Lightly oil 2 baking sheets. Roll out the dough to a fat sausage and cut
into 18 equal-sized pieces. Roll each piece into a stick 12cm (5in) long. Scatter
the seeds and Parmesan onto 3 separate plates. Beat the remaining egg.
Brush the sticks with the beaten egg and roll a third of the sticks in each
flavour. Place them a little apart on the baking sheets and bake for 15–20
minutes or until crisp and golden. Allow to cool.

STATISTICS PER SERVING

Energy 158kcals/662kJ

Protein 6g

Fat 9.5g
Saturated fat 2.5g

Carbohydrate 16g
Sugar 2.5g

Fibre 1.5g

Salt 0.4g

CHEESE STRAWS
WITH TOMATO AND BASIL DIP

GUIDELINES PER SERVING

● ● ○ CALORIES

● ● ● SATURATED FAT

● ● ○ SALT

MAKES 18 **PREP** 15 MINS **COOK** 15–20 MINS
PLUS CHILLING

Shape the cheese straw trimmings into little biscuits – they still taste great, whatever the shape.

225g (8oz) gluten-free plain flour, plus extra for dusting
100g (3½oz) butter, cubed
2 tsp mustard powder
1 tsp xanthan gum
½ tsp salt
85g (3oz) mature Cheddar cheese, grated, or blue cheese, crumbled
1 egg, beaten
milk for brushing

3 tbsp finely grated Parmesan cheese
paprika, for sprinkling

For the dip
4 medium tomatoes
2 tbsp finely chopped basil
1 tbsp olive oil
1 tbsp tomato purée
½ tsp caster sugar
salt and freshly ground black pepper

1 Place the flour, butter, mustard, xanthan, and salt in a food processor and pulse until the mixture looks like crumbs. Transfer to a bowl. Stir through the Cheddar or blue cheese, then add the egg along with 4 tablespoons cold water. Using a round-bladed knife, mix to form a ball of dough. Lightly knead on a floured surface, wrap in cling film, and chill for 30 minutes.

2 Preheat the oven to 200°C (400°F/Gas 6). Roll out the dough on a lightly floured surface to a rectangle measuring 23 x 36cm (9 x 14½in), and trim the edges. Brush with milk, then sprinkle over the Parmesan and paprika. Cut 2cm (¾in) wide strips from the dough and place them on baking trays. Bake for 15–20 minutes or until the strips are golden and puffy. Leave to cool.

3 For the dip, score the tomatoes and soak in boiling water for 30 seconds. Peel and discard the skin, then roughly chop the tomatoes on a board to make a pulp. Tip the flesh and all the juices into a small bowl. Add the remaining ingredients, stir well, and season to taste. Serve at room temperature with the cheese straws.

STATISTICS PER SERVING

Energy 133kcals/554kJ

Protein 4g

Fat 8.5g
Saturated fat 5g

Carbohydrate 10g
Sugar 1g

Fibre 0.8g

Salt 0.4g

● ● ● CALORIES

● ● ● SATURATED FAT

● ● ○ SALT

LAVOSH WITH AUBERGINE DIP

SERVES 8   **PREP** 20 MINS   **COOK** 1 HOUR 10 MINS

Iranian-style seeded crisp breads served with a sesame-scented aubergine dip make a great snack or appetiser.

150g (5½oz) gluten-free plain
  flour, plus extra for dusting
2 tsp xanthan gum
½ tsp salt
2 egg whites
15g (½oz) butter, melted
2 tbsp sesame seeds
1 tbsp poppy seeds

For the dip
2 medium aubergines
2 garlic cloves, crushed
zest and juice of 1 lemon
3 tbsp tahini paste
½ tsp salt
90ml (3fl oz) olive oil
3 tbsp finely chopped fresh coriander
4 tbsp Greek yogurt
freshly ground black pepper

1 Preheat the oven to 200°C (400°F/Gas 6). For the dip, bake the aubergines on a baking tray for 30–40 minutes or until soft and lightly charred. Cool.

2 Meanwhile, make the lavosh. Sift the flour, xanthan, and salt into a large bowl. Beat 1 egg white with 90ml (3fl oz) water, stir into the flour with the melted butter, and mix well to form a dough. Lightly knead the dough on a floured surface, divide into 6 balls, and roll out each ball until paper thin, then place on baking sheets. Repeat with all the dough.

3 Brush the remaining egg white over the lavosh, sprinkle the seeds, and bake in 2 batches for 10–15 minutes or until crisp and golden.

4 Halve the aubergines and scoop the flesh into a food processor. Add the rest of the ingredients and blend to a chunky spread. Check the seasoning, spoon into a bowl, and serve with the crisp breads.

STATISTICS PER SERVING

Energy 226kcals/994kJ

Protein 5.5g

Fat 17g
Saturated fat 3.5g

Carbohydrate 15.5g
Sugar 1.5g

Fibre 3g

Salt 0.6g

COOK'S TIP
You can also store the lavosh, after it has cooled, in an airtight container for 2–3 days. Re-crisp in a warm oven. The dip can be stored for 2–3 days in an airtight container in the fridge.

⬤⬤⬤ CALORIES

⬤⬤◯ SATURATED FAT

⬤⬤◯ SALT

SESAME RICE CRACKERS

SERVES 6   **PREP** 20 MINS   **COOK** 20 MINS
PLUS DRYING

These fiery hot crackers are perfect for serving with dips or spicy relishes and pickles.

500g (1lb 2oz) sticky rice (sushi rice), washed in cold running water, until the water runs clear
salt
2 tbsp sesame seeds

1 tsp wasabi paste
2 tsp tamari (gluten-free soy sauce)
sunflower oil, for frying
hot carrot and onion seed pickle or spicy cauliflower pickle, to serve

1 Tip the washed rice into a large pan, add 660ml (1 pint) cold water, cover with a lid, bring to the boil, and simmer for 10 minutes or until all the water has been absorbed; make sure it doesn't dry out or the rice will burn. Remove from the heat, but do not remove the lid. Leave covered for 15 minutes.

2 Season the cooked rice with salt, stir in the sesame seeds, wasabi, and tamari, and mix well until it is all combined.

3 Spread the mixture out onto a baking tray lined with baking parchment. Squash the rice a little and top with another sheet of baking parchment. Use a rolling pin to roll over the paper and flatten the rice so it is about 5mm (¼in) thick. Remove the baking parchment and place in the fridge to dry overnight.

4 Remove the rice from the fridge 20 minutes before you are ready to cook. Pour the oil to a depth of 5cm (2in) in a deep frying pan. Slice the rice into square shapes, breaking pieces off (it will be irregular), and add to the hot oil a couple at a time. Continue frying until they are all cooked. Drain on kitchen paper and serve with a hot carrot and onion seed or spicy cauliflower pickle.

STATISTICS PER SERVING

Energy 363kcals/1514kJ

Protein 7g

Fat 7g
Saturated fat 1g

Carbohydrate 62g
Sugar 1g

Fibre 0.5g

Salt 0.6g

VEGETABLE CRISPS

SERVES 4   **PREP** 20 MINS   **COOK** 30 MINS

Deliciously sweet and healthier than regular crisps, these make an ideal snack for children; omit the salt if you prefer.

2 parsnips
1 sweet potato
2 beetroots

sunflower oil, for deep-frying,
    enough to fill half the pan
sea salt (optional)

1 Peel and trim the vegetables, then cut them into wafer-thin slices using a vegetable peeler or a mandolin, if you have one.

2 Heat the oil in a heavy, deep-sided pan over a high heat until really hot. Don't leave the pan unattended, take off the heat when not using, and keep a fire blanket nearby in case of fire. Add the vegetable slices a few at a time. Fry each batch for 2–3 minutes or until crisp and golden, then remove with a slotted spoon and spread out over kitchen paper on a baking sheet. Repeat until all are cooked.

3 Sprinkle with sea salt (if using) and then sit them piled high in bowls to serve with drinks, or serve alongside meat such as game.

VARIATIONS
Sprinkle with either paprika, black pepper, or dried chilli flakes for extra flavour.

Yellow beetroot »
If you are wary of the staining juices from red beetroot, look out for Burpee's Golden, a bright yellow beet that does not bleed when cut.

● ● ● CALORIES

● ● ○ SATURATED FAT

● ○ ○ SALT

GREAT FOR KiDS

NUTRIENT BOOST
Beetroots produce nitric oxide gas in the blood, which lowers blood pressure.

STATISTICS PER SERVING

Energy 258kcals/1076kJ

Protein 3g

Fat 17.5g
Saturated fat 2g

Carbohydrate 22g

Sugar 10g

Fibre 7.5g

Salt 0.15g

● ● ○ CALORIES

● ● ● SATURATED FAT

● ● ○ SALT

OLIVE PINWHEELS

MAKES 16   **PREP** 20 MINS   **COOK** 15–20 MINS   **FREEZE** 3 MONTHS

Gluten-free puff pastry spread with tapenade, rolled and baked until golden for a delectable party snack.

400g (14oz) gluten-free rough puff pastry (see pages 46–7)
1 egg, lightly beaten, to glaze

salt and freshly ground black pepper
100ml (3½fl oz) extra virgin olive oil
juice of ½ lemon

For the tapenade
150g (5½oz) pitted black olives
2 garlic cloves, roughly chopped

1 Preheat the oven to 200°C (400°F/Gas 6). For the tapenade, whizz the olives, garlic, and seasoning in a food processor until well minced. With the blade turning, trickle in enough oil to make a soft paste; you may not need it all. Add a little lemon juice to taste, then set aside.

2 Roll the pastry out to a rectangle about 30 x 35cm (12 x 14in); this may be more easily done between sheets of cling film. Spread the tapenade over the pastry leaving a 2.5cm (1in) border all around the edge.

3 Carefully roll up the pastry from the shorter end, as tightly as you can, then cut into 16 slices. Sit the pinwheels on their sides on a lightly oiled baking sheet and brush each one with a little egg. Bake in the oven for 15 minutes or until pale golden and lightly puffed. Remove and transfer to a serving plate. Serve as a snack with drinks.

STATISTICS PER PINWHEEL

Energy 154kcals/642kJ

Protein 2g

Fat 12.5g
Saturated fat 4g

Carbohydrate 9g
Sugar 0.3g

Fibre 0.4g

Salt 0.4g

COOK'S TIPS
Make these ahead and freeze them raw, then simply bake in the oven from frozen. You can replace the tapenade with a gluten-free pesto (see page 137), a tomato sauce, or simply grated cheese.

RED ONION AND CHILLI BHAJIS WITH RAITA

GUIDELINES PER SERVING

●●○ CALORIES

●●○ SATURATED FAT

●○○ SALT

SERVES 4   **PREP** 20 MINS   **COOK** 20 MINS
PLUS RESTING

Children will love these with the chilli omitted and a mild masala used. Try adding roughly puréed peas instead.

1 medium red onion, finely sliced
1 red chilli, deseeded and
  finely chopped
pinch of turmeric
2 tsp garam masala
1 tsp black onion (nigella) seeds
salt and freshly ground black pepper
juice of ½ lemon
about 200g (7oz) gram (chickpea) flour
handful of fresh coriander leaves,
  finely chopped

sunflower or vegetable oil, for frying,
  enough to fill half the pan

For the raita
200ml (7fl oz) Greek yogurt
½ cucumber, peeled, halved
  lengthways, deseeded, and
  finely chopped
handful of mint leaves, finely chopped
salt and freshly ground black pepper

1 Place the onion and chilli in a bowl along with the turmeric, garam masala, and onion seeds. Season to taste with salt and pepper, and add the lemon juice. Sprinkle in the flour with 100–150ml (3½–5fl oz) cold water, adding both a little at a time. Keep adding until it forms a thick mixture that holds together. Be careful not to add too much water and turn it into a batter. Stir in the coriander, then allow the mixture to rest in the fridge for 5 minutes.

2 Meanwhile, make the raita. Mix together the yogurt, cucumber, and mint, and season well. Set aside.

3 Heat the oil in a deep-sided pan over a high heat until hot. Don't leave the pan unattended, take off the heat when not using, and keep a fire blanket nearby in case of fire. Drop a little mixture into the oil to check if it is hot enough; it should sizzle. Drop a loose ball (about the size of a golf ball) into the hot oil and deep-fry for 4–5 minutes or until beginning to colour. Remove with a slotted spoon and drain on kitchen paper. Repeat to use up the mixture, and serve with the raita.

GREAT FOR KIDS

STATISTICS PER BHAJI

Energy 139kcals/580kJ

Protein 5g

Fat 9g
Saturated fat 2g

Carbohydrate 10g
Sugar 3g

Fibre 2.5g

Salt 0.15g

● ○ ○ CALORIES

● ● ○ SATURATED FAT

● ○ ○ SALT

COURGETTE AND CHILLI FRITTERS

SERVES 4   **PREP** 25 MINS   **COOK** 10 MINS
PLUS RESTING

Perfect for a light supper, these fritters shouldn't be at all oily: use minimal oil and drain well.

900g (2lb) courgettes, topped
  and tailed
salt and freshly ground black pepper
150g (5½oz) rice flour
1 tbsp olive oil
2 eggs, separated

150ml (5fl oz) milk
1 tsp dried chilli flakes
sunflower oil, for frying
fresh tomato salsa or home-made
  mayonnaise, to serve

1 Finely grate the courgettes into a colander, sprinkle over a little salt, and leave for 30 minutes. Tip them into a tea towel and squeeze out the excess water (see Cook's tip).

2 For the batter, place the flour in a bowl, season, and add the olive oil, egg yolks, and milk. Mix well to combine. Leave to rest for 30 minutes, if time permits.

3 Meanwhile, whisk the egg whites until fairly stiff, then fold them into the batter mixture. Add the grated courgettes to the batter mixture along with the chilli flakes and fold them in gently.

4 Heat a little sunflower oil in a non-stick frying pan and add dollops of the batter; they will spread so add only about 3 at a time. Cook for 1–2 minutes or until they begin to turn golden, then flip and cook the other side. Drain on kitchen paper and continue until all the batter is used up. Serve with fresh tomato salsa or some home-made mayonnaise.

COOK'S TIP

It's essential that the courgettes are drained of all the excess water, so squeeze and pat them dry really well.

STATISTICS PER SERVING

Energy 370kcals/1574kJ

Protein 11g

Fat 20g
Saturated fat 4g

Carbohydrate 33g
Sugar 5.5g

Fibre 4g

Salt 0.2g

CORN AND FETA FRITTERS

SERVES 4   **PREP** 15 MINS   **COOK** 15 MINS   **FREEZE** 1 MONTH
PLUS RESTING

A very easy, light supper dish that uses only a few ingredients from the fridge and storecupboard.

○○ CALORIES

●● ○ SATURATED FAT

●●● SALT

125g (4½oz) gluten-free plain flour
2 tsp gluten-free baking powder
1 egg
100ml (3½fl oz) milk
195g can sweetcorn, drained, or the
  kernels from 2 fresh cobs (see below)

freshly ground black pepper
75g (2½oz) feta cheese, crumbled
2–3 tbsp sunflower oil, for frying
fried or grilled bacon, to serve
  (optional)

GREAT FOR KiDS

1 Sift the flour and baking powder into a bowl and make a well. Add the egg and milk, and start to incorporate the flour, whisking until smooth. Add the sweetcorn, some pepper, and mix. Rest in the fridge for 15 minutes.

2 When ready to cook, stir in the feta, then heat a little oil in a non-stick frying pan over a medium heat. Spoon in 2 tablespoons of the mixture and flatten together to form each fritter, leaving plenty of space between them; you will have to cook them in batches.

NUTRiENT BOOST
The phytochemicals in canned sweetcorn are more easily absorbed than in fresh.

3 Fry for 1–2 minutes or until the underside is pale golden, then turn and cook the other side for a further 1–2 minutes. Remove and drain on kitchen paper. Serve alone or with bacon, as a main meal or breakfast.

VARIATIONS
Once you've mastered the batter mix, try varying it with grated Cheddar cheese and spring onion, peas and chopped mint, or blue cheese and chopped red onion.

STATISTICS PER SERVING

Energy 294kcals/1230kJ

Protein 8g

Fat 13g
Saturated fat 4.5g

Carbohydrate 36g
Sugar 5.5g

Fibre 0.8g

Salt 1.9g

Corn on the cob »
To prepare fresh sweetcorn, pull off the husk and silk, hold upright, and slice straight down the sides to cut off the kernels. Steam or boil for 2–3 minutes.

● ● ○ CALORIES

● ● ● SATURATED FAT

● ● ○ SALT

BLINIS WITH SMOKED TROUT AND HOT AND SOUR CUCUMBER

SERVES 10 **PREP** 15 MINS **COOK** 10-15 MINS **FREEZE** 6 MONTHS
PLUS MARINATING BLINIS ONLY

Serve these little pancakes as smart canapés daintily topped with the cucumber, trout, and soured cream.

85g (3oz) buckwheat flour
85g (3oz) gluten-free plain flour
½ tsp gluten-free baking powder
1 tsp fast-action dried yeast
salt
200ml (7fl oz) milk
1 egg, separated
15g (½oz) butter, melted
250g (9oz) cucumber, peeled, halved, deseeded, and thinly sliced

½ tsp white mustard seeds
½ tsp Sichuan peppercorns
3 tbsp cider vinegar
1 tbsp finely chopped dill
1 tbsp caster sugar
½ tsp dried chilli flakes
140g (5oz) smoked trout, finely chopped
150ml (5fl oz) soured cream
vegetable oil, for frying

1 Sift the flours, baking powder, yeast, and ½ teaspoon salt into a large bowl. Heat the milk until lukewarm, and pour into the flour with the egg yolk and melted butter. Mix well and cover. Leave to stand for 30 minutes.

2 Place the cucumber in a bowl. Lightly crush the mustard seeds and peppercorns with a mortar and pestle. Add to the cucumber with the vinegar, dill, sugar, ½ teaspoon salt, and chilli flakes, and mix. Cover and marinate for 20 minutes.

3 Stir the batter. Whisk the egg white in a clean bowl until it forms stiff peaks, then fold it into the batter. Heat a heavy non-stick frying pan, add a few drops of oil, and wipe it around the pan with kitchen paper. Drop dessertspoonfuls of the batter into the hot pan; they should be 5cm (2in) wide. Cook over a medium heat for 1–2 minutes until bubbles form and the base is golden. Flip and cook for 1 minute. Repeat to make 35–40 blinis. Serve warm with the cucumber, smoked trout, and soured cream.

STATISTICS PER SERVING

Energy 171kcals/714kJ

Protein 6.5g

Fat 8.5g
Saturated fat 4g

Carbohydrate 16g
Sugar 3.5g

Fibre 0.6g

Salt 0.9g

● ● ○ CALORIES

● ● ● SATURATED FAT

● ● ● SALT

SAUSAGE ROLLS

GREAT FOR KiDS

SERVES 6   **PREP** 20 MINS   **COOK** 30 MINS   **FREEZE** 3 MONTHS

A real favourite with everyone – perfect for parties, snacks, or picnics.

400g (14oz) gluten-free sausages, removed from their skins
½ medium onion, very finely chopped
handful of flat-leaf parsley, finely chopped
salt and freshly ground black pepper

400g (14oz) gluten-free rough puff pastry (see pages 46–7)
1 egg, lightly beaten, or more if needed
vegetable oil, for greasing

1 Preheat the oven to 200°C (400°F/Gas 6). Add the sausagemeat to a bowl and chop using a fork, stir in the onion and parsley, and season if required (the sausages may be salty enough already).

2 On a lightly floured surface, roll out the pastry to a large rectangle about 24 x 30cm (9½ x 12in) and 4mm (¼in) thick, then cut it lengthways so you have 2 rectangles. Halve the sausage mixture, roll each half into a long sausage shape, and place down the middle of each piece of pastry.

3 Brush the edges of the pastry with the beaten egg and then fold the pastry over, so it wraps the sausagemeat with the seam underneath. Press the edges together to seal. Repeat with the other rectangle of pastry. Now slice each roll into 6 pieces. Slash the tops so that steam escapes as they cook, then brush them with the remaining beaten egg. Sit them on a lightly oiled baking sheet and cook in the oven for 25–30 minutes until evenly golden and the sausagemeat is cooked through. Remove and serve hot or cold.

STATISTICS PER SERVING

Energy 428kcals/1786kJ

Protein 14g

Fat 30g
Saturated fat 12g

Carbohydrate 26g
Sugar 2g

Fibre 0.6g

Salt 1.8g

VARIATION

Cheese rolls Follow the same recipe for a non-meat version, but replace the sausagemeat with 200g (7oz) mature Cheddar cheese, grated, and 200g (7oz) gluten-free breadcrumbs, mixed with the onion and parsley. Use your hands to squeeze the mixture together into a sausage shape, fill the pastry rectangles, and seal. Brush with beaten egg and bake for 20–25 minutes or until golden.

FISH FINGERS

SERVES 4   **PREP** 20 MINS   **COOK** 20 MINS   **FREEZE** 3 MONTHS
PLUS CHILLING

So much better than ready-made ones, and you have complete control over what goes into them and coats them.

GREAT FOR KiDS

400g (14oz) white fish fillets or loin, such as haddock, skin and pinbones removed
150g (5½oz) polenta or fine cornmeal, plus extra if needed
50g (1¾oz) fresh Parmesan cheese, grated

5 tbsp gluten-free plain flour or gram flour, plus extra if needed
salt and freshly ground black pepper
1 egg, lightly beaten
2–3 tbsp sunflower oil
lemon wedges and gluten-free tartare sauce, to serve

1 Cut the fish into 12–16 lengths to form fingers and then trim to neaten. The number will depend on the size and shape of the fish.

2 Mix the polenta with the Parmesan, then season the plain or gram flour with salt and pepper. Tip the flour out onto a plate, the beaten egg onto another plate, and the polenta mix onto a third.

3 Dip each fish finger into the flour and turn to cover so the egg will stick, then dip into the egg to coat, and roll in the polenta until completely covered. Sit the fingers on a baking tray and put in the fridge to firm up for 20 minutes. When ready to cook, heat a little oil in a non-stick frying pan and add a few at a time, frying on a medium-high heat for 5–6 minutes on each side or until golden. Repeat with all fingers, topping up the pan with more oil as needed. Serve with lemon wedges and gluten-free tartare sauce.

COOK'S TIPS
You could oven-bake these if you prefer: sit them on a lightly oiled baking sheet and cook in the oven at 200°C (400°F/Gas 6) for 20 minutes, turning them halfway through. Excellent for children: serve sandwiched between slices of gluten-free bread for the perfect fish-finger sandwich.

STATISTICS PER SERVING

Energy 406kcals/1700kJ

Protein 30g

Fat 13g
Saturated fat 4g

Carbohydrate 40g
Sugar 0.2g

Fibre 0.8g

Salt 0.6g

● ● ○ CALORIES

● ○ ○ SATURATED FAT

● ○ ○ SALT

CHICKEN NUGGETS

SERVES 4   **PREP** 20 MINS   **COOK** 20-30 MINS   **FREEZE** 1 MONTH

Processed nuggets are justly criticised for the poor quality of their meat; with these home-made versions you know exactly what has gone into them.

900g (2lb) chicken breast, skinless, cut
  into cubes or bite-sized pieces
2-3 tbsp gluten-free plain flour,
  rice flour, or cornflour, plus extra
  if needed
salt and freshly ground black pepper
1 egg, lightly beaten, or more
  if needed

150-200g (5½-7oz) polenta or
  fine cornmeal
2 tsp paprika
oil, for greasing
green salad and fresh tomato relish,
  to serve

1 Preheat the oven to 200°C (400°F/Gas 6). Toss the chicken pieces in the flour until they are evenly coated, then season well with salt and pepper. Tip the beaten egg out onto a plate. Mix the polenta with the paprika and tip this out onto a separate plate.

2 Dip the chicken pieces into the beaten egg, transfer them to the polenta, and toss to coat.

3 Sit all the coated pieces on a lightly oiled baking sheet and bake in the oven for 20–30 minutes until golden, turning them halfway through cooking so they colour evenly. Remove and serve with a lightly dressed green salad and a fresh tomato relish.

COOK'S TIP
Prepare these ahead and freeze uncooked on a baking sheet, transfer to a plastic bag, and seal. To eat, defrost overnight in the fridge and cook as per recipe.

STATISTICS PER SERVING

Energy 424kcals/1785kJ

Protein 60g

Fat 5.5g
Saturated fat 1g

Carbohydrate 31g
Sugar 0.5g

Fibre 1g

Salt 0.5g

CHICKEN SATAY KEBABS

GUIDELINES PER SERVING

● ● ● CALORIES

● ● ● SATURATED FAT

● ● ● SALT

SERVES 4   **PREP** 15 MINS   **COOK** 35–50 MINS
PLUS MARINATING

The spicy cubes of chicken in these kebabs are charred on the outside but remain juicy and tender on the inside.

3 chicken breasts, skinless, cut into
  bite-sized cubes
1 tbsp sunflower oil
3 tbsp tamari (gluten-free soy sauce)
1 red chilli, deseeded and
  finely chopped
juice of ½ lemon
2 tsp palm or demerara sugar
salt and freshly ground black pepper

For the satay sauce
400ml can coconut milk
1–2 tbsp gluten-free red curry paste
300ml (10fl oz) hot gluten-free
  vegetable stock

1 tbsp tamari (gluten-free soy sauce)
1–2 tbsp palm or demerara sugar
200g (7oz) ground freshly shelled
  peanuts, or 5 tbsp gluten-free
  peanut butter
salt
2 tsp tamarind paste or juice of
  1 lemon or 1 lime

SPECIAL EQUIPMENT 8 wooden
  skewers, soaked in cold water for
  30 minutes; griddle pan

1 Put the chicken pieces in a bowl, add the oil, tamari, chilli, lemon juice, and sugar, and season. Stir to combine and leave to marinate for 30 minutes.

2 For the sauce, place the coconut milk in a medium pan and bring to the boil. Reduce the heat, stir in the curry paste, stock, tamari, and sugar, and cook gently for 10 minutes, stirring occasionally. Add the peanuts, stir until they melt into the sauce, bring to the boil, and simmer for 10–15 minutes or until thickened. Season with salt and add the tamarind paste or lemon or lime juice to taste. Set aside to cool and for all the flavours to mingle. The sauce can be prepared ahead and kept in the fridge for up to 3 days.

3 Meanwhile, mix the marinade around a little, then thread the chicken pieces onto the skewers, so they sit tightly. Heat the griddle pan to hot. Cook 4 at a time for about 4–6 minutes until golden, then turn and cook the other side for about the same time or until the chicken begins to char at the edges. Repeat to cook the remaining kebabs and serve with the satay sauce.

STATISTICS PER SERVING

Energy 647kcals/2703kJ

Protein 44g

Fat 45g
Saturated fat 20g

Carbohydrate 17g
Sugar 10g

Fibre 3g

Salt 3g

● ● ○ CALORIES

● ○ ○ SATURATED FAT

● ● ○ SALT

VEGETABLE SPRING ROLLS

MAKES 10   **PREP** 30 MINS   **COOK** 15-20 MINS

You can fry these ahead and crisp them up in a hot oven just before serving. Look for rice pancakes in Asian stores.

15g (½oz) dried shiitake mushrooms, soaked in boiling water for 20 mins
1 small carrot, cut into matchsticks
3 spring onions, cut into matchsticks
85g (3oz) white cabbage, shredded
2 garlic cloves, crushed
2cm (¾in) piece of fresh root ginger, peeled and grated
2 tbsp tamari (gluten-free soy sauce)
1 tbsp Chinese cooking wine
½ tsp Chinese five-spice powder
1 tbsp vegetable oil

60g (2oz) beansprouts
20 rice pancakes
vegetable oil, for deep-frying

For the chilli dipping sauce
60g (2oz) caster sugar
90ml (3fl oz) rice wine vinegar
2 garlic cloves, chopped
2 red chillies, finely chopped

SPECIAL EQUIPMENT deep-fat fryer, or large pan plus cooking thermometer

1 Drain and finely chop the mushrooms and mix together with the next 5 ingredients. In a small jug, mix the tamari, wine, and five-spice powder. Heat the oil in a frying pan or wok, add the vegetable mix, mushrooms, and beansprouts, and stir-fry for 1 minute. Add the tamari mix and simmer for 30 seconds. Remove from the heat and leave to cool.

2 For the sauce, place the ingredients in a medium pan with 4 tablespoons water, boil, then simmer for 5 minutes or until slightly thickened. Cool.

STATISTICS PER ROLL

Energy 105kcals/440kJ

Protein 1.1g

Fat 6g
Saturated fat 0.7g

Carbohydrate 12g
Sugar 8g

Fibre 1g

Salt 0.7g

3 Dip a pancake in a bowl of warm water for 10–15 seconds or until soft. Lay it on a damp tea towel and blot until slightly sticky. Place a heaped dessertspoonful of filling in the centre. Fold the bottom of the pancake up over the filling, fold in the sides, rolling up the pancake tightly. Soak a second pancake, wrap it around the first layer, and set aside. Repeat until the filling is used up. Heat the oil in a deep-fat fryer or large pan until it reaches 180°C (350°F). Do not leave the fryer or pan unattended, switch off when not using, and keep a fire blanket nearby in case of fire. Cook the spring rolls in the hot oil, 2 at a time, for 3–4 minutes or until golden. Remove with a slotted spoon and drain on kitchen paper. Keep warm while you fry the remainder. Serve the rolls hot with the chilli dipping sauce.

VEGETABLE TEMPURA

SERVES 6　　**PREP** 25 MINS　　**COOK** 10 MINS

Don't let the batter for these Japanese snacks sit: it needs to be used immediately, so prepare the vegetables ahead.

1 red pepper, deseeded and
　cut into strips
1 small head of broccoli, broken
　into florets
1 medium onion, cut into eighths
2 carrots, cut into batons
1 tbsp cornflour
sunflower oil, for frying

For the dipping sauce
2 tbsp gluten-free mirin
3 tbsp tamari (gluten-free soy sauce)

1–2 tsp sugar, or to taste
1 tbsp lime juice

For the batter
1 egg yolk
120ml (4fl oz) sparkling mineral water,
　ice cold
100g (3½oz) rice flour, sieved
salt and freshly ground black pepper

SPECIAL EQUIPMENT wok or large, deep,
　non-stick frying pan

1 To make the sauce, place the mirin, tamari, and sugar in a bowl and mix. Then add the lime juice and 3 tablespoons water to dilute it. Mix again, taste, and add more water if needed. Set aside. For the batter, place the egg yolk in a bowl and mix with a fork. Pour in the mineral water and mix. Add the rice flour and seasoning and mix lightly.

2 Toss the prepared vegetables in the cornflour. Pour the oil into a wok, to a depth of 7.5cm (3in). Heat on high until hot. Don't leave the wok or pan unattended, take off the heat when not using, and keep a fire blanket nearby in case of fire. Dip the vegetables, one by one, into the batter until just coated, then place them in the oil. Don't overcrowd the pan. Remove with a slotted spoon as soon as the batter is crispy and golden, about 2–3 minutes, and drain on kitchen paper. Continue with the rest of the vegetables and batter. Serve hot with the dipping sauce.

STATISTICS PER SERVING

Energy　221kcals/918kJ

Protein　3g

Fat　13g
Saturated fat　2g

Carbohydrate　22g
Sugar　0.5g

Fibre　3g

Salt　0.3g

« Tamari
Most soy sauce is made by fermenting soya beans with roasted wheat. Tamari, however, is made only with beans and is naturally gluten-free.

SESAME PRAWN TOASTS

MAKES 32   **PREP** 15 MINS   **COOK** 15-20 MINS

Ready in minutes and great to serve as a canapé with drinks. If you omit the chilli from the prawn mixture, they make a delicious home-from-school snack for children.

GUIDELINES PER SERVING

● ○ ○ CALORIES

● ○ ○ SATURATED FAT

● ○ ○ SALT

250g (9oz) ready-cooked prawns
1 red chilli, deseeded and
 finely chopped
handful of fresh coriander leaves,
 finely chopped
salt and freshly ground black pepper
8 slices of gluten-free white bread
 (see page 38), lightly toasted

4 tbsp sesame seeds, or more
 if needed
4-5 tbsp sunflower oil, or more
 if needed

SPECIAL EQUIPMENT food processor

GREAT FOR KIDS

1 Place the prawns in a food processor along with the chilli, coriander, salt, and pepper and whizz until really well minced. Slice the crusts off the bread and reserve (see Cook's tip).

2 Spread the minced prawn mixture over the toast slices and press down well to make sure it sticks. Cut the toasts into quarters and then triangles. Tip the sesame seeds out onto a plate and dip each toast, prawn-side down, into them to cover.

3 Heat 1 tablespoon oil in a frying pan over a medium heat. Add a few toasts at a time, plain-side down, and cook for 1–2 minutes, then turn and cook the topped side for 1–2 minutes or until golden. Remove and place on kitchen paper. Remove excess sesame seeds from the pan and continue until all the toasts are done, topping up with the remaining oil as needed.

COOK'S TIP
Use the bread crusts to make breadcrumbs: whizz in a food processor and keep sealed in the fridge for a few days or in the freezer for up to 3 months.

STATISTICS PER TOAST

Energy 43kcals/182kJ

Protein 2g

Fat 3g
Saturated fat 0.5g

Carbohydrate 3g
Sugar 0.2g

Fibre 0.3g

Salt 0.2g

● ● ● CALORIES

● ● ○ SATURATED FAT

● ● ● SALT

CRISPY KING PRAWNS WITH TERIYAKI SAUCE

SERVES 4   **PREP** 15 MINS   **COOK** 10 MINS

Use good-quality, juicy prawns for this simple dish as they are the star of the show.

3 tbsp tamari (gluten-free soy sauce)
1 tbsp gluten-free mirin
1 tsp caster sugar
2–3 tbsp cornflour
salt and freshly ground black pepper
pinch of dried chilli flakes

12 large raw king prawns, shelled and de-veined, but tail left intact
5 tbsp sunflower oil

SPECIAL EQUIPMENT wok or large, deep, non-stick frying pan

1 First make the teriyaki sauce by mixing together the tamari, mirin, and caster sugar. Taste, adjust if necessary, and set aside.

2 Mix together the cornflour, salt and pepper, and chilli flakes, then add the prawns and toss well so they all get thoroughly coated.

3 Heat the oil in the wok or pan until hot, add a few prawns, and cook until they turn pink, about 3–5 minutes. Remove with a slotted spoon and continue until all the prawns are cooked. Serve with the teriyaki sauce, either spooned over the prawns or as a dip.

STATISTICS PER SERVING

Energy 234kcals/971kJ

Protein 11g

Fat 17g
Saturated fat 2g

Carbohydrate 8g
Sugar 2g

Fibre trace

Salt 2.4g

COOK'S TIP
You could also use rice flour or potato flour to coat the prawns.

« King or Tiger prawns
Meaty, tropical prawns found mainly in the Pacific or Indian oceans. To prepare, snip off the legs and antennae, then twist and pull out the tail section.

CRAB CAKES WITH SWEET AND SOUR SAUCE

SERVES 4   **PREP** 15 MINS
PLUS CHILLING   **COOK** 30 MINS   **FREEZE** 3 MONTHS
CRAB CAKES ONLY

Succulent bites of minced crab flavoured with chilli and coriander make a perfect culinary treat.

400g (14oz) fresh or canned crab meat
1 bunch of spring onions, trimmed
  and finely chopped
handful of fresh coriander,
  roughly chopped
1 chilli, deseeded and finely chopped
1 egg, lightly beaten
1-2 tbsp rice flour, for dusting
sunflower oil, for frying

For the sweet and sour sauce
5 tbsp rice vinegar
2 tsp cornflour
150ml (5fl oz) pineapple juice
2 tbsp passata
1-2 tsp sugar, or more to taste
salt and freshly ground black pepper

SPECIAL EQUIPMENT food processor

1 First make the sauce. Place all the ingredients in a small pan and gently bring to the boil, stirring well as you go. Reduce to a simmer and cook for 10 minutes, until thickened. Season to taste, then set aside.

2 For the crab cakes, place the crab meat, spring onion, coriander, and chilli in a food processor and pulse until well minced. Season and pulse again. Spoon the mixture into a bowl and mix in the egg, a little at a time. Keep adding until the mixture is soft and pliable but not too mushy; it is best to mix with your hands.

3 Lightly flour your hands, scoop out balls of the mixture, and flatten them into about 16 mini rounds. Place them on a baking sheet lined with baking parchment and chill in the fridge for 30 minutes to firm up.

4 Heat a little oil in a non-stick frying pan and add the cakes a few at a time. Cook on each side until golden, about 5–6 minutes in total. Place on kitchen paper to drain, then serve with the sweet and sour sauce.

STATISTICS PER SERVING

Energy 248kcals/1037kJ

Protein 22g

Fat 13g
Saturated fat 2g

Carbohydrate 10g
Sugar 5g

Fibre 0.5g

Salt 1.1g

● ● ● CALORIES

● ● ● SATURATED FAT

● ● ○ SALT

MINI FISHCAKES WITH CORIANDER MAYONNAISE

SERVES 4 **PREP** 30 MINS
PLUS CHILLING **COOK** 30 MINS **FREEZE** 3 MONTHS
FISHCAKES ONLY

GREAT FOR KIDS

Omit the mayonnaise if you are in a vulnerable group as it contains raw eggs, which have a risk of salmonella.

2 egg yolks
1 tsp Dijon mustard
salt and freshly ground black pepper
300ml (10fl oz) sunflower oil,
  plus extra for frying
1 tbsp white wine vinegar
handful of fresh coriander,
  leaves only, finely chopped
450g (1lb) salmon fillet, skinned
300ml (10fl oz) milk
200g (7oz) mashed potato

small handful of dill, finely chopped
zest and juice of ½ lemon
¼–½ tsp cayenne pepper
½ green pepper, finely chopped
2–3 tbsp rice flour
1 egg, lightly beaten
100g (3½oz) gluten-free white bread
  (see page 38), whizzed into
  fine breadcrumbs

SPECIAL EQUIPMENT food processor

NUTRIENT BOOST
Oily fish like salmon are rich in omega-3 fats that help keep your heart healthy.

STATISTICS PER SERVING

Energy 766kcals/2534kJ

Protein 32g

Fat 37g
Saturated fat 7.5g

Carbohydrate 37g
Sugar 7g

Fibre 2.5g

Salt 1g

1 For the mayonnaise, place the egg yolks, mustard, some seasoning, and the vinegar in the bowl of a food processor. With the motor running, add the oil in a thin, steady stream until the mixture emulsifies and thickens. Taste and add more seasoning or vinegar, if required. Transfer to a serving bowl, stir in the coriander, cover, and set aside.

2 For the fishcakes, add the salmon to a deep-sided frying pan and pour over the milk, season, bring to the boil, and simmer gently for 4–6 minutes until the fish starts to turn opaque. Transfer the salmon with a slotted spoon to a bowl. Flake the fish, add the mashed potato, dill, lemon zest and juice, cayenne, and green pepper, and season. Stir, then scoop out ½ tablespoon of mixture and flatten into a mini cake. Repeat to make about 20 cakes. Place on a baking sheet lined with baking parchment.

3 Dredge the fishcakes in flour, dip in egg, and coat with breadcrumbs. Chill for 30 minutes. Heat 1 tablespoon oil in a non-stick frying pan and cook a few cakes at a time, 3–4 minutes each side, until golden. Serve with the coriander mayonnaise.

SOUPS AND SALADS

FRENCH ONION SOUP

SERVES 6   **PREP** 25 MINS   **COOK** 1 HOUR 25 MINS–1 HOUR 40 MINS

An extremely satisfying soup and filling enough for a main meal with delicious cheese toasties on top.

2 tbsp olive oil
6 medium onions, peeled, halved, and thinly sliced
salt and freshly ground black pepper
1 bay leaf
1 tbsp demerara sugar
120ml (4fl oz) dry white wine
1.2 litres (2 pints) hot gluten-free beef or vegetable stock (see page 115)

For the toasties
4–6 slices of gluten-free white bread (see page 38), crusts removed and lightly toasted
150g (5½oz) Gruyère cheese, grated

1 Heat the oil in a large flameproof casserole or ovenproof pot, add the onions, and stir well. Season and add the bay leaf. Cook on a low heat for about 15 minutes until they begin to soften. Raise the heat a little, sprinkle in the sugar, and stir. Cook for a further 35 minutes until the onions are golden and caramelized. Stir them occasionally, watching that they don't burn; turn the heat down, if required.

2 Over a medium-high heat, add the wine, and stir to get all the sticky bits of onion up from the bottom of the casserole. Cook for 1–2 minutes, then pour in the stock. Bring to the boil, then reduce to a simmer and cook uncovered for 20–30 minutes. Remove the bay leaf and season to taste.

3 Preheat the oven to 180°C (350°F/Gas 4). Sprinkle a handful of cheese into the soup and stir well. Pop the slices of toast on the top of the soup and divide the remaining cheese over the toast. Cook in the oven, uncovered, until the cheese begins to bubble and turns golden. Divide between bowls, topped with a cheese toastie.

COOK'S TIPS

The trick for rich-tasting French onion soup is to let the onions caramelize. Use a wide, heavy flameproof casserole - cast iron is ideal - so there is little chance of burning. This is a perfect recipe for using up any leftover bread.

STATISTICS PER SERVING

Energy 298kcals/1249kJ

Protein 13g

Fat 13g
Saturated fat 6g

Carbohydrate 28g
Sugar 9g

Fibre 3g

Salt 0.9g

MINESTRONE SOUP

GREAT FOR KiDS

SERVES 8   **PREP** 40 MINS   **COOK** 1¾–2¼ HOURS   **FREEZE** 3 MONTHS

This soup can use up a glut of seasonal vegetables, simply change them depending on the time of the year.

NUTRiENT BOOST

Canned beans and pulses are an excellent source of soluble fibre.

1 ham knuckle or "hock", or 1 pack
  of bacon, roughly chopped
1 tbsp olive oil
1 medium onion, finely chopped
2 bay leaves
3 large carrots, diced
1 fennel bulb, finely chopped
2 garlic cloves, finely chopped
freshly ground black pepper
4 large ripe tomatoes, chopped
leaves from a few thyme sprigs
pinch of freshly grated nutmeg
400g can chickpeas, drained
  and rinsed

400g can cannellini or butter beans,
  drained and rinsed
100g (3½oz) broad beans, fresh
  or defrosted, shelled weight
100g (3½oz) peas, fresh or defrosted,
  shelled weight
200g (7oz) small gluten-free
  pasta shapes (shop-bought or
  see pages 42–3)
100g (3½oz) spinach
grated Parmesan or Pecorino cheese

1 Put the ham pieces in a large pan and add enough cold water to nearly fill the pan. Bring to the boil, reduce to a medium-low heat, partially cover the pan with a lid, and cook for 1–1½ hours or until the ham begins to soften. Strain the stock, reserving the bones and meat. Strain the stock again, through a fine sieve, into a measuring jug; you will need 1.2 litres (2 pints), adding water if needed. Set aside. Strip the meat from the bones, discard the bones, and set the meat aside.

2 Heat the oil in a large, heavy pan. Add the onion and bay leaves, and cook over a medium-low heat for 5–7 minutes until soft. Add the carrots and fennel and cook for 8 more minutes until soft. Stir in the garlic and season with pepper, add the tomatoes, and cook on a low heat for 10 minutes. Ladle in a little stock if it starts to get dry. Add the thyme leaves, nutmeg, chickpeas, beans, and peas, and stir. Add enough stock to cover and simmer gently for 10 minutes. Add the pasta shapes, the reserved meat, and remaining stock. Bring to the boil, then simmer until the pasta is cooked. Add the spinach and stir. Taste and season again, if needed. Serve with the grated cheese.

STATISTICS PER SERVING

Energy 215kcals/910kJ

Protein 11g

Fat 4g
Saturated fat 0.5g

Carbohydrate 34g
Sugar 7g

Fibre 9.5g

Salt 0.8g

○○ CALORIES

●○ SATURATED FAT

●○ SALT

MEXICAN SWEETCORN SOUP WITH TORTILLA CRISPS

SERVES 6 **PREP** 15 MINS **COOK** 25 MINS

Make this easy-to-prepare soup as hot and spicy as you like, and use gluten-free crisps as an alternative topping.

GREAT FOR KIDS

2 x 326g cans sweetcorn, drained
1 tbsp olive oil
50g (1¾oz) butter
1 onion, finely chopped
2 garlic cloves, finely chopped
½ tsp cumin seeds
3–4 red or green jalapeños in brine, drained and finely chopped
salt and freshly ground black pepper

pinch of cayenne pepper (optional)
leaves from a few sprigs of thyme
1 tbsp gluten-free plain flour
1 litre (1¾ pints) hot gluten-free vegetable stock (see page 115)
2 corn tortillas (see page 233)
handful of fresh coriander leaves, roughly chopped
lime wedges, to serve

NUTRIENT BOOST
Sweetcorn provides a useful amount of fibre, vitamin B6, and magnesium.

STATISTICS PER SERVING

Energy 330kcals/1384kJ

Protein 4g

Fat 11g
Saturated fat 5g

Carbohydrate 32g
Sugar 12g

Fibre 2.5g

Salt 1.4g

1 Pulse half the sweetcorn in a food processor until smooth. Heat the oil and butter in a large, heavy pan, add the onion, and cook over a low heat for 2–3 minutes until beginning to soften. Stir in the garlic, cumin, and jalapeños, cook for 1 minute, and season.

2 Add the cayenne and thyme and cook gently for 1 minute. Then remove from the heat, stir in the flour, and tip in the pulsed and whole sweetcorn. Pour in a little stock and return the pan to the heat. Bubble and stir, then add the remaining stock and bring to the boil. Reduce to a simmer and cook gently for about 15 minutes or until the soup begins to thicken.

3 Preheat the grill to medium and lightly grill the tortillas for about 1 minute on each side or until they start to crisp and bubble. Cut the tortillas into small triangles. Taste the soup and season again if necessary. Divide between bowls, top with the tortilla triangles and coriander, and serve with lime wedges.

COOK'S TIP

If you don't have a food processor, substitute a can of creamed sweetcorn instead of pulsing.

QUINOA VEGETABLE SOUP

GUIDELINES PER SERVING

● ○ ○ CALORIES

● ○ ○ SATURATED FAT

● ○ ○ SALT

SERVES 6   **PREP** 20 MINS   **COOK** 1½ HOURS

A light soup flavoured with orange, basil, and chilli – great when served with seeded brown rolls. Prepare the stock the night before for a more intense flavour.

1 tbsp olive oil
1 onion, finely chopped
salt and freshly ground black pepper
1 garlic clove, finely chopped
½ tsp dried oregano
zest of 1 orange
3 carrots, diced
2 celery sticks, diced
150g (5½oz) broad beans, fresh
  or frozen, shelled weight
125g (4½oz) quinoa
handful of torn basil leaves
pinch of dried chilli flakes

grated Parmesan cheese and Seeded
  brown rolls (see page 218), to serve

For the stock
1 onion
2 cloves
1 carrot, cut into 4 pieces
1 celery stick, cut into 4 pieces
2 bay leaves
2 leeks, trimmed and roughly chopped
pinch of salt
1 tsp black peppercorns

1 For the stock, stud the onion with the cloves and place in a large pan with the carrot, celery, bay leaves, leeks, salt, and peppercorns. Add 1.4 litres (2½ pints) water and bring to the boil. Reduce to a simmer, partially cover with a lid, and cook for 1 hour on a low heat. Turn off the heat, cover, and leave for the flavours to infuse.

2 In a large, clean pan, heat the oil, add the onion, and cook for 5–6 minutes over a low heat until soft. Season, add the garlic, oregano, orange zest, carrots, and celery, and cook over a low heat for about 10 minutes or until the carrots soften. Stir in the broad beans and the quinoa. Strain the stock through a sieve into a large jug and discard the strained vegetables.

3 Add the stock, a ladleful at a time, to the pan with the softened vegetables and quinoa. Cook on a gentle simmer, adding enough stock until the desired consistency is reached. Bring to the boil and cook gently, uncovered, for 10 minutes, adding more stock if necessary, or until the quinoa is cooked. Stir through the basil and sprinkle with chilli flakes. Taste and season, if needed, and serve with grated Parmesan and seeded brown rolls.

STATISTICS PER SERVING

Energy 140kcals/587kJ

Protein 6g

Fat 4g
Saturated fat 0.5g

Carbohydrate 21g
Sugar 9g

Fibre 6g

Salt 0.28g

NUTRiENT BOOST
Beetroot is rich in antioxidants and folate.

BEETROOT AND GINGER SOUP

SERVES 4   **PREP** 10 MINS   **COOK** 55 MINS

Earthy beetroot always makes a colourful soup. Here, ginger adds a pleasant zing and the wasabi cream, swirled in at the last minute, gives a fiery kick.

500g (1lb 2oz) raw beetroot,
   stalks removed
salt
pinch of sugar
1 tbsp olive oil
bunch of spring onions, trimmed and
   finely chopped
5cm (2in) piece of fresh root ginger,
   peeled and grated

salt and freshly ground black pepper
750ml (1¼ pints) hot gluten-free
   vegetable stock (see page 115)
3 tbsp soured cream
¼ tsp wasabi paste, or more
   if you like it hot

SPECIAL EQUIPMENT food processor
   or stick blender

1 To cook the beetroot, place them in a pan of salted water, add the sugar, and bring to the boil. Cook on a low-medium heat with the lid ajar for 40 minutes or until the beetroot is tender when poked with a sharp knife. Drain and, when cool enough to handle, peel and roughly chop the beetroot.

2 In a clean pan, heat the oil and add the spring onions. Cook for 2–3 minutes on a medium heat, just enough for them to soften, then add the ginger and cook for a further minute. Add the chopped beetroot and stir well to coat with the oil. Season, pour in the stock, and bring to the boil.

3 Reduce to a simmer and cook gently for about 10 minutes, then ladle into a food processor and blend until smooth, or use a stick blender. Taste and season some more, if needed. Mix the soured cream with the wasabi. Ladle the soup into bowls with a swirl of the wasabi cream.

COOK'S TIP
If you don't have wasabi paste, use gluten-free hot horseradish sauce instead.

STATISTICS PER SERVING

Energy 113kcals/475kJ

Protein 4g

Fat 5.5g
Saturated fat 2g

Carbohydrate 12g
Sugar 12g

Fibre 4g

Salt 0.7g

EGYPTIAN LENTIL SOUP

SERVES 6   **PREP** 15 MINS   **COOK** 30 MINS   **FREEZE** 3 MONTHS

The gentle spice flavours of this hearty vegetarian soup are greatly enhanced by a squeeze of lemon before serving.

1 tbsp olive oil
50g (1¾oz) butter
1 onion, finely chopped
salt and freshly ground black pepper
1 tsp cumin seeds
1 tsp turmeric
1 tsp paprika
2 garlic cloves, finely chopped
2 carrots, diced
2 potatoes, diced

125g (4½oz) red lentils
900ml (1½ pints) hot gluten-free
   vegetable stock (see page 115)
lemon wedges and 2 warmed
   gluten-free pitta breads
   (see page 232), to serve

SPECIAL EQUIPMENT food processor
   or stick blender

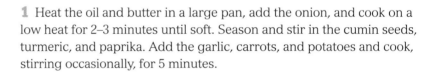

1 Heat the oil and butter in a large pan, add the onion, and cook on a low heat for 2–3 minutes until soft. Season and stir in the cumin seeds, turmeric, and paprika. Add the garlic, carrots, and potatoes and cook, stirring occasionally, for 5 minutes.

2 Stir in the lentils, making sure they get coated with any buttery juices. Ladle in a little stock, bring to the boil, stir, and then add the rest of the stock. Boil again, reduce to a simmer, and cook gently for 15–20 minutes or until the soup thickens and the potatoes are cooked. Top up with hot water, if required.

3 Season to taste. Transfer to a food processor and blend until smooth, in batches if necessary, or use a stick blender. Pour the soup into a clean pan and top up with hot water if required. Heat through until piping hot and serve in shallow bowls with lemon wedges and warmed gluten-free pitta breads.

COOK'S TIPS

You could top the soup with a sprinkling of dukkah, an Egyptian spice blend made with toasted nuts and herbs. For a sweeter version that will appeal to kids, add a 400g can of chopped tomatoes with the stock.

NUTRIENT BOOST Lentils are an excellent source of fibre and count towards your 5-a-day.

STATISTICS PER SERVING

Energy 245kcals/1028kJ

Protein 7g

Fat 9g
Saturated fat 5g

Carbohydrate 25g
Sugar 4g

Fibre 4g

Salt 0.6g

INDIAN SPLIT PEA SOUP WITH PANEER CROUTONS

GUIDELINES PER SERVING

⬤◯◯ CALORIES

⬤⬤⬤ SATURATED FAT

⬤◯◯ SALT

SERVES 4   **PREP** 25 MINS   **COOK** 50 MINS

This rich, creamy soup is topped with spicy croutons made from Indian paneer. The ghee gives it an authentic touch.

1 tbsp ghee or 1 tbsp sunflower oil
1 onion, finely chopped
1 tsp turmeric
seeds of 4 cardamom pods, crushed
2 garlic cloves, finely chopped
1-2 green chillies, deseeded and
  finely chopped
salt and freshly ground black pepper
150g (5½oz) yellow split peas, rinsed
  and drained
400g can coconut milk
900ml (1½ pints) hot gluten-free
  vegetable stock (see page 115)

For the croutons
1 tbsp ghee or 1 tbsp sunflower oil
1-2 pinches of dried chilli flakes
½ tsp ground cumin
½ tsp ground cinnamon
100g (3½oz) paneer, cut
  into small cubes
fresh coriander leaves, to garnish
2 warmed gluten-free pitta breads
  (see page 232), to serve

SPECIAL EQUIPMENT food processor
or stick blender

1 Heat the ghee or oil in a large pan. Add the onion, turmeric, and crushed cardamom seeds. Cook on a low heat for 2–3 minutes until the onion softens. Stir in the garlic, chilli, and seasoning and cook for a further 1–2 minutes.

2 Stir in the split peas and turn, so they soak up any liquid and get coated with spices. Pour in a little coconut milk, raise the heat, and stir. Pour in the remaining coconut milk with half the stock and bring to the boil. Reduce to a simmer and cook uncovered for 30–35 minutes until the peas are soft, topping up with the stock if required. Season to taste and blend in a food processor until smooth, or use a stick blender.

3 For the croutons, place the ghee or oil in a small frying pan along with the spices, season, and heat gently over a low heat. Add the paneer, turn the heat up a little, and fry for 10 minutes until golden on all sides.

4 Heat the soup through until piping hot and top with the paneer croutons and coriander leaves. Serve with warmed gluten-free pitta breads.

STATISTICS PER SERVING

Energy 397kcals/1666kJ

Protein 16g

Fat 25g
Saturated fat 16g

Carbohydrate 27g
Sugar 3g

Fibre 4g

Salt 0.23g

FENNEL SOUP WITH PARMESAN THINS

SERVES 4   **PREP** 20 MINS   **COOK** 45 MINS

Parmesan thins are simplicity itself to make and elevate this rich, creamy soup to dinner party sophistication.

1–2 tbsp olive oil
50g (1¾oz) butter
1 onion, finely chopped
salt and freshly ground black pepper
1 celery stick, finely chopped
1 carrot, finely chopped
2 garlic cloves, finely chopped
3–4 fennel bulbs, trimmed and finely chopped, fronds reserved to garnish

750ml (1¼ pints) hot gluten-free vegetable stock (see opposite)
4 tbsp finely grated Parmesan cheese
200ml (7fl oz) double cream
pinch of freshly grated nutmeg

SPECIAL EQUIPMENT food processor or stick blender

1 Heat 1 tablespoon oil and the butter in a large pan, add the onion, cook over a low heat for 5–6 minutes until soft, and season. Add the celery and carrot, and cook over a low heat for 10 minutes or until nicely golden. Add the garlic and fennel and cook over a very low heat for 5 minutes until the fennel begins to soften, adding more oil if needed. Pour over a little stock and bring to the boil. Add the remaining stock and bring to the boil again. Reduce to a simmer and cook for 20 minutes until the fennel is tender.

2 For the Parmesan thins, place 4 equal heaps of the grated Parmesan into a large, non-stick frying pan. Cook over a low heat and flatten each heap with the back of a spoon. Cook for a few minutes until the Parmesan begins to melt and forms a crust. Once it has started to crisp on the bottom and tiny bubbles start to appear around the edges, carefully flip each over using a palette knife. Cook for a further minute or so, then remove the pan from the heat, leaving the thins in the pan to keep warm.

3 Transfer the soup to a food processor and blend until smooth, then return to the pan, or use a stick blender. Season to taste, pour in the cream, and heat gently. Serve in wide bowls with a pinch of nutmeg and topped with a Parmesan thin. Garnish with the reserved fennel fronds.

STATISTICS PER SERVING

Energy 465kcals/1917kJ

Protein 9g

Fat 45g
Saturated fat 26g

Carbohydrate 6g
Sugar 5g

Fibre 4g

Salt 0.6g

TOMATO PANZANELLA SOUP

SERVES 4   **PREP** 15 MINS   **COOK** 25-30 MINS

This rustic soup is a great way to use up leftover bread.
Make it in summer when tomatoes are flavoursome.

2 tbsp olive oil
1 onion, finely chopped
salt and freshly ground black pepper
2 garlic cloves, finely chopped
900g (2lb) tomatoes, skinned and
　roughly chopped (see page 163)
4 chunky slices of stale gluten-free
　bread (see page 38), roughly torn
handful of basil leaves
extra virgin olive oil, for drizzling

For the vegetable stock
4 carrots, roughly chopped
4 onions, rougly chopped
4 celery stalks, roughly chopped
2 bay leaves
large handful of peppercorns
salt

GREAT FOR KiDS

1 For the vegetable stock, place all the ingredients in a large stock pan and pour in 2 litres (3½ pints) water. Season with salt and bring to the boil, then reduce to a simmer and cook gently for 1 hour with the lid ajar. Drain into a large jug ; you should have about 1.2 litres (2 pints). If making ahead, keep the stock in the fridge and use within 3 days.

2 Heat the olive oil in a large pan, add the onion, and cook over a low heat for 5–6 minutes until soft. Season with salt and pepper, stir in the garlic, and cook for a further minute. Add the tomatoes with any juices to the pan, and cook on a low heat for 5 minutes. Pour in 750ml (1¼ pints) of the stock (see Cook's tip) and add the bread, pushing it down with a spoon to immerse.

3 Partially cover the pan with a lid and cook gently for about 15 minutes. The soup should be fairly dense, so you could almost eat it with a fork, but top up with hot water if required. Season to taste. Stir through the basil, ladle into bowls, and drizzle with the olive oil to serve.

NUTRiENT BOOST
Tomatoes are rich in lycopene, believed to protect against some cancers.

COOK'S TIP
Freeze the leftover stock by first boiling rapidly for about 10 minutes to intensify the flavour. Leave to cool then transfer to a freezer bag and seal or freeze in ice cube trays. Use within 1 month.

STATISTICS PER SERVING

Energy 225kcals/947kJ

Protein 6.5g

Fat 10g
Saturated fat 1.5g

Carbohydrate 27g
Sugar 9g

Fibre 4g

Salt 0.6g

CALORIES

SATURATED FAT

SALT

SMOKED HADDOCK CHOWDER

SERVES 4   **PREP** 20 MINS   **COOK** 30 MINS

This hearty, creamy soup with delicate white fish and meaty prawns is a meal in itself.

25g (scant 1oz) butter
1 onion, finely chopped
salt and freshly ground black pepper
200g (7oz) smoked pancetta, chopped, or smoked bacon bits
1 bay leaf
3 medium waxy potatoes, such as Charlotte or Maris Peer, peeled and cut into bite-sized pieces
2 tbsp rice flour

1 large glass of dry white wine
300ml (10fl oz) single cream
600ml (1 pint) hot gluten-free fish or vegetable stock (see page 115)
400g can sweetcorn, drained and rinsed
350g (12oz) smoked, undyed haddock, skinned and roughly chopped
250g (9oz) raw, shelled prawns

1 Heat the butter in a large pan, add the onion, and season. Cook on a low heat for 2–3 minutes until softened, then increase the heat a little, add the pancetta and bay leaf, and cook for 4–5 minutes.

2 Turn the heat down, add the potatoes, and stir well to coat with the juices. Tip in the flour and mix thoroughly. Add the wine, increase the heat, and let the wine bubble for 1–2 minutes, stirring occasionally. Stir in the cream and stock, and bring to the boil.

3 Reduce the heat, add the sweetcorn, and simmer gently for about 15 minutes or until the potatoes are cooked. Add the haddock and prawns, cover with a lid, and cook for 4–6 minutes until the fish is just turning opaque and the prawns are pink. Taste and season if necessary.

COOK'S TIP
The secret to a good chowder lies in not overcooking the fish. It will be ready in minutes and will continue cooking in the hot stock once taken off the hob.

STATISTICS PER SERVING

Energy 693kcals/2908kJ

Protein 44g

Fat 33.5g
Saturated fat 17g

Carbohydrate 43g
Sugar 10g

Fibre 3.5g

Salt 3g

ASIAN CRAB AND NOODLE SOUP

SERVES 4　　**PREP** 15 MINS　　**COOK** 30 MINS
PLUS CHILLING

Prepare this soup a day in advance to allow the flavours
to develop, then add the noodles and crab before serving.

1 tbsp sunflower oil
1 bunch of spring onions,
　sliced at an angle
1–2 red chillies, deseeded and
　finely chopped
1–2 garlic cloves, finely chopped
3 carrots, sliced at an angle
326g can sweetcorn, drained
salt and freshly ground black pepper

2 tbsp tamari (gluten-free soy sauce)
750ml (1¼ pints) hot gluten-free
　vegetable stock (see page 115)
100g (3½oz) dried fine rice noodles
400g (14oz) white crab meat
small bunch of chives, finely chopped
small bunch of fresh coriander,
　roughly chopped (see Cook's tip)

1　Heat the oil in a large pan and swirl it around. Add the spring onions
and cook over a medium heat for 1 minute until softened. Add the chilli,
garlic, carrots, and sweetcorn. Stir and season with salt and pepper.

2　Add the tamari and stir it around so everything gets coated, then add
a little of the stock and bring to the boil. Add the rest of the stock, bring to
the boil again, partially cover with a lid, reduce to a simmer, and gently cook
over a low heat for 15–20 minutes or until the carrots are soft. Set aside to
cool, then chill overnight in the fridge to allow the flavours to develop.

3　Place the noodles in a large bowl and pour over enough boiling water
to cover. Leave to soak according to pack instructions, then drain.

4　Gently warm the soup, add the noodles, and stir through the crab meat
and half the herbs until piping hot. Ladle the soup into bowls and sprinkle
with the remaining herbs to serve.

STATISTICS PER SERVING

Energy 369kcals/1550kJ

Protein 24g

Fat 9.5g

Saturated fat 1g

Carbohydrate 44g

Sugar 13g

Fibre 4g

Salt 3g

COOK'S TIP

As well as the leaves, use the coriander stalks, which are full of flavour and give
a much more distinctive taste than the leaves alone.

CHINESE CHICKEN SOUP WITH PRAWN DUMPLINGS

GUIDELINES PER SERVING

●○○ CALORIES

●○○ SATURATED FAT

●●● SALT

SERVES 4   **PREP** 20 MINS   **COOK** 50 MINS

If you don't have time to make dumplings, simply chop the prawns and stir them straight into the soup.

2 large chicken breasts, skinless
salt and freshly ground black pepper
5 spring onions, sliced at an angle
5cm (2in) piece of fresh root ginger,
  peeled and sliced into matchsticks
1–2 tbsp tamari (gluten-free soy sauce)
½–1 red chilli, thinly sliced at an angle
150g (5½oz) shiitake mushrooms, sliced
125g (4½oz) cooked rice

For the dumplings
350g (12oz) prawns, cooked and peeled
5cm (2in) piece of fresh root ginger,
  peeled and roughly chopped
1 red chilli, deseeded, finely chopped
small handful of coriander leaves,
  plus extra to garnish
2 tsp gluten-free nam pla (fish sauce)
2 tbsp cornflour, plus extra for rolling

1 For the stock, pour 1.5 litres (2¾ pints) water into a large pan and add the chicken breasts and seasoning. Bring to a steady simmer and cook on a low-medium heat, partially covered, for 15–20 minutes until the chicken is cooked. Remove with a slotted spoon and set aside to cool. Strain the stock into a clean pan; you will need about 1.2 litres (2 pints). Shred the chicken and set aside.

2 For the dumplings, place all the ingredients in a food processor, season, and pulse until minced. Scoop up small handfuls and roll into balls; you may need more cornflour. Place the dumplings on a plate and chill in the fridge.

3 Heat the stock over a low-medium heat, add the spring onions, ginger, tamari, chilli, and the mushrooms, and cook for about 20 minutes. Taste and adjust the seasoning as needed.

4 Stir in the rice and shredded chicken and simmer gently for 2 minutes. Add the dumplings, cover, and cook for about 5–8 minutes. Ladle into bowls and top with coriander leaves to serve.

STATISTICS PER SERVING

Energy 250kcals/1047kJ

Protein 36g

Fat 2g
Saturated fat 0.5g

Carbohydrate 19g
Sugar 1g

Fibre 0.9g

Salt 2.5g

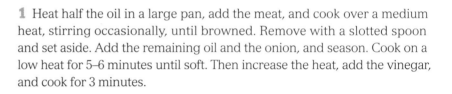

⬤◯◯ CALORIES

⬤⬤◯ SATURATED FAT

⬤◯◯ SALT

RICH BEEF AND QUINOA SOUP

SERVES 4 **PREP** 20 MINS **COOK** 1 HOUR 20 MINS–1 HOUR 50 MINS
FREEZE 3 MONTHS

A filling soup with a splash of heat that makes an ideal family supper. Go easy on the Tabasco if you prefer it mild.

2 tbsp olive oil
675g (1½lb) braising steak, cut into
   small pieces (see Cook's tip)
1 onion, finely chopped
salt and freshly ground black pepper
1 tbsp white wine vinegar
400g can chopped tomatoes

750ml (1¼ pints) hot gluten-free
   vegetable stock (see page 115)
good splash of smoked or regular
   Tabasco sauce, plus extra for
   serving (optional)
pinch of dried oregano
100g (3½oz) quinoa

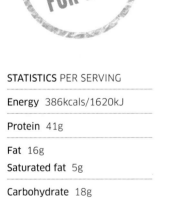

GREAT FOR KIDS

1 Heat half the oil in a large pan, add the meat, and cook over a medium heat, stirring occasionally, until browned. Remove with a slotted spoon and set aside. Add the remaining oil and the onion, and season. Cook on a low heat for 5–6 minutes until soft. Then increase the heat, add the vinegar, and cook for 3 minutes.

2 Return the meat to the pan with the tomatoes, stock, Tabasco, and oregano. Cover and simmer gently for 1–1½ hours or until the beef is tender, topping up with a little hot water if needed.

3 While the soup is cooking, prepare the quinoa according to pack instructions and set aside.

4 Taste the soup and season if necessary. Transfer to a food processor and whizz to form a thick purée, retaining some texture. Return the soup to a clean pan, stir in the quinoa, and gently heat through until piping hot. Serve with a splash of Tabasco sauce, if you like.

COOK'S TIP
Any stewing steak will work well in this recipe – look out for the best offer at your supermarket or butcher.

STATISTICS PER SERVING

Energy 386kcals/1620kJ

Protein 41g

Fat 16g
Saturated fat 5g

Carbohydrate 18g
Sugar 6g

Fibre 1g

Salt 0.4g

MOROCCAN HARIRA SOUP

SERVES 4   PREP 20 MINS   COOK 1 HOUR 20 MINS   FREEZE 1 MONTH

This rich, main-course soup is traditionally eaten to break the fast during the Muslim holy month of Ramadan.

GUIDELINES PER SERVING

⬤⬤◯ CALORIES

⬤⬤◯ SATURATED FAT

⬤◯◯ SALT

1 tbsp olive oil
1 onion, finely chopped
500g (1lb 2oz) stewing lamb,
  finely chopped
salt and freshly ground black pepper
1 tbsp garam masala
1 tsp turmeric
1 tbsp dried mint

1 tbsp tomato purée
750ml (1¼ pints) hot gluten-free
  vegetable stock (see page 115)
400g can chickpeas, drained
  and rinsed
100g (3½oz) dried fine rice noodles
lemon wedges and fresh mint leaves,
  to serve

1 Heat the oil in a large pan, add the onion, and cook on a low heat for 5–6 minutes until soft. Add the lamb, raise the heat a little, and cook for 10 minutes until the lamb takes on some colour. Season and stir through the garam masala, turmeric, and dried mint, then cook for 1 minute.

2 Stir through the tomato purée and a little of the stock. Bring to the boil and stir to get any bits up from the bottom of the pan, add the rest of the stock, and boil again. Reduce to a simmer, add the chickpeas, and cook, partially covered, on a gentle heat for 1 hour or until the lamb is tender. Top up with hot water, if required. Meanwhile, place the noodles in a bowl and cover with hot water, according to pack instructions. Drain and set aside.

3 Taste the soup and adjust the seasoning, then transfer to a food processor and whizz briefly just to break it up, but leave plenty of texture; you can omit this step and leave chunks, if preferred. Return to a clean pan, stir through the noodles, and heat until piping hot. Ladle into bowls, top with fresh mint leaves, and serve with lemon wedges.

COOK'S TIP
You could use leftover roast lamb for this soup: simply shred it and add to the soup just before processing.

STATISTICS PER SERVING

Energy 413kcals/1730kJ

Protein 33g

Fat 16g
Saturated fat 5g

Carbohydrate 32g
Sugar 2g

Fibre 4g

Salt 0.6g

QUINOA SALAD WITH MANGO, LIME, AND TOASTED COCONUT

SERVES 4   **PREP** 15 MINS   **COOK** 10 MINS

A healthy salad full of big, tropical flavours and bright colours. Try to get Alphonso mangoes, if possible, which are famed for their sweetness.

50g (1¾oz) desiccated or
  flaked coconut
300g (10oz) quinoa
400g can butter beans, drained
  and rinsed
½ red onion, finely chopped
1 large mango, peeled, stoned, and cut
  into bite-sized pieces
1 lime, peeled, segmented, and
  segments halved

handful of mint, finely chopped
handful of flat-leaf parsley,
  finely chopped

For the dressing
3 tbsp olive oil
1 tbsp white wine vinegar
pinch of sugar
salt and freshly ground black pepper

NUTRIENT BOOST

Mango is an excellent source of betacarotene.

1 Toast the coconut by dry frying it in a pan over a medium heat for 2–3 minutes until golden, stirring so that it doesn't burn. Remove from the heat and allow to cool.

2 To make the dressing, place all the ingredients in a small bowl or jug and whisk. Taste and adjust the seasoning as needed.

3 Cook the quinoa according to pack instructions. Drain well and tip into a large serving bowl. While the quinoa is still warm, stir through the butter beans, onion, mango, lime, mint, and parsley, and season.

4 Pour over the dressing and stir well. Sprinkle the toasted coconut on top and serve immediately.

STATISTICS PER SERVING

Energy 460kcals/1935kJ

Protein 15g

Fat 20g
Saturated fat 8g

Carbohydrate 54g
Sugar 12.5g

Fibre 7.5g

Salt 0.8g

⬤◯◯ CALORIES

⬤◯◯ SATURATED FAT

⬤◯◯ SALT

QUINOA, BROAD BEAN, AND DILL SALAD

SERVES 4   **PREP** 15 MINS   **COOK** 20 MINS

If possible, prepare this salad at least an hour in advance so that the flavours have time to develop.

200g (7oz) quinoa
250g (9oz) broad beans, fresh
  or frozen, shelled weight
salt and freshly ground black pepper
1 tbsp olive oil
3 small courgettes, trimmed, halved
  lengthways, and chopped

2 garlic cloves, finely chopped
pinch of dried chilli flakes
zest and juice of 1 lemon
handful of sultanas (optional)
bunch of dill, finely chopped
1 tbsp fruity extra virgin olive oil
gluten-free bread, to serve

1 Put the quinoa in a pan, cover with water, bring to the boil, and cook according to pack instructions. Drain well, rinse under cold running water, and transfer to a large serving dish.

2 Cook the broad beans in a pan of boiling salted water for 2 minutes, until tender. Drain and rinse under cold water. If using fresh beans, peel the outer skin of any larger than your thumbnail. Add to the quinoa in the serving dish.

3 Heat the olive oil in a large frying pan, add the courgettes, and season well. Stir in the garlic, chilli flakes, and lemon zest, and cook on a medium heat for 5–6 minutes until golden. Stir the courgettes into the quinoa and beans. Add the sultanas (if using) and dill, and mix well. Add the lemon juice and extra virgin olive oil. Taste and season, if necessary. Serve with some gluten-free bread.

STATISTICS PER SERVING

Energy 290kcals/1215kJ

Protein 12g

Fat 9g
Saturated fat 1g

Carbohydrate 40g
Sugar 13g

Fibre 6g

Salt trace

PANZANELLA

SERVES 4 **PREP** 10 MINS

This classic Italian salad combines torn bread tossed with fresh tomatoes and basil.

GUIDELINES PER SERVING

● ○ ○ CALORIES

● ○ ○ SATURATED FAT

● ● ○ SALT

GREAT FOR KIDS

8 slices of gluten-free white bread, preferably home-made (see page 38), crusts removed
handful of basil leaves, torn
extra virgin olive oil, for drizzling
1–2 tbsp balsamic vinegar
sea salt and freshly ground black pepper
5 tomatoes, skinned and roughly chopped (see Cook's tip)
handful of pitted black olives

1 Tear the bread into chunky pieces and sit them in a bowl. Cover with a little cold water and leave to soak for 2 minutes. Remove and squeeze away any excess water, then place in a serving bowl.

2 Add the basil leaves and a drizzle of olive oil. Sprinkle balsamic vinegar to taste, and season well.

3 When ready to serve, add the tomatoes and olives, and toss together well. Season to taste and drizzle over more oil if required.

COOK'S TIP
Use firm tomatoes for this salad. It's best made in the summer when full-flavoured tomatoes are plentiful.

Golden Queen tomatoes »
To add extra visual appeal, look out for colourful varieties of tomatoes, such as Golden Queen. Yellow tomatoes tend to have a milder flavour, however, so mix with the stronger-tasting red varieties.

STATISTICS PER SERVING

Energy 225kcals/953kJ

Protein 7g

Fat 6g
Saturated fat 1g

Carbohydrate 37g
Sugar 6g

Fibre 3.5g

Salt 1g

⬤◯◯ CALORIES

⬤◯◯ SATURATED FAT

⬤◯◯ SALT

FATTOUSH WITH CORN TORTILLAS

SERVES 4   **PREP** 20 MINS   **COOK** 10 MINS

This salad is based on the Lebanese dish fattoush, which means "moistened bread" – and this is what you should aim for, rather than letting it turn soggy!

4 corn tortillas (see page 233)
½ tbsp olive oil, for greasing
6 flavoursome tomatoes, quartered
½ cucumber, halved lengthways,
  seeds removed, and chopped
1 small red onion, finely chopped
small bunch of flat-leaf parsley,
  leaves only, roughly chopped
small bunch of mint, leaves only,
  roughly chopped

For the dressing
3 tbsp extra virgin olive oil
juice of ½ lemon
2 garlic cloves, finely chopped
salt and freshly ground black pepper
3 tsp sumac (optional)

1 Preheat the oven to 200°C (400°F/Gas 6). Cut each tortilla into 4 triangles, then divide the pieces between 2 lightly oiled baking sheets. Bake for about 5–10 minutes until they begin to turn golden. Remove and set aside.

2 To make the dressing, place all the ingredients in a bowl and whisk. Season to taste and set aside.

3 Place the tomatoes, cucumber, onion, and herbs in a serving bowl. Drizzle over the dressing and toss gently with your hands. Add the tortilla pieces, toss once more, and serve immediately.

STATISTICS PER SERVING

Energy 281kcals/1182kJ

Protein 6g

Fat 11g
Saturated fat 1.5g

Carbohydrate 40g
Sugar 7g

Fibre 5g

Salt 0.5g

« Sumac
Sumac is a spice derived from the fruit of a shrub native to the Middle East, where its pleasantly tart taste is used in cooking to bring out other flavours, much like salt.

TUNA AND VEGETABLE PASTA SALAD

GUIDELINES PER SERVING

● ● ○ CALORIES

● ○ ○ SATURATED FAT

● ● ○ SALT

SERVES 4   **PREP** 15 MINS   **COOK** 10–15 MINS

Tuna and green beans mix well with pasta in this simple salad. The addition of artichokes makes it extra special.

150g (5½oz) green beans
salt and freshly ground black pepper
250g (9oz) gluten-free pasta shapes
  (shop-bought or see pages 42–3)
150g (5½oz) cherry tomatoes, halved
8 artichoke halves in oil, drained
  and halved

75g (2½oz) pitted green olives, sliced
juice of ½ lemon
2 x 120g cans tuna in oil, drained
  and roughly flaked
extra virgin olive oil, for drizzling
gluten-free bread, to serve

1 Place the beans in a pan of boiling salted water and cook for about 5 minutes until tender. Drain, refresh in cold water, and drain again. Cut each bean into 3 pieces and set aside.

2 Cook the pasta in a large pan of boiling salted water according to instructions. Drain and return to the pan with a little of the cooking water.

3 Place the pasta and beans in a serving bowl, add the tomatoes, artichokes, olives, and lemon juice, and toss together. Add the tuna, drizzle with olive oil, and season to taste with salt and pepper. Serve with some gluten-free bread.

COOK'S TIP

Refreshing the beans in cold water just after cooking helps retain their vibrant colour and keeps them crisp by halting the cooking process.

STATISTICS PER SERVING

Energy 420kcals/1768kJ

Protein 23g

Fat 15g
Saturated fat 2g

Carbohydrate 46g
Sugar 4g

Fibre 5g

Salt 1.2g

GREAT FOR KIDS

SOBA NOODLE AND PRAWN SALAD

SERVES 4   **PREP** 15 MINS   **COOK** 25 MINS

Nutty-flavoured soba noodles are here teamed with Tiger prawns and drizzled with an orange and ginger dressing.

200g (7oz) soba noodles
  (see Cook's tip)
salt and freshly ground black pepper
1 tbsp sunflower oil
250g (9oz) raw Tiger prawns, shelled
  and tails removed
300g (10oz) frozen soya beans
4 spring onions, finely chopped
1 red chilli, deseeded and finely sliced
handful of fresh coriander leaves,
  roughly chopped

handful of mint leaves,
  roughly chopped

For the dressing
juice of 1 orange
5cm (2in) piece fresh root ginger,
  peeled and grated
1 tbsp tamari (gluten-free soy sauce)
2 garlic cloves, grated
pinch of sugar

NUTRiENT BOOST
Soya beans provide fibre, protein, and useful amounts of iron and folate.

STATISTICS PER SERVING

Energy 396kcals/1670kJ

Protein 27g

Fat 12g
Saturated fat 1.5g

Carbohydrate 45g
Sugar 5g

Fibre 4g

Salt 1.2g

1 Place the noodles in a large pan of boiling salted water and cook according to pack instructions. Drain well and transfer to a serving dish. In a bowl, whisk all the dressing ingredients together. Season, taste, and adjust as needed. Set aside.

2 Heat the oil in a frying pan, add the prawns, and season. Cook on a fairly high heat for 3–4 minutes or until the prawns are pink. Remove with a slotted spoon and leave to cool slightly. Slice them in half lengthways and add to the noodles.

3 Place the soya beans in a medium pan of boiling salted water and cook for 3–5 minutes until tender. Drain and refresh in cold water. Add the beans, spring onions, and chilli to the serving bowl along with half the herbs. Drizzle over the dressing and toss, so everything gets coated. Sprinkle over the remaining herbs and serve.

COOK'S TIP
Soba noodles are a naturally gluten-free Japanese noodle made from buckwheat.

SPINACH AND PINE NUT SALAD

SERVES 4   **PREP** 15 MINS   **COOK** 10 MINS

Crispy breadcrumbs and toasted nuts top this leafy salad. Good on its own or as a side dish to accompany grilled lamb cutlets.

250g (9oz) baby spinach leaves
handful of juicy raisins (optional)
100g (3½oz) SunBlush tomatoes,
   roughly chopped
50g (1¾oz) pine nuts, toasted

For the dressing
3 tbsp extra virgin olive oil
1 tbsp orange juice

pinch of sugar
salt and freshly ground black pepper

For the breadcrumb topping
2–3 slices of gluten-free bread
   (see page 38), torn
pinch of dried chilli flakes

NUTRIENT BOOST
Spinach is rich in betacarotene, which the body converts into vitamin A.

1 For the dressing, mix the ingredients together in a bowl, taste, and adjust the seasoning as needed. Set aside. Preheat the oven to 200°C (400°F/Gas 6).

2 For the breadcrumb topping, put the bread in a food processor and whizz to form crumbs. Tip the crumbs into a roasting tin and bake for 5–10 minutes or until golden. Don't let them brown. Stir the chilli flakes and salt and pepper into the crumbs. Set aside.

3 To assemble the salad, pour the dressing into a large salad bowl and swirl it around. Add the spinach leaves and shake so they get coated. Add the raisins (if using) and SunBlush tomatoes and toss gently. Top with the pine nuts, sprinkle over the breadcrumbs, and serve.

COOK'S TIP
For a more substantial salad, add some cheese: Parmesan shavings, crumbled feta, or torn buffalo mozzarella all work well.

STATISTICS PER SERVING

Energy 270kcals/1124kJ

Protein 6g

Fat 19g
Saturated fat 2g

Carbohydrate 17.5g
Sugar 9.5g

Fibre 4g

Salt 0.8g

● ● ○ CALORIES

● ● ○ SATURATED FAT

● ○ ○ SALT

CHICKPEA, RED RICE, AND ARTICHOKE SALAD

SERVES 4 **PREP** 10 MINS **COOK** 35 MINS

A substantial main meal salad, it's also good as a side dish to accompany grilled or barbecued salmon or chicken.

400g (14oz) Camargue red rice
400g can chickpeas, drained
 and rinsed
280g jar roasted artichokes, drained
1 red chilli, deseeded and
 finely chopped
handful of fresh coriander,
 finely chopped
handful of flat-leaf parsley,
 finely chopped
2 tbsp pine nuts, toasted
75g (2½oz) feta cheese, crumbled

**For the coriander and
orange dressing**
6 tbsp extra virgin olive oil
2 tbsp white wine vinegar
juice of 1 large orange
1½ tsp coriander seeds,
 lightly crushed
1 tsp Dijon mustard
pinch of sugar
salt and freshly ground black pepper

NUTRIENT BOOST
Soluble fibre in chickpeas helps balance blood sugar and reduce cholesterol.

1 For the dressing, place all the ingredients in a small bowl or jug and mix well. Taste and adjust the seasoning as required.

2 Place the rice in a large pan of salted water and cook according to pack instructions until tender. Drain well and transfer to a serving bowl.

3 While the rice is still warm, stir through the chickpeas, artichokes, chilli, and herbs, and mix well. Pour the dressing over the rice mixture and toss together. Taste and adjust the seasoning. Top with the pine nuts and feta cheese and serve.

STATISTICS PER SERVING

Energy 710kcals/2958kJ

Protein 17g

Fat 28g
Saturated fat 5.5g

Carbohydrate 90g

Sugar 7g

Fibre 5g

Salt 1.3g

COOK'S TIP
Camargue red rice has a slightly nutty taste. You can also use half Camargue rice and half basmati rice.

⬤◯◯ CALORIES

⬤⬤⬤ SATURATED FAT

⬤⬤◯ SALT

NUTRiENT BOOST
Beetroot helps produce nitric oxide in the body, which can lower blood pressure.

BEETROOT AND HAZELNUT SALAD WITH BLUE CHEESE

SERVES 4   **PREP** 15 MINS   **COOK** 1 HOUR

A mix of earthy flavours and a classic combination of blue cheese and nuts makes this a substantial salad.

500g (1lb 2oz) beetroot, trimmed
few sprigs of thyme
2 tbsp olive oil
2 red onions, thickly sliced into rings
150g (5½oz) salad leaves, such as
  lamb's lettuce, watercress, or rocket
sea salt and freshly ground
  black pepper
50g (1¾oz) hazelnuts, toasted
  and roughly chopped

100g (3½oz) Gorgonzola
  cheese, crumbled
gluten-free bread, to serve

For the dressing
3 tbsp extra virgin olive oil
1 tbsp white wine vinegar

1 Preheat the oven to 200°C (400°F/Gas 6). Line a roasting tin with foil, then add the beetroot, thyme, and half the oil. Mix with your hands, so that the beetroot is coated. Bring the ends of the foil together to form a sealed packet, and roast for 40 minutes until the beetroot is tender when pierced with a knife. Unwrap the beetroot, add the onions and the remaining oil, seal the foil again, and cook for another 20 minutes. Remove, leave to cool, then peel away the skin from the beetroot, and slice into quarters.

2 For the dressing, whisk together the oil and vinegar, and season.

3 Place the salad leaves on a serving plate or large shallow bowl and top with the beetroot and onion mix. Sprinkle with salt and pepper, then scatter over the hazelnuts and cheese. Spoon over a little dressing, leaving some on the side for people to help themselves, and serve with gluten-free bread.

COOK'S TIP
Try swapping the Gorgonzola for a mild Stilton or some slightly warmed slices of goat's cheese.

STATISTICS PER SERVING

Energy 370kcals/1525kJ

Protein 10g

Fat 30g
Saturated fat 8g

Carbohydrate 14g
Sugar 12g

Fibre 6g

Salt 1.2g

CHORIZO AND WATERCRESS SALAD

SERVES 4   **PREP** 20 MINS   **COOK** 15-20 MINS

This warm salad makes a light main meal or hearty lunch, with lots of gutsy flavours on a bed of fresh leaves.

400g (14oz) baby new potatoes
250g (9oz) gluten-free cooking
  chorizo sausages, roughly chopped
leaves from a few sprigs of thyme
175g (6oz) watercress,
  thick stalks removed
½ red onion, finely diced

For the dressing
3 tbsp olive oil
1 tbsp white wine vinegar
juice of 1 orange
leaves from a few sprigs of thyme
pinch of sugar
salt and freshly ground black pepper

1 Place all the dressing ingredients in a jug, whisk well to combine, and set aside.

2 Cook the baby potatoes in a pan of boiling salted water for about 15–20 minutes until tender when pierced with a knife. Drain well, and halve any large ones. Set aside.

3 Meanwhile, place the chorizo in a large frying pan and cook over a medium heat for 5–6 minutes or until just turning golden brown on both sides. Sprinkle over the thyme leaves and fry for 1 minute. Remove with a slotted spoon and drain on kitchen paper.

4 Tip the watercress into a large shallow bowl, add the potatoes and chorizo, toss them together, sprinkle over the onion, and spoon over a little of the dressing, leaving some on the side for people to help themselves.

NUTRiENT BOOST
"Superfood" watercress is full of vitamins B and C, iron, and phytochemicals.

STATISTICS PER SERVING

Energy 352kcals/1468kJ

Protein 14.5g

Fat 23g
Saturated fat 7.5g

Carbohydrate 20.5g
Sugar 6.5g

Fibre 2.5g

Salt 0.9g

Chorizo sausage »
This Spanish delicacy is usually made with pork and always generously seasoned with paprika. Look for the uncured cooking chorizo, or *chorizo fresco*, for this recipe.

PASTA, NOODLES, AND RICE

● ○ ○ CALORIES

● ○ ○ SATURATED FAT

● ○ ○ SALT

LEMON AND ASPARAGUS PASTA

SERVES 4   **PREP** 5 MINS   **COOK** 10-12 MINS

Try to get the freshest new season asparagus for this simple supper dish.

250g (9oz) asparagus, trimmed
  and halved
90ml (3fl oz) olive oil
salt and freshly ground black pepper
350g (12oz) gluten-free tagliatelle
  (shop-bought or see pages 42-3)
2 garlic cloves, crushed
zest and juice of 1 large lemon

1 red chilli, deseeded and
  finely chopped
½ tsp freshly grated nutmeg
3 tbsp finely chopped flat-leaf parsley
freshly grated Parmesan cheese,
  to serve

SPECIAL EQUIPMENT griddle pan

1 Bring a small pan of salted water to the boil. Blanch the asparagus in the boiling water for 2 minutes. Drain and refresh in cold water.

2 Place a griddle pan on the hob to heat up. Drizzle the blanched asparagus with a little of the olive oil and season well with salt and pepper. Cook the asparagus on the hot griddle for 5–6 minutes, turning it occasionally until chargrilled. Set aside.

3 Bring a large pan of salted water to the boil. Add the pasta to the pan and cook according to instructions, giving it a stir at the beginning to prevent it from sticking together.

4 Heat the remaining olive oil in a large frying pan and add the garlic, lemon zest, and chilli. Sauté for 30 seconds, then add the lemon juice, plenty of black pepper, and the nutmeg. Remove from the heat.

5 Drain the pasta and add it to the frying pan along with the asparagus and parsley. Toss well to mix. Divide between plates and serve sprinkled with Parmesan cheese.

STATISTICS PER SERVING

Energy 420kcals/1770kJ

Protein 12g

Fat 13g
Saturated fat 2g

Carbohydrate 63g
Sugar 3g

Fibre 5g

Salt trace

PASTA GENOVESE

SERVES 4   **PREP** 10 MINS   **COOK** UP TO 12 MINS

A quick home-made pesto is tossed with linguine for this timeless classic from the Italian city of Genoa.

GUIDELINES PER SERVING

● ● ○ CALORIES

● ● ● SATURATED FAT

● ● ○ SALT

2 garlic cloves, roughly chopped
large handful of basil leaves
100g (3½oz) Parmesan cheese, finely grated
100g (3½oz) Pecorino cheese, finely grated
85g (3oz) pine nuts, toasted
salt and freshly ground black pepper

about 200ml (7fl oz) extra virgin olive oil
350g (12oz) gluten-free linguine (shop-bought or see pages 42–3)
tomato salad, to serve

SPECIAL EQUIPMENT food processor

1 To prepare the pesto, place the garlic in a food processor and whizz until minced. Then add the basil leaves, Parmesan, Pecorino, pine nuts, and seasoning, and pulse a few times until it reaches your preferred texture.

2 Slowly trickle in the olive oil, pressing the pulse button as you go, adding as much or little to get the correct consistency – avoid a sloppy pesto. Taste and season if required. Set aside. Alternatively, make the pesto in a pestle and mortar for a coarser texture.

3 Put the pasta in a large pan of boiling salted water and cook according to instructions, giving it a stir at the beginning to prevent it from sticking together. Drain well and return to the pan with a little of the cooking water. Add enough pesto to just coat and toss well. Serve with a fresh tomato salad.

COOK'S TIP
For a more substantial supper, add some cooked, chopped green beans and cooked, diced potatoes.

STATISTICS PER SERVING

Energy 658kcals/2766kJ

Protein 32g

Fat 31g
Saturated fat 11g

Carbohydrate 63g
Sugar 3g

Fibre 4g

Salt 1g

RICOTTA AND SQUASH RAVIOLI

SERVES 4   **PREP** 30 MINS   **COOK** 50-55 MINS   **FREEZE** 1 MONTH
PLUS CHILLING

Make the ravioli a day in advance. Dust them with polenta, place them on a tray covered with cling film, and chill.

175g (6oz) butternut squash, peeled, deseeded, and cut into 5cm (2in) cubes
1 tbsp olive oil
salt and freshly ground black pepper
85g (3oz) ricotta cheese
30g (1oz) Parmesan cheese, finely grated
1 garlic clove, crushed
½ tsp freshly grated nutmeg
350g (12oz) gluten-free pasta dough (see pages 42-3)
gluten-free plain flour, for dusting
polenta or fine cornmeal, for dusting

For the sage butter
3 tbsp olive oil
60g (2oz) butter
zest of ½ lemon
2 tsp roughly chopped sage leaves
finely grated Parmesan cheese, to serve

SPECIAL EQUIPMENT 6cm (2½in) round metal cutter

1 For the filling, preheat the oven to 200°C (400°F/Gas 6). Place the butternut cubes in a roasting tin and drizzle over the oil, 3 tablespoons water, and seasoning. Cover with foil and roast for 30–35 minutes or until tender. Transfer to a food processor and blitz until smooth. Spread in the roasting tin and leave until cold. Place the ricotta, Parmesan cheese, garlic, and nutmeg in a bowl. Stir in the butternut squash and season to taste. Chill.

Energy 640kcals/2670kJ

Protein 16g

Fat 40g
Saturated fat 15g

Carbohydrates 53g
Sugar 3g

Fibre 3g

Salt 1.2g

2 Roll out the pasta dough onto a lightly floured surface to 3mm (⅛in) thick. Cut out 64 rounds using a cutter. Top half the rounds with ½ teaspoon filling. Brush a little water around the filling and place a plain pasta round on top. Pinch the edges to seal. This will make 32 ravioli. Dust with polenta to prevent them from sticking together. Cover and chill until required.

3 Bring a large pan of salted water to the boil. Add the pasta and cook for 4–5 minutes or until al dente. For the sage butter, heat a large frying pan, add the olive oil, butter, lemon zest, and sage, and sauté for 30 seconds. Remove and add plenty of pepper. Drain the pasta in a colander, add to the frying pan, and toss well to mix. Serve sprinkled with Parmesan.

GREAT FOR KiDS

PASTA PRIMAVERA

SERVES 4   **PREP** 15 MINS   **COOK** 30 MINS

Serve this light and fresh vegetarian dish in spring, when young, tender vegetables are easily available.

200g (7oz) green beans, trimmed
1 bunch of fine asparagus, trimmed
350g (12oz) gluten-free linguine
  or other pasta shapes (shop-bought
  or see pages 42–3)
1 tbsp olive oil
3 courgettes, halved lengthways
  and chopped

salt and freshly ground black pepper
pinch of saffron threads (optional)
4 tomatoes, roughly chopped
grated Parmesan or Pecorino cheese,
  to serve

1 Place the beans in a pan of boiling salted water and cook for 4–5 minutes until tender but still with some bite. Remove with a slotted spoon (reserve the water in the pan), refresh in cold water, and roughly chop. Add the asparagus to the reserved boiling water and cook for 6–8 minutes until almost tender. Drain, refresh, and roughly chop.

2 Put the pasta in a large pan of boiling salted water and cook according to instructions. Give it a stir at the beginning of cooking to prevent it from sticking together. Drain well, return to the pan with a little of the cooking water, and toss together to combine.

3 Meanwhile, heat the oil in a large frying pan, add the courgettes, and season. Add the saffron threads (if using) and cook on a low-medium heat for about 10 minutes until the courgettes turn golden.

4 Add the beans, asparagus, and tomatoes to the frying pan. Stir and cook over a low heat for 5 minutes. Tip the vegetables into the pasta and toss to combine. Serve with the Parmesan or Pecorino and more freshly ground black pepper, if you wish.

COOK'S TIP
Swap the asparagus for frozen peas, if asparagus is not in season.

STATISTICS PER SERVING

Energy 384kcals/1629kJ

Protein 15g

Fat 5g
Saturated fat 1g

Carbohydrate 68g
Sugar 6g

Fibre 8g

Salt 0.1g

CRAB AND TOMATO PASTA

SERVES 4   **PREP** 15 MINS   **COOK** 30 MINS

Pasta absorbs wonderfully the sweet flavour of crab.
This is an easy dish for last-minute entertaining.

1 tbsp olive oil
1 onion, very finely chopped
1 celery stick, very finely chopped
1 bay leaf
salt and freshly ground black pepper
2 garlic cloves, finely chopped
1 red chilli, deseeded and
  finely chopped

100ml (3½fl oz) dry white wine
150ml (5fl oz) passata
350g (12oz) gluten-free linguine
  or other pasta shapes (shop-bought
  or see pages 42–3)
250g (9oz) fresh white crab meat
handful of flat-leaf parsley,
  finely chopped

1 Heat the oil in a large pan, add the onion, and cook over a low heat for 5–6 minutes until soft. Add the celery, bay leaf, and salt and pepper, and cook gently on a low heat, stirring, for about 10 minutes, making sure the vegetables don't brown. Stir in the garlic and chilli, and cook for another minute.

2 Raise the heat, add the wine, and let it bubble for 1 minute. Add the passata and let this bubble for 2–3 minutes. Reduce to a low heat and simmer gently for about 15 minutes.

3 Put the pasta in a large pan of boiling salted water and cook according to instructions. Give it a stir at the beginning of cooking to prevent it from sticking together. Drain and return to the pan with a little of the cooking water. Stir the crab meat into the tomato sauce and warm through. Pour the sauce over the linguine and toss to combine. Sprinkle over the parsley and serve straight away.

Fresh crab »
If buying whole crab or cooking your own crab, the white meat can be found in the central body, legs, and claws. Use a lobster or nut-cracker to break the shell and extract the flesh with a lobster pick or skewer.

STATISTICS PER SERVING

Energy 446kcals/1888kJ

Protein 23g

Fat 8g
Saturated fat 1g

Carbohydrate 66g
Sugar 3.5g

Fibre 4.5g

Salt 0.7g

SMOKED SALMON PASTA

SERVES 4   **PREP** 10 MINS   **COOK** 15 MINS

Cream cheese makes an instant and cheap pasta sauce for this easy mid-week supper dish.

350g (12oz) gluten-free linguine or
  other pasta shapes (shop-bought
  or see pages 42–3)
200g (7oz) cream cheese
250g (9oz) smoked salmon
  trimmings, chopped

2–3 sprigs of dill, finely chopped
salt and freshly ground black pepper
wild rocket leaves dressed with olive
  oil and lemon juice, to serve

1 Put the pasta in a large pan of boiling salted water and cook according to instructions. Give it a stir at the beginning of cooking to prevent it from sticking together. Drain and return to the pan with a little of the cooking water.

2 Stir the cream cheese through the pasta, so it melts to form a sauce. Add the salmon and stir again.

3 Sprinkle over the dill and season. Serve with a lightly dressed, lemony wild rocket salad.

COOK'S TIP
For a more sophisticated version, swap the cream cheese for fresh ricotta.

STATISTICS PER SERVING

Energy 636kcals/2669kJ

Protein 26g

Fat 31g
Saturated fat 16g

Carbohydrate 62g
Sugar 2g

Fibre 3.5g

Salt 2.5g

MUSHROOM AND HAM PASTA

SERVES 4   **PREP** 15 MINS   **COOK** 40 MINS

This is flavour-packed comfort food at its best, perfect for the whole family.

GUIDELINES PER SERVING

CALORIES

SATURATED FAT

SALT

300g (10oz) chestnut mushrooms
2 tbsp olive oil
1 onion, finely chopped
salt and freshly ground black pepper
2 garlic cloves, grated
3 sage leaves, finely chopped
100ml (3½fl oz) dry white wine
150ml (5fl oz) double cream

handful of finely grated Parmesan cheese, plus extra to serve
200g (7oz) good-quality, gluten-free ham, cut into bite-sized chunks
350g (12oz) gluten-free linguine or other pasta shapes (shop-bought or see pages 42–3)

1 Chop 200g (7oz) of the mushrooms into quarters and grate the remainder (see Cook's tip). Heat half the oil in a large frying pan, add the onion, and cook on a low heat for 5–6 minutes until soft. Season with salt and pepper, stir through the garlic and chopped sage, and cook for 1 more minute.

2 Add the quartered and grated mushrooms and the remaining oil, and cook over a low-medium heat, stirring occasionally. Let the mushrooms warm gently for about 10 minutes until they begin to release their juices.

3 Raise the heat, add the wine, and bubble for 2–3 minutes. Reduce the heat a little and stir through the cream. Cook for 1–2 minutes, add the Parmesan, and stir. Season to taste again if necessary. Stir in the ham and heat gently.

4 Put the pasta in a large pan of boiling salted water and cook according to instructions. Give it a stir at the beginning of cooking to prevent it from sticking together. Drain well and return to the pan with a little of the cooking water. Add the sauce to the pasta and toss gently to coat. Serve with grated Parmesan cheese.

GREAT FOR KIDS

COOK'S TIP
Grating the mushrooms really enriches the sauce – you could always add some soaked dried porcini to add further depth and richness.

STATISTICS PER SERVING

Energy 681kcals/2855kJ

Protein 26g

Fat 33g
Saturated fat 17g

Carbohydrate 65g
Sugar 4.5g

Fibre 5g

Salt 1.8g

PASTA AND MEATBALLS

SERVES 4   **PREP** 20 MINS   **COOK** 40 MINS
PLUS CHILLING

Anchovies add richness to the meatballs without giving them a "fishy" flavour. Replace the red wine with 150ml (5fl oz) gluten-free beef stock for a child-friendly version.

GREAT FOR KIDS

NUTRIENT BOOST
Lean red meat is an excellent source of iron.

1 red onion, finely chopped
300g (10oz) minced beef
pinch of dried chilli flakes
handful of flat-leaf parsley, finely chopped
3 anchovy fillets, chopped (optional)
rice flour, for dusting
2–3 tbsp olive oil
300g (10oz) gluten-free spaghetti or tagliatelle (see pages 42–3)

For the sauce
1 tbsp olive oil
1 onion, finely chopped
salt and freshly ground black pepper
1 small glass red wine
400g can chopped tomatoes
pinch of dried oregano
freshly grated Parmesan cheese, to serve

1 Place the onion, beef, chilli flakes, parsley, and anchovies (if using) in a large bowl, and mix well with your hands, so that the mixture is tightly packed. With floured hands, scoop out golf-ball sized portions and roll until neat. It should make about 12. Sit them on a baking sheet lined with parchment paper and chill in the fridge to firm up.

2 Heat a little oil in a large non-stick frying pan with a lid and add the meatballs a few at a time. Cook on a medium-high heat until browned on all sides, about 6–8 minutes. Repeat with all the meatballs, adding more oil as needed. Transfer to a plate lined with kitchen paper to drain.

3 For the sauce, use the same frying pan to heat the oil, add the onion, season, and cook over a low heat for 3–4 minutes until soft. Tip in the wine, raise the heat, and let it bubble for 2–3 minutes. Reduce to a simmer. Add the tomatoes and oregano and cook gently for 5 minutes. Add the meatballs to the sauce and cook on a low heat with the lid ajar for 20 minutes, turning occasionally and topping up with hot water, if it appears to be drying out. Cook the pasta according to instructions. Season the sauce as needed. Serve with the pasta, topped with grated Parmesan cheese.

STATISTICS PER SERVING

Energy 601kcals/2521kJ

Protein 28g

Fat 24g
Saturated fat 7.5g

Carbohydrate 61g
Sugar 8g

Fibre 5g

Salt 0.7g

● ● ○ CALORIES

● ● ● SATURATED FAT

● ○ ○ SALT

MACARONI CHEESE

GREAT FOR KiDS

SERVES 4   **PREP** 15 MINS   **COOK** 50 MINS   **FREEZE** 1 MONTH

A cheese sauce made with gluten-free flour bubbles away with pasta until golden. Raw onion is added to the mix to cut through the richness of the sauce.

350g (12oz) gluten-free macaroni
  or penne pasta
½ red onion, very finely chopped

For the cheese sauce
50g (1¾oz) butter
1 tbsp gluten-free plain flour
  or rice flour

450ml (15fl oz) milk
salt and freshly ground black pepper
1 tsp English mustard (optional)
125g (4½oz) mature Cheddar cheese,
  grated, plus an extra handful to top

1 Preheat the oven to 190°C (375°F/Gas 5). For the cheese sauce, melt the butter in a medium pan, remove it from the heat, and stir in the flour. When combined, add a splash of the milk and stir, then put the pan back on the heat and add more milk, a little at a time. Cook on a low heat, stirring constantly with a wooden spoon. When it starts to thicken slightly, switch to a balloon whisk and stir until smooth and lump-free; the sauce will not thicken as much as with regular flour. Season well, then stir in the mustard (if using) and the cheese until it melts. Remove from the heat and set aside.

2 Add the macaroni or penne to a large pan of boiling salted water, stir, and cook for 12 minutes or as per pack instructions. Drain and return to the pan with a little of the cooking water.

3 Transfer the macaroni to a baking dish, add the onion, mix, and season to taste with pepper. Pour over the cheese sauce and turn to coat, then sprinkle more cheese over the top. Bake for 25–30 minutes until golden and bubbling.

STATISTICS PER SERVING

Energy 631kcals/2651kJ

Protein 23g

Fat 28g
Saturated fat 17g

Carbohydrate 70g
Sugar 8g

Fibre 4g

Salt 1.3g

COOK'S TIP
To freeze, cook as per recipe and cool completely. To reheat, defrost overnight in the fridge, then reheat as portions in the microwave on high for 3 minutes, or return to room temperature, cover with foil, and bake at 180°C (350°F/Gas 4) until piping hot.

PUMPKIN, SPINACH, AND GORGONZOLA LASAGNE

SERVES 4   **PREP** 25-30 MINS   **COOK** 1-1¼ HOURS   **FREEZE** 1 MONTH

This vegetarian lasagne is rich and satisfying, with fresh sage and nutmeg bringing the flavours alive.

GUIDELINES PER SERVING

●●○ CALORIES

●●● SATURATED FAT

●●○ SALT

about 800g (1¾lb) small pumpkin or butternut squash, peeled, deseeded, and chopped into bite-sized pieces
1 tbsp olive oil
salt and freshly ground black pepper
8 sage leaves, roughly chopped
pinch of freshly grated nutmeg
pinch of dried chilli flakes (optional)
pinch of allspice
200g (7oz) spinach
10 gluten-free pre-cooked lasagne sheets (shop-bought or see pages 42–3)

125g (4½oz) Gorgonzola cheese, chopped
lightly dressed green salad, to serve

For the sauce
100g (3½oz) butter
2 tbsp gluten-free plain flour or rice flour
900ml (1½ pints) milk

SPECIAL EQUIPMENT 20 x 30cm (8 x 12in) ovenproof dish

1 Preheat the oven to 200°C (400°F/Gas 6). Place the pumpkin in a large roasting tin, add the oil and plenty of seasoning, and stir to coat; the tin must be large or the pumpkin will steam rather than roast. Sprinkle over the sage, nutmeg, chilli (if using), and allspice and stir. Roast for 20–30 minutes, stirring halfway, until golden, then remove. Stir in the spinach, which will wilt in a few minutes. Set aside. Reduce the oven temperature to 190°C (375°F/Gas 5).

2 For the sauce, melt the butter in a medium pan. Remove, add the flour, and stir. Add a little milk, stir, and return to the heat. Cook over a low heat, adding the milk and stirring with a wooden spoon. As it thickens, switch to a balloon whisk and stir to remove any lumps. Season well and set aside.

3 For the lasagne, spoon half the pumpkin mixture into the ovenproof dish. Seasoning well between each layer, add half the lasagne sheets, half the sauce, and half the Gorgonzola. Repeat to use up all the ingredients. Place on a baking tray and bake for 30–40 minutes until golden and bubbling. Serve with a lightly dressed green salad.

NUTRIENT BOOST
Spinach is a good source of vitamin K, which is important for healthy bones.

STATISTICS PER SERVING

Energy 531kcals/2221kJ

Protein 19g

Fat 30g
Saturated fat 16g

Carbohydrate 47g
Sugar 10g

Fibre 6g

Salt 1.8g

SPLIT PEA, NOODLE, AND VEGETABLE POT

SERVES 4 **PREP** 15 MINS **COOK** 1 HOUR **FREEZE** 1 MONTH

Split peas need a fair amount of seasoning to bring out their flavours, so don't skimp on the salt and pepper in this nourishing dish.

85g (3oz) dried rice noodles
1 tbsp olive oil
1 onion, finely chopped
salt and freshly ground black pepper
2 garlic cloves, finely chopped
1 tsp turmeric
1 tsp coriander seeds, crushed
3 carrots, diced

2 courgettes, diced
225g (8oz) yellow split peas, rinsed
200ml (7fl oz) coconut milk
1 litre (1¾ pints) hot gluten-free
  vegetable stock (see page 115)
large handful of fresh coriander
  leaves, roughly chopped, to garnish

NUTRiENT BOOST
Soluble fibre in split peas balances blood sugar and reduces cholesterol.

1 Soak the noodles in boiling water for 5 minutes, or as per instructions, then drain and set aside. Heat the oil in a large, heavy pan, add the onion, and cook on a low heat for 2–3 minutes. Season well with salt and pepper, stir in the garlic, turmeric, and coriander seeds, and cook for 2 minutes.

2 Add the carrots and courgettes, turn to coat, and cook for 5 minutes. Stir in the split peas, add the coconut milk, raise the heat, and bubble for 1 minute, then add the stock and bring to the boil.

3 Reduce to a simmer and cook on a low heat, partially covered, for 40–50 minutes or until the split peas begin to soften. Top up with hot water as needed; you want it to have plenty of liquid and not be all dry. For the last 5 minutes of cooking, add the noodles to heat through. Season well to taste and serve garnished with the chopped coriander.

STATISTICS PER SERVING

Energy 474kcals/1996kJ

Protein 17g

Fat 13g

Saturated fat 8g

Carbohydrate 57g

Sugar 8g

Fibre 8g

Salt 0.8g

« Fresh coriander
Coriander leaves are delicate, and high or prolonged heat diminishes their flavour, so unless using in a paste, always add right at the end of the cooking time.

THAI-STYLE AUBERGINE CURRY

SERVES 4   **PREP** 20-25 MINS   **COOK** 40 MINS

Hot, sweet, and sour flavours mingle in this subtle, light curry that is mild enough for children to enjoy.

GUIDELINES PER SERVING

● ○ ○ CALORIES

● ● ● SATURATED FAT

● ○ ○ SALT

GREAT FOR KIDS

2 tbsp sunflower oil
1 onion, finely chopped
3 garlic cloves, finely chopped
1 cinnamon stick
1 star anise
1 red chilli, deseeded and finely chopped
1 stalk of lemongrass, trimmed, outer leaves removed, and finely chopped
4 kaffir lime leaves, stems removed and leaves shredded
salt and freshly ground black pepper

4 baby aubergines, sliced into quarters lengthways, or 2 regular aubergines, roughly chopped
400ml can coconut milk
pinch of palm sugar or demerara sugar
600ml (1 pint) hot gluten-free vegetable stock (see page 115)
gluten-free nam pla (fish sauce), to taste
200g (7oz) dried rice noodles
handful of fresh coriander leaves
1 lime, cut into wedges, to serve

1 Heat half the oil in a large, heavy pan, add the onion, and cook on a low heat for 2–3 minutes. Stir in the garlic, cinnamon stick, star anise, chilli, lemongrass, and lime leaves, and season to taste. Add the remaining oil and the aubergine. Cook on a medium heat for 5 minutes or until the aubergine begins to turn slightly golden.

2 Add a little coconut milk, sprinkle in the sugar, stir, and bring to the boil. Add the remaining coconut and the stock, and bring to the boil. Reduce the heat, add a splash of nam pla, and simmer, uncovered, for 20 minutes. In a separate bowl, cook the noodles according to instructions. Drain.

3 Taste the curry and add more nam pla or sugar if needed. Cook for 1 minute. Remove the star anise and cinnamon stick, add half the coriander, and stir. Divide the noodles between 4 bowls, ladle over the curry, top with the remaining coriander, and serve with the lime wedges.

COOK'S TIP
Kaffir lime leaves can be found in Asian supermarkets. Fresh leaves can be frozen and used straight from the freezer, or buy them dried in jars.

STATISTICS PER SERVING

Energy 464kcals/1940kJ

Protein 6.5g

Fat 23g

Saturated fat 16g

Carbohydrate 46g

Sugar 3g

Fibre 2.5g

Salt 0.7g

GREAT FOR KiDS

MEE GORENG

SERVES 4   **PREP** 25–30 MINS   **COOK** 20 MINS

This classic Malaysian dish is traditionally made with wheat egg noodles but works just as well with rice noodles.

4 garlic cloves, roughly chopped
10 black peppercorns
1 red chilli, deseeded and
  roughly chopped
3 tbsp sunflower oil
225g (8oz) firm tofu, cut into cubes
  or strips
3 tbsp tamari (gluten-free soy sauce)
300ml (10fl oz) hot gluten-free
  vegetable stock (see page 115)

300g (10oz) dried vermicelli
  rice noodles
½ small, firm white cabbage,
  finely shredded
handful of beansprouts
4 spring onions, finely sliced
4 eggs, fried, to serve (optional)

SPECIAL EQUIPMENT wok or large,
  deep, non-stick frying pan

1 Grind the garlic, pepper, and chilli to a paste in a pestle and mortar, or put in a small food processor and whizz until minced. Heat the oil in a wok on a medium-high heat, add the garlic mixture, and cook for a few seconds. Add the tofu and cook for 5–8 minutes until it starts to turn golden. Add the tamari and stir carefully, then let it bubble for 2–3 minutes. Add the stock, bubble again, and cook until the mixture has reduced by half.

2 Meanwhile, sit the noodles in a bowl, cover with boiling water, and leave for 5 minutes until beginning to soften, then drain.

3 Add the cabbage to the mixture and mix quickly, then add the noodles and mix well. Add the beansprouts and spring onions, toss together, and remove from the heat. Serve hot, topped with a fried egg and more tamari, if needed.

COOK'S TIPS

Make this with chicken and prawns if you're not keen on tofu. If making for kids, add more vegetables, such as green beans or broccoli, to increase their intake.

STATISTICS PER SERVING

Energy 534kcals/2226kJ

Protein 20g

Fat 20g
Saturated fat 4g

Carbohydrate 62g
Sugar 4.5g

Fibre 2.5g

Salt 2.2g

SWEET PRAWN AND COURGETTE NOODLES

GUIDELINES PER SERVING

⬤◯◯ CALORIES

⬤◯◯ SATURATED FAT

⬤⬤◯ SALT

SERVES 4   **PREP** 20 MINS   **COOK** 25 MINS

Succulent prawns with courgettes and a little spice are all that this easy dish requires.

200g (7oz) dried rice noodles
400g (14oz) raw Tiger prawns,
  shells removed and tails on
2 tbsp olive oil
2 courgettes, sliced lengthways,
  and finely diced
sea salt and freshly ground
  black pepper
pinch of chilli flakes
3 garlic cloves, finely chopped
handful of beansprouts
handful of fresh coriander
  leaves, chopped
sesame seeds (optional)

For the marinade
1 tbsp clear honey
1 tbsp tamari (gluten-free soy sauce)
juice of 1 lime
1 red chilli, deseeded and
  finely chopped
splash of gluten-free nam pla
  (fish sauce)

1 Place the rice noodles in a bowl, cover with boiling water, and leave for 10 minutes or as per instructions. Drain, separate the strands, and set aside.

2 Mix together the marinade ingredients, season to taste, and add the prawns. Stir until combined, then set aside while you cook the courgettes.

3 Heat half the oil in a large frying pan, add the courgettes, season with salt and pepper, and add the chilli flakes. Cook on a low heat for 5–6 minutes until lightly golden, then add the garlic and cook for another minute. Stir through the beansprouts, spoon out, and set aside.

4 Heat the remaining oil in the pan, add the prawns and the marinade, and cook on a medium-high heat for about 5–6 minutes or until pink. Turn them occasionally and make sure that the honey doesn't burn. Plate up the noodles, spoon over the courgettes, and top with the prawns. Sprinkle over the coriander and sesame seeds (if using), before serving.

STATISTICS PER SERVING

Energy 327kcals/1366kJ

Protein 22g

Fat 6.5g
Saturated fat 1g

Carbohydrate 41g
Sugar 3g

Fibre 0.7g

Salt 1.9g

SPICED NOODLES WITH AROMATIC RED SNAPPER

SERVES 4   **PREP** 15 MINS   **COOK** 25-30 MINS
PLUS MARINATING

Sambal oelek, an Indonesian hot chilli condiment, is the perfect partner for this delicate fish.

1 red snapper, filleted, skinned, and chopped into large chunks
250g (9oz) dried fine rice noodles
1 tbsp sunflower oil
bunch of spring onions, sliced
300g (10oz) French beans, trimmed and chopped
1 red pepper, deseeded and finely chopped
2 garlic cloves, finely chopped
1-2 tsp sambal oelek, or 1 chopped red chilli, or ½-1 tsp dried chilli flakes mixed with 1 tsp vegetable oil
1 tbsp tamari (gluten-free soy sauce)

handful of fresh coriander, leaves only
1 orange, peeled and segmented

For the marinade
zest and juice of 1 orange
2 tsp finely chopped thyme leaves
1 red chilli, deseeded and finely chopped
2 garlic cloves, finely chopped
1 tbsp olive oil
salt and freshly ground black pepper

SPECIAL EQUIPMENT wok or large, deep, non-stick frying pan

1 Place the fish in a shallow dish. Combine all the marinade ingredients in a jug, stir well, and pour over the fish, turning the pieces to coat. Set aside to marinate for up to 1 hour. Preheat the oven to 180°C (350°F/Gas 4). Remove the fish using a slotted spoon and place in a roasting tin. Roast for 20–25 minutes or until the fish is cooked through and turning opaque. Set aside.

2 Cover the noodles with boiling water and leave for 10 minutes or as per pack instructions. Drain. Add the oil to the wok or pan and swirl it around. Add the spring onions and cook on a medium-high heat for 2–3 minutes until soft. Add the beans and stir. Cook for about 5 minutes until they begin to soften. Stir in the pepper and garlic and cook for 2–3 minutes.

3 Add the sambal oelek and tamari. Add the noodles and toss. Cook for 3–5 minutes and transfer to a serving dish. Top with the fish and coriander. Serve with the orange segments.

STATISTICS PER SERVING

Energy 473kcals/1982kJ

Protein 35g

Fat 8g
Saturated fat 1g

Carbohydrate 59g
Sugar 11g

Fibre 4g

Salt 1g

●●○ CALORIES

●○○ SATURATED FAT

●●○ SALT

CHICKEN, CASHEW, AND CORIANDER NOODLE STIR-FRY

SERVES 4   **PREP** 20 MINS   **COOK** 20 MINS

A simple stir-fry, zinging with fresh flavours. Use the best-quality chicken you can find – it will make all the difference.

GREAT FOR KiDS

200g (7oz) dried rice noodles
3 chicken breasts, skinless, cut into
  bite-sized pieces
salt and freshly ground black pepper
1 tbsp cornflour
2 tbsp sunflower oil
2 red peppers, deseeded and
  sliced into strips
bunch of spring onions,
  sliced at an angle
5cm (2in) piece of fresh root ginger,
  peeled and grated

3 garlic cloves, grated
2 tbsp tamari (gluten-free soy sauce)
1 tbsp gluten-free mirin (Chinese rice
  wine) or dry sherry
100g (3½oz) unsalted cashew nuts,
  toasted and roughly chopped
large bunch of fresh coriander,
  finely chopped

SPECIAL EQUIPMENT wok or large, deep
  non-stick frying pan

NUTRiENT BOOST
Cashew nuts are rich in essential fatty acids and a good source of protein.

STATISTICS PER SERVING

Energy 543kcals/2268kJ

Protein 35g

Fat 19g
Saturated fat 3.5g

Carbohydrate 51g
Sugar 7g

Fibre 3g

Salt 1.5g

1 Put the rice noodles in a bowl and cover with boiling water. Leave for 10 minutes or as per instructions. Drain, separate the strands, and set aside.

2 Season the chicken and toss in the cornflour. Heat half the oil in a wok on a medium-high heat and add the chicken. Fry for 8–10 minutes or until the chicken is cooked through. Remove and set aside. Add the remaining oil and the peppers and fry for 2–3 minutes. Add the spring onions and toss the ingredients around the wok on a fairly high heat. Add the ginger and garlic and cook for another 2–3 minutes. Add the tamari and mirin or sherry and bubble for 1 minute. Add a splash of water to loosen the sauce if necessary.

3 Return the chicken to the wok, add the cashews and coriander, and stir to coat. Remove from the heat and serve with the rice noodles.

COOK'S TIP
Stir-fries require a little speed so that everything remains crisp. Have the ingredients prepped and chopped, ready to throw in.

CHICKEN CHILLI NOODLES

GUIDELINES PER SERVING

SERVES 4   **PREP** 15 MINS   **COOK** 20 MINS

⬤◯◯ CALORIES

⬤◯◯ SATURATED FAT

⬤⬤◯ SALT

The simplicity of ingredients works well in this dish. If you would like more greenery on the plate, add 200g (7oz) sugar snap peas or mangetout at the same time as the chillies.

3 chicken breasts, skinless, cut into strips
salt and freshly ground black pepper
1 tbsp cornflour
pinch of dried chilli flakes
4 tbsp sunflower oil
4 nests of dried vermicelli rice noodles
1 red chilli, deseeded and sliced into fine strips

1 green chilli, deseeded and sliced into fine strips
3 garlic cloves, grated
2 tbsp tamari (gluten-free soy sauce)
handful of basil leaves, torn

SPECIAL EQUIPMENT wok or large, deep non-stick frying pan

1 Toss the chicken in the salt and pepper, cornflour, and chilli flakes. Heat 1 tablespoon oil in a wok and swirl it around. Add the coated chicken pieces and fry on a medium-high heat for 10 minutes or until the chicken is cooked through. Remove and set aside.

2 Add the remaining oil, sit the rice noodle nests in the wok, and fry on a medium-high heat for 1–2 minutes on each side until pale golden. Remove from the wok with a slotted spatula and drain on kitchen paper.

3 Add the chillies to the wok and cook for 2–3 minutes, then add the garlic and stir. Add the tamari, bubble for a minute, return the noodles and chicken to the wok, and simmer gently for 5 minutes or until the noodles have softened. Stir through the basil and serve.

STATISTICS PER SERVING

Energy 487kcals/2036kJ

Protein 31g

Fat 12g
Saturated fat 2g

Carbohydrate 57g
Sugar 0.5g

Fibre 0g

Salt 1.5g

● ○ ○ CALORIES

● ○ ○ SATURATED FAT

● ○ ○ SALT

MINCED PORK AND NOODLES WITH CARROT PICKLE

SERVES 4   **PREP** 15 MINS   **COOK** 30 MINS

Fresh carrot pickle cuts through the richness of the pork. Omit the chilli if making this dish for children.

GREAT FOR KIDS

200g (7oz) dried rice noodles
1 tbsp olive oil
1 onion, finely chopped
salt and freshly ground black pepper
3 garlic cloves, finely chopped
2 green chillies, deseeded and
  finely chopped
pinch of dried mint
pinch of allspice
350g (12oz) minced pork meat
1 tbsp tamari (gluten-free soy sauce)

1 tsp caster sugar
green beans, lightly steamed, to serve

For the pickle
3 medium carrots
1 tbsp white wine vinegar
1-2 tsp caster sugar
handful of fresh mint leaves, finely
  chopped, plus extra to garnish
  (optional)

1 Place the noodles in a bowl, cover with boiling water, and leave for 10 minutes or as per pack instructions. Drain and set aside.

2 For the carrot pickle, peel the carrots and finely slice on the diagonal using a mandolin to make thin rounds. In a separate bowl, whisk together the vinegar and sugar and pour the mixture over the carrots. Stir in the mint leaves, season to taste, and set aside.

3 Heat the oil in a large, heavy frying pan. Add the onion and some seasoning. Fry for 2–3 minutes on a low heat, stir through the garlic, chilli, dried mint, and allspice, and cook for 1 minute.

4 Add the minced pork, increase the heat a little, and cook for 8–10 minutes, stirring occasionally, until the pork is cooked through. Stir in the tamari and sugar and cook for 1–2 minutes more. Taste and add more seasoning and tamari if needed. Spoon the pork over a bed of noodles with some carrot pickle on the side. Scatter over more chopped mint leaves for colour, if desired, and serve with steamed green beans.

STATISTICS PER SERVING

Energy 396kcals/1653kJ

Protein 20g

Fat 12g
Saturated fat 4g

Carbohydrate 48g
Sugar 9g

Fibre 3g

Salt 0.9g

SALT-AND-PEPPER BEEF NOODLES

GUIDELINES PER SERVING

○○ CALORIES

○○ SATURATED FAT

●○ SALT

SERVES 4   **PREP** 15 MINS   **COOK** 20 MINS

Succulent strips of beef are stir-fried in a Chinese-style sauce with crisp mangetout.

200g (7oz) dried rice noodles
600g (1lb 5oz) sirloin steak, thinly sliced
salt and freshly ground black pepper
1 tsp Sichuan pepper
1 tbsp sunflower oil
3 garlic cloves, finely sliced
5cm (2in) piece of fresh root ginger, peeled and finely sliced
1 green chilli, deseeded and sliced into fine strips
200g (7oz) mangetout or sugarsnap peas, sliced (optional)

3 spring onions, finely sliced, to garnish

For the sauce
2 tbsp tamari (gluten-free soy sauce)
1 tbsp gluten-free nam pla (fish sauce)
1 tbsp cornflour
1 tsp caster sugar

SPECIAL EQUIPMENT wok or large, deep non-stick frying pan

1 Place the noodles in a bowl, cover with boiling water, and leave for 10 minutes or as per pack instructions. Drain and set aside.

2 For the sauce, mix together the tamari, nam pla, cornflour, and sugar and set aside.

3 Toss the beef with the salt and pepper and Sichuan pepper. Heat the oil in a wok, add the beef, and stir-fry on a medium-high heat for 3–4 minutes or until browned all over, then remove.

4 Add the garlic, ginger, chilli, and mangetout or sugarsnap peas (if using) to the wok, adding a little more oil if needed, and stir-fry for 2 minutes on a medium-high heat. Pour in the sauce and let it bubble. Add 2–3 tablespoons water – more if it is still too thick – and let it cook for 2 more minutes. Return the beef to the wok and stir to coat, then add the noodles and stir again. Spoon out into a serving dish and top with the spring onion.

STATISTICS PER SERVING

Energy 450kcals/1884kJ

Protein 40g

Fat 10g
Saturated fat 3g

Carbohydrate 46g
Sugar 4g

Fibre 1.2g

Salt 1.9g

● ● ○ CALORIES

● ○ ○ SATURATED FAT

● ○ ○ SALT

HOT SPICED RICE WITH CHICKEN AND POMEGRANATE

SERVES 4   **PREP** 15 MINS
PLUS MARINATING   **COOK** 35-40 MINS

The heady spice mix elevates this easy chicken dish – plus it's a real feast for the eyes!

½ tsp ground cinnamon
½ tsp ground allspice
½ tsp ground cloves
½ tsp ground coriander
salt and freshly ground black pepper
juice of 1 orange
150ml (5fl oz) pomegranate juice
  (see Cook's tip)

2 garlic cloves, finely chopped
8 chicken thighs, skin on
3 courgettes, thickly sliced
300g (10oz) basmati rice
1-2 Scotch bonnet chillies, left whole
150g (5½oz) pomegranate seeds,
  or seeds from 1 pomegranate

1 Preheat the oven to 200°C (400°F/Gas 6). Mix all the spices with the salt and pepper, orange juice, pomegranate juice, and garlic. Place the chicken pieces in a roasting tin and pour over half the mixture to coat. Cover and marinate for 30 minutes, then roast in the oven for 20–25 minutes. Add the courgettes to the roasting tin and cook for another 15 minutes or until the chicken is golden and the skin begins to char slightly.

2 Meanwhile, place the rice and chillies in a pan, and top up with water so it just covers the rice. Season with salt and tip in the remaining spice mix. Cook on a medium heat with the lid ajar for 15 minutes until the rice has absorbed all the water and is just cooked. Turn off the heat, sit the lid on top, and leave for 10 minutes to steam.

3 Transfer the rice to a serving dish, top with the chicken and any juices, and the courgettes, and sprinkle with the pomegranate seeds to serve. Use Scotch bonnets for garnish, or chop and scatter over the dish for some heat.

COOK'S TIP
Make fresh pomegranate juice by squashing the seeds from 3 fresh pomegranates through a sieve. Alternatively, try pomegranate molasses for a more intense flavour.

Energy 518kcals/2174kJ

Protein 38g

Fat 8g
Saturated fat 2g

Carbohydrate 68g
Sugar 13g

Fibre 2g

Salt 0.35g

● ○ ○ CALORIES

● ○ ○ SATURATED FAT

● ○ ○ SALT

TURKISH RICE WITH YOGURT

SERVES 4   **PREP** 15 MINS   **COOK** 30 MINS

This fragrant dish of gently spiced rice with creamy yogurt can be baked in the oven or cooked on the hob.

2 tbsp olive oil
knob of butter
1 onion, very finely chopped
salt and freshly ground black pepper
2 garlic cloves, finely chopped
1 tsp sumac (see page 126)
pinch of paprika
½ tsp ground cumin
250g (9oz) mixed basmati
  and wild rice

500ml (16fl oz) hot gluten-free
  vegetable stock (see page 115)
8 tbsp Greek or plain yogurt
110g pack pomegranate seeds
few sprigs of dill, finely chopped,
  to garnish

SPECIAL EQUIPMENT heavy, lidded,
  cast-iron frying pan

1 Preheat the oven to 200°C (400°F/Gas 6). Heat the oil and butter in the frying pan, add the onion, and cook on a low heat until softened. Season, stir through the garlic and spices, and cook for a few more seconds.

2 Stir in the basmati and wild rice, ensuring it gets coated with the juices, and season again if needed. Pour over the stock, cover with a lid, and bake in the oven for 20 minutes or until the rice is soft. Check that it isn't drying out too much and top up with a little hot water if necessary.

3 Remove from the oven and leave covered for 10 minutes, then spoon over the yogurt, scatter over the pomegranate seeds and dill, and serve hot.

STATISTICS PER SERVING

Energy 349kcals/1457kJ

Protein 7.5g

Fat 10g

Saturated fat 3g

Carbohydrate 53g

Sugar 6g

Fibre 1.7g

Salt 0.2g

VARIATIONS

Some feta would be nice scattered over this. You can also make little wells in the cooked rice, crack an egg into each one, cover, and bake again for 3–4 minutes. Remove and leave covered for a further 10 minutes.

COOK'S TIP

If cooking on the hob, cook over a low heat for 20 minutes and check frequently that the rice isn't drying out.

HADDOCK AND TURMERIC RICE

SERVES 4   **PREP** 20 MINS   **COOK** 25 MINS

Children will love this kedgeree-style dish, just go easy on the garam masala – a pinch will suffice.

300g (10oz) basmati rice
salt and freshly ground black pepper
350g (12oz) undyed smoked
  haddock fillet
300ml (10fl oz) milk
1 tbsp olive oil
knob of butter
1 onion, finely chopped

2 tsp turmeric
2 tsp garam masala or mild
  curry powder
75g (2½oz) frozen peas, defrosted
4 eggs, hard boiled and halved
fresh coriander or flat-leaf parsley
  leaves, roughly chopped, lemon
  wedges, and mango chutney, to serve

1 Put the rice in a large pan and pour in enough water to cover. Season with salt and simmer gently with the lid ajar for 10–15 minutes until tender and cooked. Drain and set aside.

2 Lay the fish in a frying pan, skin-side down, and cover with milk or 300ml (10fl oz) water. Cover the pan and cook on a low heat for 4–5 minutes until the fish just begins to flake. Remove with a slotted spoon, discard the skin, and set aside, keeping warm.

3 Heat the oil and butter in a large frying pan and add the onion. Cook on a low heat for 2–3 minutes. Season to taste. Stir in the turmeric and garam masala and cook for 1–2 minutes. Stir in the rice and add the peas. On a very low heat, stir to combine and warm the peas through, then flake the fish into chunky pieces and add to the pan. Top with the eggs and season to taste. Sprinkle over the coriander or parsley and add a squeeze of lemon. Serve with mango chutney on the side.

Ground turmeric »
Turmeric imparts a slightly sweet, warm, and musky flavour, and is often used as the base spice in a curry as it binds and harmonizes the other spices.

GREAT FOR KiDS

NUTRiENT BOOST
Peas contain protein and good amounts of soluble and insoluble fibre.

STATISTICS PER SERVING

Energy 545kcals/2281kJ

Protein 34g

Fat 15g
Saturated fat 5g

Carbohydrate 64g

Sugar 6g

Fibre 1.6g

Salt 2g

NUTRIENT BOOST
Beans contain soluble fibre, which can help control blood cholesterol.

BRAZILIAN-STYLE RICE, BLACK BEANS, AND CHORIZO

SERVES 4   **PREP** 25–30 MINS   **COOK** 2 HOURS
PLUS SOAKING

Rice absorbs beautifully the flavours of cured chorizo sausage, whose smokiness deepens the fresh taste of green chilli and coriander leaves.

225g (8oz) black turtle beans or black-eyed beans, soaked overnight and refreshed with clean water
600ml (1 pint) hot gluten-free beef stock
150g (5½oz) basmati rice
2 tbsp olive oil
1 onion, finely chopped
salt and freshly ground black pepper

2 green chillies, deseeded and finely chopped
1 bay leaf
100g (3½oz) gluten-free cured chorizo sausage, roughly chopped
100g (3½oz) pancetta, cubed
handful of fresh coriander leaves, finely chopped
orange slices, to serve

1 Drain the beans and place them in a large pan, then add the beef stock and more hot water to cover if needed. Cover with a lid, bring to the boil, and cook for 10 minutes, then reduce to a simmer and cook partly covered for 1–1½ hours until the beans are soft. Take off the heat and set aside.

2 Meanwhile, cook the rice in a medium pan of boiling salted water for 10–15 minutes or as per pack instructions, drain, and set aside. Heat the oil in a large, heavy frying pan, add the onion, and season with a little salt and pepper. Cook on a low heat for 6–8 minutes, stirring so they don't brown too much. Cook until soft, then add the chilli and the bay leaf and stir. Increase the heat a little, add the chorizo and pancetta, and cook for a further 10 minutes or until golden.

3 Ladle in the beans, taking in a little of the stock too, and simmer gently for 5 minutes, then stir through the rice and the coriander. Remove the bay leaf and serve with some fresh orange slices.

STATISTICS PER SERVING

Energy 543kcals/2274kJ

Protein 25g

Fat 18g
Saturated fat 5.5g

Carbohydrate 59g
Sugar 3.5g

Fibre 7g

Salt 1.6g

LAMB AND FIG PILAF

SERVES 4   **PREP** 15 MINS   **COOK** 40 MINS

The mix of spices blends perfectly with the lamb and the fruit adds just enough sweetness to this dish.

GUIDELINES PER SERVING

●●○ CALORIES

●●○ SATURATED FAT

●○○ SALT

3 tbsp olive oil
500g (1lb 2oz) lamb leg steaks,
  cut into bite-sized pieces
salt and freshly ground black pepper
1 onion, finely chopped
2 tbsp pine nuts
200g (7oz) basmati rice
2 tomatoes, peeled and chopped

pinch of sugar
100g (3½oz) dried figs, chopped
  fairly small
1 tsp cinnamon
½ tsp allspice
handful of dill, finely chopped
handful of mint leaves, finely chopped

1 Heat half the oil in a large, heavy pan, season the lamb with salt and pepper, and cook on a medium-high heat for 10 minutes, turning the lamb halfway through so it all becomes golden. Remove with a slotted spoon and set aside.

2 Heat the remaining oil in the pan, add the onion, and cook on a low heat for 5 minutes or until just starting to turn golden. Throw in the pine nuts and cook for 2–3 minutes until they begin to colour, then stir in the rice so it gets well coated in the oil. Stir in the tomatoes and sugar and cook for a further 1–2 minutes.

3 Add the figs and pour in 400ml (14fl oz) boiling water. Season well, add the cinnamon and allspice, and stir. Cover with a lid and cook on a low heat for 10–15 minutes or until the rice is tender. Now, remove the lid, add the lamb, and cook for a further 5 minutes or until the mixture begins to thicken up. Stir through half the dill and mint and season to taste. Sprinkle with the remaining dill and mint to serve.

Peeling tomatoes »
To peel tomatoes, place them in a heatproof jug or bowl and pour on boiling water to cover completely. Count 10 seconds, drain, wait for them to cool slightly and then peel; the skins will slip away easily.

STATISTICS PER SERVING

Energy 573kcals/2392kJ

Protein 32g

Fat 24g
Saturated fat 6g

Carbohydrate 54g
Sugar 16g

Fibre 4g

Salt 0.3g

MEAT AND FISH

● ● ○ CALORIES

● ● ● SATURATED FAT

● ○ ○ SALT

SALMON EN CROÛTE

SERVES 6   **PREP** 30 MINS   **COOK** 25-30 MINS   **FREEZE** 1 MONTH
PLUS CHILLING   UNCOOKED

This classic summer dinner party dish looks impressive
and is surprisingly easy to make.

100g (3½oz) spinach leaves
salt and freshly ground black pepper
800g (1¾lb) salmon fillet, skinned
1-2 tbsp gluten-free hot horseradish
  sauce (optional)
bunch of dill, finely chopped
zest of 1 lemon

oil, for greasing
gluten-free plain flour, for dusting
400g (14oz) gluten-free rough puff
  pastry (see pages 46-7)
1 egg, lightly beaten
green beans and new potatoes,
  to serve

NUTRIENT BOOST
Try to eat at least one
serving of oily fish
each week.

1 Place the spinach in a medium pan and sprinkle over a few drops of
water, sit the pan on a low heat, cover, and cook for 2 minutes until the
spinach wilts. Drain and, when cool enough to handle, squeeze out as
much water from the leaves as possible. Set aside.

2 Season the salmon, place it between sheets of cling film and gently bash
to flatten it to about 1cm (½in) thick. Remove the top layer of the cling film
and spread the horseradish over the salmon (if using), then the spinach.
Mix the dill with the lemon zest and sprinkle evenly over the spinach.

3 Using the cling film to pull the salmon towards you, carefully roll it into
a thick roll (approximately 25 x 10cm/10 x 4in). Tighten the cling film at the
edges to form a secure roll. Chill in the refrigerator for about 1 hour.

4 Lightly oil a baking sheet. On a lightly floured surface, roll out the
pastry into a 35cm (14in) square, about 3mm (⅛in) thick. Remove the cling
film and place the salmon in the middle of the pastry, seam up (the pastry
and salmon seam should be aligned). Fold in and seal the edges with
water to form a closed parcel. Sit it on the baking sheet, sealed side down.
Brush with half the beaten egg and chill for 30 minutes. Preheat the oven
to 200°C (400°F/Gas 6). Brush with the remaining beaten egg and bake until
the pastry is cooked and golden, about 25–30 minutes. Slice and serve
with green beans and new potatoes.

STATISTICS PER SERVING

Energy 516kcals/2151kJ

Protein 32g

Fat 32g
Saturated fat 10g

Carbohydrate 23g
Sugar 1.5g

Fibre 0.5g

Salt 0.8g

⬤◯◯ CALORIES

⬤◯◯ SATURATED FAT

⬤◯◯ SALT

POLENTA FISHCAKES

GREAT FOR KiDS

SERVES 4   **PREP** 20 MINS   **COOK** 50 MINS   **FREEZE** 1 MONTH
PLUS CHILLING

Polenta makes a crunchy, gluten-free alternative to breadcrumbs for coating fishcakes.

400g (14oz) floury potatoes
400g (14oz) white fish, skin on
200ml (7fl oz) milk
1 bay leaf
knob of butter
1 onion, finely chopped
salt and freshly ground black pepper
handful of flat-leaf parsley,
  finely chopped
2 tsp capers, rinsed and chopped

2 gherkins, roughly chopped
100g (3½oz) polenta or fine cornmeal,
  to coat
leaves from a few sprigs of thyme,
  finely chopped
2 tbsp gluten-free plain flour
1 egg, lightly beaten
3-4 tbsp sunflower oil, for frying
gluten-free tartare sauce and salad,
  to serve

1 In a large pan, cook the potatoes, still in their skins, in boiling water for 20–30 minutes until soft. Drain and cool, then remove the skins and mash well. Set aside. Sit the fish in a frying pan, add the milk and the bay leaf, then cover and simmer on a gentle heat for 5 minutes until the fish begins to flake. Remove from the heat and discard the bay leaf and most of the milk; keep some back for the potato mix. Discard the skin and bones. When cool enough to handle, pull apart into chunky flakes and set aside.

2 Melt the butter in a frying pan, add the onion, season, and cook on a low heat for 5 minutes until soft. Leave to cool. In a large bowl, add the fish, potatoes, onions, parsley, capers, and gherkins, and stir gently until combined; if the mixture is stiff, add 1–2 tablespoons of the cooking milk to help bind it. Season, divide the mixture into 8 balls, and flatten into cakes.

3 Take 3 plates. Mix the polenta and the thyme and add to 1 plate, the flour to another, and the egg to a third. Dip the cakes into the flour for a light dusting, then dip in the egg, and coat in the polenta. Put on a baking tray and chill in the fridge for 20 minutes; if freezing, do so at this point. To cook, heat a little oil in a non-stick frying pan, add the cakes a few at a time, and cook on a medium heat for 3–4 minutes on each side until golden all over. Top up with oil as needed. Serve with tartare sauce and a lightly dressed mixed salad.

STATISTICS PER SERVING

Energy 409kcals/1715kJ

Protein 28g

Fat 14.5g
Saturated fat 3g

Carbohydrate 40g
Sugar 4g

Fibre 3g

Salt 0.5g

CHEESE-CRUSTED SALMON

SERVES 4   **PREP** 10 MINS   **COOK** 20 MINS

The cheesy coating adds real flavour to the salmon; it's rather like a rarebit mixture roasted with the fish and is a great way to get children to eat fish.

4 large salmon fillets, about
   150g (5½oz) each, skin on
oil, for greasing
salt and freshly ground black pepper
125g (4½oz) Cheddar cheese, grated
25g (scant 1oz) Parmesan cheese,
   grated

splash of gluten-free Worcestershire
   sauce or tamari (gluten-free soy sauce)
2 slices of gluten-free bread, whizzed
   into breadcrumbs
beetroot salad, to serve

GREAT FOR KIDS

1 Preheat the oven to 200°C (400°F/Gas 6). Sit the fish in a large, lightly oiled roasting tin, and season with salt and pepper.

2 Mix together the cheeses, Worcestershire sauce or tamari, and breadcrumbs, then spoon equal amounts onto each salmon fillet.

3 Press the mixture evenly onto the fillets to coat and bake in the oven for 20 minutes, or until the top begins to turn golden and the fish is flaky and cooked through. Cover with foil if it starts to brown too much. Remove and serve with a chopped beetroot salad.

NUTRIENT BOOST
Aim to eat 2 portions of fish a week, including an oil-rich fish like salmon.

VARIATION
Substitute the salmon for white fish, such as cod.

Salmon fillets »
Try to get large loin fillets for this dish, which are thicker than the tail. If using tail fillets you may need to reduce the baking time.

STATISTICS PER SERVING

Energy 490kcals/2046kJ

Protein 42g

Fat 30g
Saturated fat 11g

Carbohydrate 13g
Sugar 1g

Fibre 2g

Salt 1.3g

⬤⬤◯ CALORIES

⬤◯◯ SATURATED FAT

⬤◯◯ SALT

BEER-BATTERED FISH AND CHIPS

SERVES 4   **PREP** 15 MINS   **COOK** 40 MINS

A favourite classic – the batter serves as a protective casing while the fish cooks, leaving it flaky and delicate.

GREAT FOR KIDS

800g (1¾lb) potatoes, peeled and cut into thickish fingers
3 tbsp olive oil
pinch of sea salt
4 haddock or cod fillets, skin on
salt and freshly ground black pepper
juice of ½ lemon
225g (8oz) gluten-free self-raising flour, sifted, plus extra for dusting

300ml (10fl oz) gluten-free beer
vegetable oil, for frying
lemon wedges, to serve

SPECIAL EQUIPMENT deep-fat fryer (optional)

1 For the chips, preheat the oven to 200°C (400°F/Gas 6). Tip the potatoes into a large roasting tin, add the olive oil, and coat them well. Spread them out so they roast rather than steam, and sprinkle with sea salt. Cook in the oven for 30–40 minutes until golden, turning them halfway through cooking.

2 Meanwhile, season the fish, squeeze a little lemon juice over each fillet, and dust with a little flour. Place the remaining flour along with a pinch of salt to a bowl and slowly pour in the beer, whisking as you go. You may not need all the beer, as the mixture should be thick. If it is too runny, it won't stick to the fish, so stop when you reach the required consistency.

3 Fill a deep-fat fryer with the vegetable oil, or pour it into a large pan so that it is one-third full, and heat to 190°C (375°F); maintain this temperature throughout. Do not leave the pan or fryer unattended, switch off when not using, and keep a fire blanket nearby in case of fire. Hold the fish by the tail and pass it through the batter so that it's completely coated, then add it to the oil. Cook 2 fillets at a time for 2–3 minutes, turn over, and cook for a further 2–3 minutes until crisp and golden. Transfer to kitchen paper to drain and repeat with the remaining fish, keeping the finished pieces warm in a low oven. Serve with the chips and lemon wedges.

STATISTICS PER SERVING

Energy 703kcals/2955kJ

Protein 37g

Fat 26g
Saturated fat 3.5g

Carbohydrate 73g
Sugar 3.5g

Fibre 5.8g

Salt 1.3g

MONKFISH CATAPLANA

GUIDELINES PER SERVING

⬤◯◯ CALORIES

⬤◯◯ SATURATED FAT

⬤◯◯ SALT

SERVES 4   **PREP** 15 MINS   **COOK** 15 MINS

Quick and impressive, this Portuguese dish is named after the special pan used to prepare it – you can also use an ordinary, large lidded pan. Good-quality fresh fish is key.

3 tbsp olive oil
2 onions, finely chopped
4 tomatoes, chopped, or 200g can
  chopped tomatoes
500g (1lb 2oz) monkfish tail fillets,
  cut into chunky bite-sized pieces
200g (7oz) clams, well washed,
  (see below)
200g (7oz) raw shelled prawns
4 garlic cloves, finely chopped

120ml (4fl oz) dry white wine
1 tsp thyme leaves
1 bay leaf
2 tsp paprika
4 chunky slices of gluten-free bread
lemon wedges and rice, to serve

SPECIAL EQUIPMENT cataplana dish
  (optional)

1 In a large lidded pan or cataplana dish, heat the oil on a medium heat, add the onion, and cook for 2–3 minutes until beginning to soften.

2 Now add the next 9 ingredients and combine well. Cover tightly and simmer over a medium heat for 10–15 minutes until the prawns are pink, the clams have opened, and the monkfish is cooked. Taste and season if needed and carefully remove the bay leaf.

3 To serve, roughly tear 1 slice of bread into each bowl (ideally rustic-style shallow bowls), then ladle over the fish and plenty of sauce. Serve with a lemon wedge and some rice.

Clam safety »
Clams must be alive before cooking or they can be unsafe to eat. Tap any that are slightly open; throw away those clams that don't close. Also discard any that remain shut after cooking.

STATISTICS PER SERVING

Energy 393kcals/1661kJ

Protein 44.5g

Fat 11g
Saturated fat 1.5g

Carbohydrate 25g

Sugar 5g

Fibre 2.2g

Salt 1.1g

● ○ ○ CALORIES

● ○ ○ SATURATED FAT

● ○ ○ SALT

ASIAN-STYLE CRISPY FISH

SERVES 4   **PREP** 20 MINS   **COOK** 15 MINS

A medley of vegetables topped with pan-fried red mullet and seasoned with a Vietnamese-style dressing.

4 red mullet, gurnard or sea bass
  fillets, skinned
1 tbsp rice flour
1 tbsp sunflower oil

For the noodles and vegetables
250g (9oz) vermicelli rice noodles
200g (7oz) pak choi, trimmed
  and shredded
2 carrots, grated
handful of beansprouts
4 spring onions, finely sliced
handful of mint leaves, torn

handful of Thai basil leaves or
  regular basil, torn
handful of fresh coriander leaves
1 tbsp sesame seeds, to garnish

For the dressing
juice of 2 limes
2 tbsp rice wine vinegar
gluten-free nam pla (fish sauce)

SPECIAL EQUIPMENT wok or large, deep
  non-stick frying pan

1 For the dressing, mix together the lime juice and rice wine vinegar. Add the nam pla to taste, and set aside.

2 Toss the fish fillets in the rice flour, heat the oil in the wok or pan, and add them to the hot oil. Cook 2 at a time on a medium-high heat for about 4–6 minutes turning halfway until golden and crispy. Remove with a fish slice and set aside on a plate layered with kitchen paper, to drain. Repeat to cook the remaining fillets.

3 Sit the noodles in a bowl, pour over boiling water to cover, and leave for 3–4 minutes, or as per pack instructions. Drain well, separate the strands if needed, and set aside to cool. In a large bowl, place the shredded pak choi, grated carrot, and half the dressing and toss. Add the beansprouts, spring onions, and cooled noodles and toss again with the remaining dressing. Add half the herbs, toss, and transfer to a serving dish. Top with the fish fillets and sprinkle over the remaining herbs and sesame seeds.

STATISTICS PER SERVING

Energy 488kcals/2043kJ

Protein 34g

Fat 11g
Saturated fat 1g

Carbohydrate 56g
Sugar 5g

Fibre 4g

Salt 0.6g

NUTRiENT BOOST
Sweetcorn contains the phytochemical zeaxanthin for healthy eyes.

FISH TACOS

GREAT FOR KiDS

SERVES 4   **PREP** 10 MINS   **COOK** 20 MINS

Crunchy corn tacos filled with lightly sautéed vegetables and shredded roasted fish – a great gluten-free stand-by supper.

2 haddock loins or fillets, skin on
3 tbsp olive oil
salt and freshly ground black pepper
1 tsp coriander seeds, ground
1 red onion, finely chopped
2 garlic cloves, finely chopped
1 green chilli, deseeded and
 finely chopped

2 courgettes, finely chopped
200g can sweetcorn, drained
handful of flat-leaf parsley,
 finely chopped
8 crunchy corn taco shells
juice of ½ lemon or lime
smoked chipotle Tabasco sauce,
 to serve (optional)

1 Preheat the oven to 190°C (375°F/Gas 5). Sit the fish in a roasting tin, drizzle over half the oil, and rub it all over the fish, then sprinkle with salt and pepper and the coriander. Roast in the oven for 15–20 minutes or until the fish is cooked and flaky. Remove and set aside.

2 Meanwhile, heat the remaining oil in a frying pan on a low-medium heat, add the onion, and season. Cook for 3–4 minutes, stir through the garlic and chilli, and cook for a further 2–3 minutes.

3 Add the courgettes and cook for 6–8 minutes until they just begin to turn golden, but not too soft. Stir in the sweetcorn and heat through, then stir in the parsley, taste, and season again if needed. Remove the skin from the fish and discard, then flake the fish into chunky pieces. Fill the tacos with the courgette mixture, top with the flaked fish, add a squeeze of lemon or lime, and serve with a drop of smoked chipotle Tabasco sauce (if using).

STATISTICS PER SERVING

Energy 304kcals/1276kJ

Protein 18g

Fat 15g
Saturated fat 1.4g

Carbohydrate 24g
Sugar 6g

Fibre 1.8g

Salt 0.4g

« Chipotle chillies
Chipotles are smoke-dried jalapeño chillies. They give chipotle Tabasco a distinctive smoky-sweet taste that works brilliantly with these fish tacos – well worth seeking out.

CHICKEN TIKKA MASALA

SERVES 4   **PREP** 15 MINS   **COOK** 50 MINS
PLUS MARINATING

A takeaway favourite, the marinade gives this home-made version quite a kick that's softened by the creamy sauce.

4 chicken breasts, skinless, cut into 2.5cm (1in) cubes

For the marinade
4 tbsp natural yogurt
juice of ½ lemon
2 tsp ground cumin
1 tsp ground cinnamon
1-2 tsp cayenne pepper
2 tsp freshly ground black pepper
5cm (2in) piece of fresh root ginger, peeled and grated
pinch of salt

For the sauce
25g (scant 1oz) butter
1 onion, finely chopped

2 garlic cloves, grated
1 red chilli, deseeded and finely chopped
1 tsp ground cumin
2 tsp paprika
400ml (14fl oz) passata
150ml (5fl oz) double cream
salt and freshly ground black pepper
handful of fresh coriander leaves, roughly chopped
rice, to serve

SPECIAL EQUIPMENT 4 skewers; if wooden, soak for 30 minutes before use

NUTRIENT BOOST
Lycopene in tomatoes protects against certain cancers.

1 Mix all the ingredients for the marinade and transfer to a rectangular dish. Thread the chicken onto the skewers, sit them in the dish, and cover with the marinade. Then cover the dish and marinate in the fridge for 2 hours.

2 For the sauce, melt the butter in a medium pan, add the onion, and cook over a medium heat for 2–3 minutes or until soft. Add the garlic and chilli and cook for 2 minutes. Add the cumin and paprika and combine, then add the passata and the cream and simmer on a gentle heat for 20–25 minutes until it thickens. Season, add half the coriander, and stir well.

3 Remove the skewers from the marinade and cook under a medium grill for 15–20 minutes until golden brown. Remove the chicken, add to the sauce, and cook for a further 2 minutes. Garnish with the remaining coriander and serve with rice.

STATISTICS PER SERVING

Energy 495kcals/2065kJ

Protein 51g

Fat 28g
Saturated fat 17g

Carbohydrate 9g

Sugar 3g

Fibre 1.5g

Salt 0.9g

⬤◯◯ CALORIES

⬤◯◯ SATURATED FAT

⬤⬤⬤ SALT

CHINESE-COATED CHICKEN WINGS

SERVES 4   **PREP** 15 MINS   **COOK** 40-45 MINS
PLUS MARINATING

GREAT FOR KiDS

Chicken wings have plenty of succulent meat on them and are economical. If you can't find them in supermarkets, you should be able to buy them from your butcher.

24 chicken wings
juice of 1 lemon
8 tbsp gluten-free plain flour
  or rice flour
2 tsp salt
1½ tsp five-spice powder
1½ tsp freshly ground black pepper
120ml (4fl oz) sunflower oil
3 chillies, deseeded and finely sliced
  at an angle (omit if making for kids)

5 garlic cloves, sliced
6 spring onions, trimmed and cut into
  2.5cm (1in) lengths at an angle
tamari (gluten-free soy sauce) and
  rice, to serve

SPECIAL EQUIPMENT wok or large, deep
  non-stick frying pan

1 Put the chicken wings in a large bowl, add the lemon juice, combine well, and allow to stand for 20 minutes. Mix the flour, salt, five-spice, and pepper together in another large bowl and add the chicken wings and juice. Combine well and marinate in the flour mixture for 5 minutes, turning over occasionally.

2 Heat the oil in the wok or pan. Add the wings, 4 at a time, and cook on a medium-high heat for 8–10 minutes until golden and crisp, then transfer to a plate lined with kitchen paper to drain. Cook the remaining chicken wings in the same way.

3 Leave about 3 tablespoons oil in the wok and drain the rest. Heat again on a low-medium heat, then add the chilli, garlic, and spring onion, and cook for 2–3 minutes, being careful not to burn them. Return the chicken wings to the wok, toss together, then serve piled up on a plate with tamari and some rice on the side.

STATISTICS PER SERVING

Energy 446kcals/1856kJ

Protein 22.5g

Fat 29g
Saturated fat 4.5g

Carbohydrate 23g
Sugar 1.5g

Fibre 1.5g

Salt 2.4g

SWEET AND SOUR CHICKEN

GUIDELINES PER SERVING

● ○ ○ CALORIES

● ○ ○ SATURATED FAT

● ○ ○ SALT

SERVES 4   **PREP** 15 MINS   **COOK** 20 MINS

Unlike most takeaway versions, this sweet and sour dish is delicate, refreshing, and guaranteed gluten-free.

300g (10oz) fine green beans,
  trimmed and cut in half at an angle
3 tbsp gluten-free plain flour
½ tsp salt
6 tbsp sparkling mineral water, ice cold
400g (14oz) chicken breast, skinless,
  cut into strips
sunflower oil, for frying
1 red pepper and 1 yellow pepper,
  deseeded and cut into thin strips
1 onion, finely chopped
2 tbsp fresh coriander leaves,
  finely chopped, to serve
rice, to serve

For the sauce
3 tbsp gluten-free rice wine
  or medium-sweet sherry
½ tsp dried chilli flakes
2 garlic cloves, grated
1 tbsp gluten-free nam pla (fish sauce)
3 tsp caster sugar
juice of 1 lime

SPECIAL EQUIPMENT wok or large, deep
  non-stick frying pan

1 Blanch the beans in a large pan of boiling water for 3 minutes, then drain and refresh in cold water to halt the cooking process.

2 For the sauce, place all the ingredients in a bowl, mix well, and set aside.

3 In a large bowl, add the flour, salt, and mineral water, then beat with a hand whisk to make a smooth batter. Add the chicken pieces and combine well to coat. Pour the oil into the wok to a depth of 2.5cm (1in) and heat until hot. Add the battered chicken pieces, several pieces at a time, and cook for 4–5 minutes on a medium-high heat until golden. Remove and drain on kitchen paper. Repeat to cook all the chicken.

4 Leave about 3 tablespoons oil in the wok and drain the rest. On a low-medium heat, add the peppers and beans and stir-fry for 2 minutes. Add the onion and cook for 1 minute. Add the sauce and cook for 1 minute to let it thicken slightly. Add the chicken pieces and turn to coat well. Scatter over the coriander and serve with rice.

STATISTICS PER SERVING

Energy 245kcals/1028kJ

Protein 27.5g

Fat 7.5g

Saturated fat 1.1g

Carbohydrate 16.7g

Sugar 7.5g

Fibre 4.7g

Salt 0.7g

NUTRIENT BOOST
Peanuts are a good source of vitamin E and fats beneficial to the heart.

CHICKEN AND PEANUT STEW

SERVES 4   **PREP** 30 MINS   **COOK** 45–50 MINS

Full of Caribbean flavours, this spicy stew works well with polenta-coated croquettes and can also be served with rice.

2 tbsp olive oil
500g (1lb 2oz) chicken breast, skinless, cut into bite-sized pieces
salt and freshly ground black pepper
2 onions, finely chopped
2 tsp ground allspice
pinch of freshly grated nutmeg
leaves from a few sprigs of thyme
2 carrots, sliced at an angle
2 red peppers, finely chopped
50g (1¾oz) peanuts (shelled weight) from whole, unshelled peanuts, roughly chopped
2 red chillies, deseeded and finely chopped

3 garlic cloves, finely chopped
1 tbsp tomato purée
300ml (10fl oz) hot gluten-free chicken or vegetable stock (see page 115)
handful of fresh coriander leaves, roughly chopped
plain yogurt, to serve (optional)

For the croquettes

500g (1lb 2oz) floury potatoes, boiled and mashed with salt and pepper and 50g (1¾oz) butter
2 tbsp finely chopped flat-leaf parsley
100g (3½oz) polenta or fine cornmeal

1 Heat half the oil in a heavy pan, season the chicken, and add to the pan. Cook on a medium-high heat for 6–8 minutes or until starting to colour. Remove and set aside. Heat the remaining oil, add the onion, and cook on a low heat for 2–3 minutes. Stir through the allspice, nutmeg, and thyme, add the carrots, and cook for 5 minutes. Add the peppers and cook for 2–3 minutes. Return the chicken to the pan and stir in the peanuts, chilli, and garlic. Cook for 2 minutes, then add the tomato purée and combine well.

2 Add the stock and bring to the boil. Reduce to a simmer, cover, and cook on a low heat for 25–30 minutes, stirring occasionally, until slightly thick. Top up with a little hot water if needed. Season to taste and stir in the coriander.

3 Meanwhile, for the croquettes, preheat the oven to 190°C (375°F/Gas 5). Mix the potato and parsley, divide the mixture into 16 balls and roll each into a sausage. Sprinkle the polenta onto a plate and roll each croquette in it so that they are coated evenly. Place on a lightly greased baking tray and bake in the oven for 25–30 minutes until golden brown and crisp.

STATISTICS PER SERVING

Energy 610kcals/2552kJ

Protein 40g

Fat 25g
Saturated fat 9g

Carbohydrate 51g
Sugar 13g

Fibre 7g

Salt 0.7g

CASSOULET

SERVES 6   PREP 15 MINS   COOK 2½ HOURS

This intensely rich French stew is well worth the wait and lovely to cook on a cold winter's day.

4 duck legs
3 tbsp olive oil
salt and freshly ground black pepper
1kg (2¼lb) rindless belly pork, cut into bite-sized pieces
6 gluten-free Toulouse sausages, each cut into 4
3 carrots, sliced
2 onions, finely sliced
4 garlic cloves, finely chopped
4 tomatoes, skinned and finely chopped

2 x 400g cans haricot beans, drained and rinsed
1 bouquet garni
300–400ml (10–14fl oz) hot gluten-free chicken stock
handful of gluten-free breadcrumbs
Savoy cabbage or green beans, to serve

SPECIAL EQUIPMENT large flameproof casserole or lidded ovenproof pan

NUTRIENT BOOST
All canned beans are a great source of fibre, protein, and minerals.

1 Preheat the oven to 220°C (425°F/Gas 7). Rub the duck legs with 1 tablespoon oil and then sprinkle and rub all over with salt. Put in a roasting tin and bake in the oven for 15–20 minutes until brown and crisp. Remove and set aside. Reduce the oven temperature to 170°C (340°F/Gas 3½).

2 In the large flameproof casserole, heat the remaining oil on a medium heat, add the pork and cook, stirring frequently, until it begins to brown. Add the sausages and cook for 4–5 minutes, then add the carrots and cook for 5 minutes. Add the onions and cook for 2 minutes. Stir in the garlic, cook for 1 minute, then add the tomatoes, beans, and bouquet garni and season well.

3 Add 300ml (10fl oz) stock to the pan; check as it cooks and add more stock if the cassoulet looks like it's drying out. Cover and cook in the oven for 1 hour, then add the duck legs, combine well, leave uncovered, and cook for a further 1 hour. Sprinkle over the breadcrumbs for the last 30 minutes of cooking; cover loosely with foil if it begins to brown too much. Stir occasionally. When ready, remove the bouquet garni and serve piping hot with Savoy cabbage or green beans.

STATISTICS PER SERVING

Energy 700kcals/2930kJ

Protein 67g

Fat 36g
Saturated fat 11g

Carbohydrate 25g
Sugar 9g

Fibre 6g

Salt 2.9g

CREAMY CHICKEN CRUMBLE

SERVES 4   **PREP** 20 MINS   **COOK** 45 MINS–1 HOUR   **FREEZE** 1 MONTH

If serving this for children, replace the wine with gluten-free stock. You could also stir in sweetcorn kernels and replace the chicken with cooked ham.

2 large chicken breasts, skin on
1 tbsp olive oil
salt and freshly ground black pepper
steamed leeks, to serve

For the crumble topping
150g (5½oz) rice flour
pinch of salt
75g (2½oz) butter, cubed
3 tbsp grated Parmesan cheese
50g (1¾oz) Cheddar cheese, grated
1 tsp mustard seeds, crushed

For the sauce
50g (1¾oz) butter
200g (7oz) baby button mushrooms,
  left whole
1 tbsp rice flour or cornflour
125ml (4fl oz) dry white wine
  or gluten-free chicken stock
150ml (5fl oz) milk
150ml (5fl oz) single cream
1 tbsp Dijon mustard
a few tarragon leaves, chopped

STATISTICS PER SERVING

Energy 712kcals/2960kJ

Protein 33g

Fat 45g
Saturated fat 27g

Carbohydrate 34g
Sugar 3g

Fibre 1.5g

Salt 1.6g

1 Preheat the oven to 200°C (400°F/Gas 6). Place the chicken in a roasting tin, drizzle with the oil, and season. Roast in the oven for 25–35 minutes until golden and cooked through. Don't overcook or it will be dry. Leave to cool slightly, remove the skin, and shred into chunky pieces.

2 For the crumble topping, place the rice flour and salt in a medium bowl. Add the butter and rub it in with your fingers until it resembles breadcrumbs. Stir through the cheeses and mustard seeds. Set aside.

3 For the sauce, melt the butter in a medium pan, add the mushrooms, and cook on a low-medium heat for 5 minutes until golden. Remove the pan, stir in the rice flour, add the wine, and stir again. Return it to the heat and cook for 2–3 minutes, stirring continuously. Add the milk and cream and bring to a gentle boil. Reduce to a simmer, stirring continuously to remove any lumps. As it thickens, stir in the mustard and tarragon leaves, and season.

4 Remove the pan and add the shredded chicken. Stir to coat, spoon into a shallow 1 litre (1¾ pint) ovenproof dish, and top with the crumble mixture. Bake in the oven for 20–25 minutes until golden. Serve with steamed leeks.

● ● ○ CALORIES

● ● ● SATURATED FAT

● ● ○ SALT

ROAST TURKEY

SERVES 8　　**PREP** 20 MINS　　**COOK** APPROX. 3½ HOURS

Whip up this traditional juicy roast filled with delectable stuffing for a perfect gluten-free Thanksgiving or Christmas. Serve with popovers (see opposite) and roast potatoes.

1 turkey, weighing about 5kg (11lb)

For the herb butter
50g (1¾oz) salted butter, softened
2 garlic cloves, grated
1 tsp dried oregano
1 tbsp finely chopped flat-leaf parsley
1 tsp finely chopped sage leaves

For the stuffing
1 tbsp olive oil
2 celery sticks, finely chopped
1 onion, finely chopped

500g (1lb 2oz) gluten-free pork
　sausages, skinned
100g (3½oz) gluten-free breadcrumbs
5 sage leaves, finely chopped
1 tsp thyme leaves
1 crisp dessert apple, chopped
4 tbsp dried cranberries
2 tbsp chopped dried apricots
100ml (3½fl oz) hot gluten-free
　chicken stock
75g (2½oz) butter, melted

NUTRIENT BOOST
High-protein, low-fat turkey is a source of selenium, good for immune health.

STATISTICS PER SERVING

Energy 570kcals/2375kJ

Protein 46g

Fat 32g
Saturated fat 14g

Carbohydrate 19g
Sugar 6g

Fibre 2g

Salt 2g

1 Preheat the oven to 200°C (400°F/Gas 6). For the herb butter, mix all the ingredients and set aside. To make the turkey stuffing, heat the oil in a large frying pan, add the celery, and cook for 3 minutes. Add the onion and cook for 3 more minutes until soft, then add the sausagemeat. Cook for 8 minutes until the pork is no longer pink, stirring well to break up the meat. Remove and cool, transfer to a large bowl, add the remaining ingredients, and combine well. If the mixture is too wet, add some more breadcrumbs.

2 Stuff the neck of the turkey with as much mixture as you can; make a note of the bird's weight at this point. Spread the herb butter over the turkey, transfer to a large roasting tin, and roast in the oven for 15 minutes.

3 Reduce the temperature to 190°C (375°F/Gas 5) and cook for 20 minutes per 1kg (2¼lb) plus 90 minutes, or until the juices run clear when the thigh is pierced with a skewer. A 5kg (11lb) turkey would take 3¼ hours to cook; the cooking time depends on the weight of the turkey after stuffing. Baste with the juices as it cooks. If it starts looking too brown, cover loosely with foil. Leave the turkey to rest for 30 minutes before slicing to serve.

POPOVERS

MAKES 8 **PREP** 15 MINS **COOK** 20 MINS

Popovers are the US equivalent of Yorkshire puddings: savoury baked puff pancakes to accompany roast meats.

GUIDELINES PER SERVING

●●○	CALORIES
●●●	SATURATED FAT
●●○	SALT

2 eggs
250ml (9fl oz) milk
250g (9oz) gluten-free plain flour
2 tsp gluten-free baking powder
salt and freshly ground black pepper
50g (1¾oz) melted butter

SPECIAL EQUIPMENT 8-hole muffin tin

1 Preheat the oven to 200°C (400°F/Gas 6) and place the muffin tin in the oven to heat up. In a bowl, beat the eggs until foamy and whisk in the milk. Add the flour, baking powder, salt and pepper, and beat to a smooth batter.

2 Take the muffin tin out of the oven and add the butter evenly to each hole; be careful not to burn the butter. Pour in the batter mixture, return to the oven, and bake for 15–20 minutes until the popovers are golden brown. Serve immediately with roast turkey or other roast meats.

STATISTICS PER POPOVER

Energy 200kcals/819kJ

Protein 4g

Fat 8.5g
Saturated fat 4.5g

Carbohydrate 26g
Sugar 1.5g

Fibre 2g

Salt 0.7g

● ○ ○ CALORIES

● ○ ○ SATURATED FAT

● ● ○ SALT

ROAST CHICKEN WITH ORANGE AND TAMARI

SERVES 4   **PREP** 15 MINS   **COOK** 40 MINS
PLUS MARINATING

A simple sweet-and-spicy dish. Chicken drumsticks and wings would also work well.

8 chicken thighs on the bone
½ tsp ground ginger
1 tsp ground dried mint
¼ tsp ground allspice
salt and freshly ground black pepper
2 tbsp pomegranate seeds
handful of fresh coriander leaves,
  roughly chopped

steamed rice or baby roast potatoes,
  to serve

For the marinade
3 tbsp tamari (gluten-free soy sauce)
juice of 3 oranges or 4 tangerines

1 Mix together the marinade ingredients in a large bowl, then add the chicken pieces and stir to coat thoroughly. Cover and put in the fridge for 30 minutes or 2 hours if time permits.

2 Preheat the oven to 200°C (400°F/Gas 6). Mix together the ginger, mint, and allspice. Sit the chicken pieces and marinade in a roasting tin, sprinkle over the spice mixture, season, and bake in the oven for 40 minutes until golden.

3 Remove from the oven, transfer to a serving plate, and sprinkle over the pomegranate seeds and coriander. Serve the chicken with steamed rice or baby roast potatoes.

STATISTICS PER SERVING

Energy 205kcals/865kJ

Protein 33g

Fat 4g
Saturated fat 1g

Carbohydrate 9g
Sugar 9g

Fibre 0.5g

Salt 2.3g

« Preparing pomegranate
To get at the juicy seeds, cut off the spiky top of the pomegranate and score the skin into quarters. Break the fruit apart with your hands and use a spoon to remove the seeds from the membrane.

TOAD IN THE HOLE

GREAT FOR KiDS

SERVES 4   **PREP** 15 MINS   **COOK** 45 MINS

If making for kids, halve the sausages and stand them on end in the tin so they stick up, and omit the wine in the gravy.

2 tbsp olive oil
8 gluten-free sausages, pork or beef
125g (4½oz) gluten-free plain flour
pinch of salt
2 eggs
300ml (10fl oz) milk
1 tbsp Dijon mustard (optional)

For the gravy
100ml (3½fl oz) red wine
1 tbsp cornflour
300ml (10fl oz) hot gluten-free pork
  or beef stock
salt and freshly ground black pepper
few sprigs of rosemary

1 Preheat the oven to 220°C (425°F/Gas 7). Heat half the oil in a large frying pan, add the sausages, and cook on a medium-high heat for 10–15 minutes, until golden all over. Remove, put them in a baking tin, and set aside.

2 For the batter, place the flour and salt in a bowl. Make a well in the centre, add the eggs and a little milk, and stir, bringing in a little flour. Slowly add the milk and continue stirring, pulling in more flour from the edges until you have a smooth batter. Use a balloon whisk at the end to avoid lumps. Stir in the mustard (if using). Add the remaining oil to the baking tin with the sausages and heat it on the hob on medium. When hot, pour in the batter and transfer to the oven to bake for 30–35 minutes until golden.

3 For the gravy, heat the frying pan containing the leftover oil; tip away the excess oil. Add the wine and bubble on a medium heat, scraping up any bits from the base of the pan. Reduce the heat, mix the cornflour with a little water to form a paste, and add to the pan, stirring constantly. Gradually pour in the stock, season to taste, and add the rosemary. Bring to the boil, then simmer, stirring, for 10 minutes. Season to taste. Strain to remove any lumps and the rosemary, pour into a jug, and serve with the toad in the hole.

VARIATIONS
Add roasted shallots or red onions to the sausages and stir your favourite flavour into the batter mix – horseradish, fresh herbs, or dried oregano all work well.

GUIDELINES PER SERVING

● ● ○ CALORIES

● ● ● SATURATED FAT

● ● ● SALT

STATISTICS PER SERVING

Energy 577kcals/2401kJ

Protein 23g

Fat 34g
Saturated fat 11g

Carbohydrate 36g
Sugar 5g

Fibre 0g

Salt 3.5g

PORK ENCHILADAS

SERVES 4   **PREP** 20–25 MINS   **COOK** 1 HOUR
PLUS MARINATING

A rich mix of fabulous flavours: tortillas filled with smoky pork and tomato salsa, baked with cheese and cream.

350g (12oz) pork tenderloin
6 corn tortillas (see page 233)
6 tbsp soured cream, to top
75g (2½oz) mature Cheddar
  cheese, grated, to top

For the marinade
2 tbsp olive oil
1 chipotle chilli, finely chopped
  (or dried jalapeño chilli) or 1 tbsp
  adobo sauce or a generous splash
  of smoked chipotle Tabasco sauce
2 tsp coriander seeds
pinch of ground cinnamon

salt and freshly ground black pepper
pinch of sugar

For the tomato salsa
500g (1lb 2oz) vine-ripened tomatoes
1 red chilli, halved and deseeded
1 tbsp olive oil
2 spring onions, finely chopped
juice of 1 lime
salt and freshly ground black pepper
handful of fresh coriander leaves,
  finely chopped

SPECIAL EQUIPMENT griddle pan

1 Put the pork in a shallow dish, mix the marinade ingredients, and pour over the pork to cover. Leave for 20 minutes or longer if time permits. Preheat the oven to 200°C (400°F/Gas 6). Transfer the pork (with the marinade) to a roasting tin and cook for 40 minutes, basting occasionally so the pork doesn't dry out. Remove and set aside.

2 For the salsa, heat a griddle pan to hot. Toss the tomatoes and chilli with the oil and add to the pan. Cook over a medium-high heat for 5–6 minutes, turning halfway, until lightly charred. Remove and pulse with the spring onions and lime juice in a food processor until chopped. Season to taste, transfer to a bowl, and stir through the coriander.

3 Shred the pork, retaining any of the juices. Lay out the tortillas and spoon the pork into the centre of each. Spoon over the salsa and roll up the tortillas. Sit them in an ovenproof dish, spoon the soured cream on top, and sprinkle the cheese. Bake for 15–20 minutes until the cheese has melted. Serve with the remaining salsa and a splash of Tabasco sauce, if liked.

STATISTICS PER SERVING

Energy 567kcals/2382kJ

Protein 32g

Fat 24g
Saturated fat 9.5g

Carbohydrate 55g
Sugar 6.5g

Fibre 5g

Salt 1.2g

LAMB TAGINE WITH CAULIFLOWER "COUSCOUS"

GUIDELINES PER SERVING

⬤⬤◯ CALORIES

⬤⬤⬤ SATURATED FAT

⬤◯◯ SALT

SERVES 4   **PREP** 15 MINS   **COOK** 1¾ HOURS

Nutty roasted cauliflower, processed until just grainy, makes a tasty gluten-free substitute for couscous.

900g (2lb) lamb shoulder,
  cut into chunks
2 garlic cloves, finely chopped
5cm (2in) piece of fresh root ginger,
  peeled and grated
salt and freshly ground black pepper
½ tsp ground cinnamon
½ tsp turmeric
1 onion, grated
1 tbsp olive oil
450g (1lb) carrots, peeled or scrubbed
  and roughly chopped
900ml (1½ pints) hot gluten-free
  vegetable stock (see page 115)

2 preserved lemons, halved, flesh
  discarded and skin finely sliced, or
  the zest and juice of 1 fresh lemon
handful of flat-leaf parsley,
  finely chopped

For the "couscous"
1 cauliflower, broken into large florets
1 tbsp olive oil
1–2 tsp ground cumin
salt and freshly ground black pepper

1 Toss the lamb with the garlic, ginger, salt and pepper, cinnamon, turmeric, and onion. Heat the oil in a large, heavy pan, add the lamb mixture, and cook on a medium heat for 10 minutes until the lamb is sealed. Stir in the carrots so they get coated. Pour over the stock, bring to the boil, cover, and simmer on a low heat for 1–1½ hours, until the lamb is tender, topping up with hot water as needed; alternatively transfer to a casserole dish and bake in an oven preheated to 180°C (350°F/Gas 4) for 1½ hours.

2 Preheat the oven to 200°C (400°F/Gas 6). Toss the cauliflower with the oil and cumin and season. Transfer to a roasting tin and bake for 10 minutes or until just turning golden. Remove the cauliflower from the oven and leave to cool completely. Transfer to a food processor and pulse until it resembles grains; don't overwork or it will become mushy. Season to taste.

3 Stir the preserved lemons or zest and juice into the lamb for the last 15 minutes of cooking, then stir through the parsley when ready to serve.

STATISTICS PER SERVING

Energy 555kcals/2316kJ

Protein 53g

Fat 26g
Saturated fat 9g

Carbohydrate 15g
Sugar 14g

Fibre 9g

Salt 1.1g

● ● ●　CALORIES

● ● ●　SATURATED FAT

● ○ ○　SALT

SPICED LAMB AND HUMMUS WRAPS

SERVES 4　　**PREP** 30 MINS　　**COOK** 4 HOURS
PLUS MARINATING

A superb mix of textures and punchy flavours make up this Lebanese-inspired meal. If you fancy an extra side dish, mix some Greek yogurt with chopped fresh mint.

1.5kg (3lb 3oz) lamb shoulder
8 corn tortillas (see page 233), lemon
　wedges, and mixed salad, to serve

For the spice rub
½ tsp ground cinnamon
½ tsp ground coriander
¼ tsp ground cumin
1 tsp dried mint
salt and freshly ground black pepper
2 tbsp olive oil

For the hummus
400g can chickpeas, drained and rinsed
3 garlic cloves, grated
2 tbsp gluten-free tahini
juice of ½–1 lemon, to taste
4–5 tbsp olive oil, plus extra to drizzle
1 tsp paprika, plus extra to sprinkle

1 Mix together the spices, herbs, and seasoning and stir into 1 tablespoon oil. Rub into the lamb and leave for at least 30 minutes or covered in the fridge overnight. Preheat the oven to 160°C (325°F/Gas 3). In a large, heavy frying pan, heat the remaining olive oil, add the lamb, and cook on a medium-high heat for 5–10 minutes or until browned all over.

2 Place the lamb in a large roasting tin, cover it with foil, and cook for 4 hours, removing the foil for the last 15 minutes of cooking. Remove from the oven, cover, and leave to rest for at least 20 minutes.

3 For the hummus, whizz the chickpeas, garlic, and tahini in a food processor until combined. Trickle in the lemon juice and olive oil, whizzing and tasting as you go. Season to taste, add the paprika, and whizz again. Transfer to a bowl, drizzle over a little olive oil, and a dusting of paprika. Heat the wraps in the oven according to pack instructions. Shred the lamb and transfer to a serving plate. Divide the salad and lamb between the wraps, top with hummus, add a squeeze of lemon, and roll or fold to serve.

Energy 900kcals/3769kJ

Protein 58g

Fat 44g
Saturated fat 11g

Carbohydrate 65g
Sugar 2g

Fibre 7.5g

Salt 1.4g

⬤◯◯ CALORIES

⬤⬤◯ SATURATED FAT

⬤◯◯ SALT

LAMB AND BEANS SIMMERED IN WINE

SERVES 4   **PREP** 10 MINS   **COOK** 1 HOUR

An easy one-pan dish that can be served straight to the table with some gluten-free bread and steamed greens.

2 tbsp olive oil
1 red onion, finely chopped
500g (1lb 2oz) lamb leg steaks, trimmed of fat and cut into bite-sized pieces
salt and freshly ground black pepper
pinch of dried chilli flakes
pinch of dried oregano
1 tbsp gluten-free plain flour
3 garlic cloves, finely sliced

150ml (5fl oz) dry white wine
300ml (10fl oz) hot gluten-free vegetable stock
400g can cannellini beans, drained and rinsed
400g can flageolet beans, drained and rinsed
lemon wedges, steamed greens, and gluten-free crusty bread, to serve

1 Heat half the oil in a large, heavy frying pan, add the onion, and cook on a low heat for 5 minutes, then remove the onion and set aside. Add the remaining oil to the pan. Season the lamb with salt and pepper, the chilli flakes, and the oregano, then toss in the flour and add to the pan.

2 Cook on a medium-high heat for 10–15 minutes until golden on all sides, then add the onion back to the pan, add the garlic, and cook for 2 more minutes. Increase the heat, add the wine, and bubble for a minute, then add the stock and bubble for 1 more minute.

3 Reduce to a simmer and stir the beans into the mixture. Cover with a lid, leaving it slightly ajar, and cook gently for 30–40 minutes; make sure it doesn't dry out and top up with stock or hot water if needed. Season to taste and serve with lemon wedges, steamed greens, and crusty bread.

STATISTICS PER SERVING

Energy 441kcals/1842kJ

Protein 35g

Fat 17g
Saturated fat 5g

Carbohydrate 24g
Sugar 1.6g

Fibre 7.2g

Salt 0.4g

VARIATION

Add some vegetables to the pan if you like, such as 2 large or 3 medium carrots, roughly diced, at the same time as the beans, or 1 fennel bulb, trimmed and sliced, and then fried with the onions.

GREEK ROAST LEG OF LAMB

SERVES 8 **PREP** 20 MINS **COOK** 2¼ HOURS
PLUS RESTING

The sweet and sharp flavours of the tomatoey crust cut through the rich lamb perfectly.

leg of lamb, approx. 2kg (4½lb)
olive oil, for rubbing
salt and freshly ground black pepper
broad beans and baby roast potatoes,
  or hot pittas and salad, to serve

2 tsp capers
grated zest and juice of 2 lemons
pinch of dried chilli flakes
handful of flat-leaf parsley
3 garlic cloves, peeled

For the crust
4 slices of gluten-free white bread
  (see pages 38–9)
50g (1¾oz) sun-dried tomatoes

1 Preheat the oven to 200°C (400°F/Gas 6). Sit the lamb in a large roasting tin, slash it a few times, rub with oil, and season well with salt and pepper.

2 Pulse all the ingredients for the crust in a food processor until well minced. Season to taste; add more lemon or sun-dried tomatoes if you want a stronger taste. Now smother the lamb with the crust mixture, pressing it onto the meat so it sticks and pushing it into the slashes.

3 Cook the lamb in the oven for 15 minutes until it starts to turn golden, then reduce the oven temperature to 160°C (325°F/Gas 3) and continue to cook for another 1½–2 hours. Cover loosely with foil if it starts to dry out. Remove from the oven and leave to rest for 20 minutes before carving the meat. Serve with the juices from the pan and some broad beans and baby roast potatoes, or with hot pittas and a lightly dressed salad.

VARIATION
You could pour some warmed rosé wine into the roasting tin halfway through cooking – adds a wonderful flavour to the pan juices.

STATISTICS PER SERVING

Energy 377kcals/1578kJ

Protein 40g

Fat 20g
Saturated fat 7g

Carbohydrate 9.5g
Sugar 0.7g

Fibre 0.3g

Salt 0.8g

● ● ○ CALORIES

● ● ● SATURATED FAT

● ○ ○ SALT

MOUSSAKA

This version of the Greek classic uses beef instead of lamb, but feel free to swap it around. Feta cheese is a tasty addition to the topping instead of Cheddar.

3 tbsp olive oil
2 onions, finely chopped
salt and freshly ground black pepper
400g (14oz) beef mince
4 anchovies, finely chopped
3 garlic cloves, finely chopped
1 tbsp tomato purée
1 tsp dried oregano, plus extra
  for topping
leaves from a few sprigs of thyme

300ml (10fl oz) hot gluten-free
  vegetable stock (see page 115)
2 aubergines, cut into 1cm (½in) slices
200ml (7fl oz) Greek yogurt
1 egg
100g (3½oz) Cheddar cheese, grated
green salad and tomatoes, to serve

SPECIAL EQUIPMENT 22 x 28cm (8¾
  x 11in) ovenproof dish, griddle pan

1 Preheat the oven to 180°C (350°F/Gas 4). In a large, non-stick pan, heat 1 tablespoon oil, add the onions, fry over a low heat for 3–4 minutes, and season. Stir in the beef mince and anchovies and cook for 5 minutes, stirring constantly and breaking up with a fork, until all the meat is sealed and browned. Stir through the garlic and cook for 2 minutes. Add the tomato purée, oregano, and thyme and combine well. Add the stock, increase the heat a little, and bubble for 1–2 minutes. Reduce to a simmer, cover, and cook gently for 15–20 minutes or until the mixture starts to dry out.

2 While the mince is cooking, brush the aubergine slices with the remaining oil and season well. Heat a griddle pan. When hot, add a few slices at a time and cook for 5 minutes on each side or until golden. Remove and sit them on a plate lined with kitchen paper. Repeat until all are cooked.

3 Layer the beef mixture and the aubergine in the ovenproof dish and set aside. Mix together the yogurt and egg in a bowl and whisk with a fork until combined. Pour evenly over the meat mixture, then sprinkle on the cheese and scatter over the oregano. Bake in the oven for 30 minutes or until the top is golden; cover with foil if it starts to brown too much. Serve with a lightly dressed crisp green salad and a plate of fresh sliced tomatoes.

STATISTICS PER SERVING

Energy 524kcals/2175kJ

Protein 33g

Fat 38g
Saturated fat 16g

Carbohydrate 8g
Sugar 7g

Fibre 2.5g

Salt 1.4g

MEAT LOAF WITH ROMESCO

SERVES 6   **PREP** 20 MINS   **COOK** 1½–2 HOURS

Romesco, a Spanish pepper sauce, is a delicious change from the tomato sauce usually partnered with meat loaf.

750g (1lb 10oz) beef or pork mince
150g (5½oz) bacon, chopped
1 red onion, finely chopped
2 garlic cloves, finely chopped
1 tbsp finely chopped rosemary leaves
few sage leaves, finely chopped
1 tbsp tomato purée
125g (4½oz) gluten-free breadcrumbs
salt and freshly ground black pepper
1 egg

For the sauce
100ml (3½fl oz) extra virgin olive oil
2 slices of gluten-free bread

200g jar roasted red peppers, drained
100g (3½oz) blanched almonds,
  lightly toasted and roughly chopped
3 garlic cloves
1 tsp sweet smoked paprika
pinch of cayenne pepper
1 tbsp red wine vinegar
juice of 1 lemon

SPECIAL EQUIPMENT 900g (2lb) loaf
  tin, greased and lined with baking
  parchment

1 Preheat the oven to 180°C (350°F/Gas 4). With your hands, squish together the meat in a large bowl. Add the other meat loaf ingredients and combine well. Spoon it into the tin, pack it down evenly, cover with baking parchment, and top with foil. Sit the tin in a roasting tin and fill with boiling water to come just under halfway up the sides of the loaf tin.

2 Bake in the oven for 1½–2 hours or until the meat is cooked through. Top up the water in the roasting tin if needed. Remove from the oven and let it sit for 15 minutes, then loosen around the edges of the tin with a knife. Invert the meat loaf onto a serving plate and slice when ready to serve.

3 For the sauce, add 1 tablespoon oil to a frying pan and fry the bread slices on a medium heat until golden. Remove and whizz in a food processor along with the peppers, almonds, garlic, paprika, cayenne, and vinegar. Season to taste and then pulse until fairly smooth. Trickle in the remaining oil while the motor is still going, then add about 4 tablespoons water until you get the right consistency; it should be thick but spoonable. Season and add the lemon juice to taste. Serve with the meat loaf.

STATISTICS PER SERVING

Energy 709kcals/2951kJ

Protein 38g

Fat 51g
Saturated fat 13g

Carbohydrate 25g
Sugar 3g

Fibre 3g

Salt 1.8g

○○ CALORIES

●● ○ SATURATED FAT

●○○ SALT

GREAT FOR KiDS

BEEF BURGERS

MAKES 6   **PREP** 20 MINS   **COOK** 20 MINS   **FREEZE** 1 MONTH
PLUS CHILLING

Home-made burgers can't be beaten, and you know exactly what's gone into the mixture.

500g (1lb 2oz) beef mince
1 large red onion, finely diced
1 garlic clove, finely chopped
1 tsp paprika
handful of flat-leaf parsley, finely chopped
1 tbsp finely chopped fresh coriander leaves
1 large egg

salt and freshly ground black pepper
small handful of gluten-free breadcrumbs (optional)
gluten-free plain flour, for dusting
vegetable oil, for frying
gluten-free baps or rolls (see pages 218–20), lettuce, tomato, and gluten-free relish, to serve

1 Add the first 8 ingredients to a large bowl and season well. Use your hands to pound the mixture to a thick paste: this way it will stay together when you cook it. To check that the mixture has a good flavour, before you shape it into burgers break off a small piece and fry until cooked through. Taste it and then alter the seasoning accordingly. If the burgers are too dense, add the breadcrumbs to lighten the texture.

2 With floured hands, divide the mixture into 6 balls, then roll each one and flatten into a burger shape. Sit on a baking sheet and chill in the fridge for 20 minutes to firm up. If freezing, open-freeze on the tray at this point until solid, transfer to plastic bags, and label.

3 Heat a large frying pan on a high heat and add a little oil. Cook the burgers for 2–3 minutes on each side. Remove and let them rest for 2 minutes before serving on gluten-free baps or rolls with lettuce leaves, sliced tomato, and a dollop of gluten-free relish of your choice.

STATISTICS PER BURGER

Energy 212kcals/879kJ

Protein 18g

Fat 15g

Saturated fat 6g

Carbohydrate 1.5g

Sugar 1.1g

Fibre 0.5g

Salt 0.2g

STEAK WITH MUSTARD SAUCE

SERVES 4   **PREP** 15 MINS   **COOK** 10 MINS

Steak and mustard is a match made in heaven. Swap the milk for double cream if you prefer a richer sauce, and try wholegrain mustard for more texture and less heat.

NUTRIENT BOOST
Red meat provides iron, vital for the manufacture of red blood cells.

4 x 300g (10oz) beef fillet steaks
1 tbsp olive oil
salt and freshly ground black pepper
new potatoes and steamed broccoli, to serve

For the sauce
25g (scant 1oz) butter
2 tbsp gluten-free plain flour

300ml (10fl oz) milk
2 tsp English mustard, or more if you like it hot
salt and freshly ground black pepper

SPECIAL EQUIPMENT griddle pan

1 First make the sauce. In a small pan, melt the butter, remove from the heat, add the flour, and combine well. Pour in a little milk and stir again. Return to the heat and, still stirring to combine well, gradually add the remaining milk to make a fairly thin white sauce. Add the mustard and season to taste. Place over a low heat and simmer, stirring constantly, for 5 minutes to cook out the flour.

2 Heat a griddle pan on a high heat, brush the steaks with the oil, and season well. Add 2 steaks at a time to the hot pan and cook undisturbed for 2–3 minutes, then turn and cook the other side for the same amount of time.

3 Cook all the steaks as above and leave to rest for 5 minutes. Ladle over the hot mustard sauce and serve with new potatoes and steamed broccoli.

STATISTICS PER SERVING

Energy   570kcals/2378kJ

Protein   67g

Fat   29g
Saturated fat   14g

Carbohydrate   9g
Sugar   3.5g

Fibre   0g

Salt   0.8g

● ● ○ CALORIES

● ● ● SATURATED FAT

● ○ ○ SALT

BEEF AND BEER CASSEROLE

SERVES 6   **PREP** 40 MINS   **COOK** 2 HOURS

A really hearty dish with slow-cooked beef simmered in a light beer. Perfect comfort food.

1 tbsp rice flour
salt and freshly ground black pepper
1kg (2¼lb) braising steak, chuck, or
  skirt, cut into large bite-sized pieces
3 tbsp olive oil
300g (10oz) carrots, cut into chunks
1 celeriac, peeled and chopped into
  bite-sized pieces
3 leeks, trimmed, washed, and cut
  into chunks
300ml (10fl oz) gluten-free beer
750ml (1¼ pints) hot gluten-free
  vegetable stock (see page 115)
50g (1¾oz) quinoa

For the herb dumplings
½ onion, finely chopped
½ tbsp olive oil
small handful of flat-leaf parsley,
  finely chopped
a few rosemary leaves, finely chopped
75g (2½oz) gluten-free breadcrumbs
1 tsp gluten-free ready-grated
  horseradish (from a jar)
1 tsp Dijon mustard
1 egg

SPECIAL EQUIPMENT large flameproof
  casserole or lidded ovenproof pan

1 Preheat the oven to 160°C (325°F/Gas 3). Season the flour and toss the beef to coat. Heat 2 tablespoons oil in the casserole and brown the beef in batches over a medium heat for 5 minutes per batch, until sealed. Set aside.

2 Add the remaining oil to the casserole and cook the vegetables for 5–6 minutes, until golden. Pour in a little of the beer, raise the heat, and stir to scrape up any bits from the bottom of the casserole. Add the remaining beer and simmer on a medium heat for 5 minutes. Pour in the stock, bring to the boil, reduce to a simmer, return the meat to the casserole along with the quinoa. Season, cover, and cook in the oven for 1½ hours before adding the dumplings; top up with hot water if it looks dry.

3 For the dumplings, cook the onion in the oil in a medium pan over a medium heat until soft. Add the remaining ingredients, season, and stir until it comes together. Form 12 dumpling balls and set aside. When ready, remove the casserole and add the balls, pushing them down into the sauce. Re-cover and cook for 30 minutes, removing the lid for the last 5 minutes.

STATISTICS PER SERVING

Energy 691kcals/2885kJ

Protein 49g

Fat 30g
Saturated fat 12g

Carbohydrate 44g
Sugar 7.5g

Fibre 0.7g

Salt 1.4g

BEEF POT WITH DUMPLINGS

SERVES 4   **PREP** 20 MINS   **COOK** 3 HOURS   **FREEZE** 1 MONTH
NOT DUMPLINGS

Gluten-free, suet-free dumplings accompany this rich beef casserole for a hearty supper or Sunday lunch.

3 tbsp gluten-free plain flour
1 tbsp paprika
salt and freshly ground black pepper
500g (1lb 2oz) stewing beef, diced
  into bite-sized pieces
5 tbsp olive oil
3 carrots, sliced
2 celery sticks, sliced
12 whole shallots
250g (9oz) chestnut mushrooms
3 garlic cloves, finely chopped
200–250ml (7–9fl oz) red wine
300ml (10fl oz) gluten-free beef stock

1 bouquet garni
green beans, to serve

For the dumplings
150g (5½oz) gluten-free plain flour
  or cornmeal flour
75g (2½oz) butter, softened
1 tbsp chopped thyme leaves or
  1 tsp paprika

SPECIAL EQUIPMENT large flameproof
  casserole or lidded ovenproof pan

STATISTICS PER SERVING

Energy 704kcals/2940kJ

Protein 35g

Fat 38g

Saturated fat 15g

Carbohydrate 44g

Sugar 9g

Fibre 7g

Salt 0.8g

1 Preheat the oven to 160°C (325°F/Gas 3). In a large bowl, place the flour, paprika, and seasoning, and stir well. Add the beef and mix, ensuring all the meat is covered. Heat half the oil in the casserole or pan on a medium heat and add the beef. Cook for 6–8 minutes until browned. Set aside.

2 Heat the remaining oil in the pan, add the carrots, and cook for 5 minutes. Add the celery and shallots and cook for 5 more minutes until they begin to turn golden. Add the mushrooms and garlic and cook for 2 more minutes. Add the wine, stock, and bouquet garni, stir, and bring to the boil. Reduce to a simmer, add the beef, and cover. Bake in the oven for 2–2½ hours, topping up occasionally with a little hot water if it starts to dry out.

3 For the dumplings, mix the flour, butter, seasoning, and chopped thyme or paprika until the mix is flaky, then add a little cold water to form a dough. Divide and roll into balls, then drop the dumplings into the pot for the last 30 minutes of cooking, gently poking them just below the surface. Uncover the pan for the last 10 minutes to allow the dumplings to turn golden. Remove the bouquet garni and serve the beef with green beans.

BEEF AND HORSERADISH WELLINGTON

GUIDELINES PER SERVING

● ○ ○ CALORIES

● ● ● SATURATED FAT

● ○ ○ SALT

SERVES 6   **PREP** 15 MINS   **COOK** 1 HOUR

Perfectly cooked beef encased in crisp gluten-free pastry, with a surprise kick from the horseradish, this dish would make an impressive centrepiece for a dinner party.

2 tbsp olive oil
800g (1¾lb) beef fillet or loin
salt and freshly ground black pepper
400g (14oz) gluten-free rough puff
  pastry (see pages 46–7)
gluten-free plain flour, for dusting

1–2 tbsp gluten-free hot horseradish
  sauce
1 egg, lightly beaten, to glaze
watercress and roasted new potatoes,
  to serve

1 Preheat the oven to 200°C (400°F/Gas 6). In a large frying pan, heat the oil on a medium heat. Season the beef, add to the pan, and cook for 8 minutes or until evenly browned all over. Remove from the pan and set aside.

2 Carefully roll out the pastry on a lightly floured surface to a rectangle with a thickness of 3–5mm (⅛–¼in), then spread over the horseradish sauce, leaving a 2.5cm (1in) border. Sit the meat on top towards one end, then very carefully roll the pastry over the meat ensuring that it is all covered. Press and seal the seam with a little water. Transfer to a baking sheet, making sure the seam is on the underside and the ends are tucked in and sealed.

3 Brush the pastry with the beaten egg and bake in the oven for 40–50 minutes or until evenly golden. Cover loosely with foil if the pastry starts to colour too quickly. Remove from the oven and leave to rest for at least 10 minutes, then slice to serve with watercress and roasted new potatoes.

COOK'S TIP
You can prepare this ahead and keep it in the fridge until ready to bake.

VARIATION
Use a pâté instead of the horseradish sauce, if you like.

STATISTICS PER SERVING

Energy 484cals/2019kJ

Protein 32g

Fat 29g
Saturated fat 14g

Carbohydrate 22g
Sugar 1g

Fibre 1.5g

Salt 0.6g

VEGETABLE
MAINS

MUSHROOM BURGERS

SERVES 4   **PREP** 20 MINS   **COOK** 50 MINS
PLUS CHILLING

Served with miso-roasted chips and tahini dip, these burgers have lots of gutsy flavours. Make mini ones for the kids.

GREAT FOR KIDS

3 tbsp olive oil
1 onion, finely chopped
500g (1lb 2oz) chestnut mushrooms,
  pulsed in a food processor
4 anchovies, finely chopped
tamari (gluten-free soy sauce)
125g (4½oz) gluten-free breadcrumbs
1 egg, lightly beaten
salt and freshly ground black pepper

For the miso chips
4 sweet potatoes, peeled and cut
  into thin chips

1 tbsp olive oil
1 tbsp sweet miso or tamari
  (gluten-free soy sauce)

For the tahini dip
2 garlic cloves, grated
pinch of sea salt
3 tbsp tahini
juice of 1 lemon

SPECIAL EQUIPMENT food processor

1 Preheat the oven to 200°C (400°F/Gas 6). Heat 1 tablespoon oil in a large frying pan, add the onion, and cook on a low heat for 3–4 minutes. Add the mushrooms and cook for 6 minutes or until they start to release their juices. Stir through the anchovies and tamari and cook for 1 minute. Transfer to a large bowl. Add the breadcrumbs and trickle in the egg until the mixture binds well. Add more crumbs if it's too wet and season well. Make 4 large balls from the mixture and form into burgers. Sit them on a baking sheet lined with baking parchment and chill in the fridge for 30 minutes.

2 For the chips, toss the potatoes with the oil and miso or tamari, and spread out in a roasting tin. Roast in the oven for 20 minutes until the chips begin to turn golden and the thinner ones are crisp. For the tahini dip, grind the garlic and sea salt in a pestle and mortar. Add the tahini and mix. Add about 2 tablespoons water to loosen it. Stir through the lemon juice.

3 To cook the burgers, heat half the remaining oil in a large frying pan on a medium heat, add the burgers 2 at a time, and cook for 3–5 minutes on each side, until golden. Repeat to cook the remaining burgers. Serve with the sweet potato chips and tahini dip.

STATISTICS PER SERVING

Energy 509kcals/2143kJ

Protein 13.6g

Fat 21.4g
Saturated fat 3.3g

Carbohydrate 65.3g
Sugar 14g

Fibre 10.8g

Salt 2.8g

BEAN PATTIES

SERVES 4　**PREP** 20 MINS　**COOK** 50 MINS
PLUS CHILLING

Mashed bean patties are a great vegetarian alternative to burgers. If making for kids, omit the chilli and replace half the onion with grated carrot for additional sweetness.

GUIDELINES PER SERVING

●○○ CALORIES

●●○ SATURATED FAT

●●○ SALT

1 onion, quartered
2 tbsp chopped flat-leaf parsley
400g can butter beans, drained and rinsed
400g can borlotti beans, drained and rinsed
1 tsp cayenne pepper
2 tbsp gluten-free plain flour
1 egg, lightly beaten
salt and freshly ground black pepper
3 tbsp olive oil
green salad, to serve

For the avocado salsa
2 ripe avocados, stoned and diced
1 large garlic clove, grated
1 red chilli, deseeded and finely chopped
2 tbsp olive oil
1 tbsp finely chopped fresh coriander leaves
juice of 1 lime
1 tsp sugar

SPECIAL EQUIPMENT food processor

1　Place the onion in a food processor and pulse until roughly chopped. Add the parsley and pulse again a couple of times. Then add the beans and pulse again. Transfer to a large bowl and stir in the cayenne pepper, flour, and egg. Season to taste and mix well. Shape the mixture into 8 patties and chill in the fridge until firm.

2　For the salsa, place all the ingredients in a bowl and combine well. Leave for 15 minutes, then stir and season to taste, as needed.

3　Heat a little oil in a large frying pan on a medium-high heat. Add the patties a few at a time and cook for 5 minutes on each side until crisp and golden. Repeat until all are cooked, adding more oil as needed. Serve with a green salad and the salsa on the side.

VARIATION
Other beans, such as cannellini, flageolet, or red kidney beans will work just as well.

NUTRIENT BOOST
Avocados contain vitamins E and B6 for a healthy heart and nervous system.

STATISTICS PER SERVING

Energy 424kcals/1761kJ

Protein 11.5g

Fat 31g
Saturated fat 5.6g

Carbohydrate 25g
Sugar 4g

Fibre 11.5g

Salt 1.4g

GNOCCHI WITH BLUE CHEESE

SERVES 4   **PREP** 30 MINS   **COOK** 50-65 MINS   **FREEZE** 3 MONTHS
UNCOOKED GNOCCHI

A few ingredients make up this delicious dish – delicate gnocchi tossed in sage butter and topped with Gorgonzola.

1kg (2¼lb) starchy potatoes, such as King Edward, Desirée, or Maris Piper, skin on
salt and freshly ground black pepper
150g (5½oz) rice flour, plus extra for dusting

pinch of freshly grated nutmeg
sea salt
50g (1¾oz) butter
4 sage leaves, torn
125g (4½oz) Gorgonzola cheese, cubed
wild rocket and tomato salad, to serve

1 Cook the whole potatoes in a large pan of boiling salted water until tender, about 30–40 minutes. Drain and leave until cool enough to handle. Peel and press the potatoes through a potato ricer onto a lightly floured surface; if you don't have a ricer, use a medium sieve but take care not to over-work the potato. Add half the rice flour, nutmeg, and the sea salt. Lightly knead until the mixture starts to come together, adding more flour as needed. Don't over-knead or the gnocchi will be tough when cooked. Divide the dough into 4. Roll each piece into a sausage shape about 1cm (½in) thick, then slice into 2cm (¾in) pieces, about 80–90 in total.

2 Preheat the oven to 190°C (375°F/Gas 5). Bring a large pan of water to a rolling boil. Add 10 gnocchi at a time, as they need lots of room; they will float to the top once cooked, about 2 minutes. Remove with a slotted spoon, transfer to a warmed ovenproof serving dish, and season with sea salt.

3 Heat the butter in a small frying pan, add the sage leaves, and cook on a medium heat for 2–3 minutes until the butter melts. Pour over the gnocchi and turn to coat. Sprinkle over the cubed cheese, then bake in the oven for 5–6 minutes. Serve with a wild rocket and tomato salad.

COOK'S TIP
To freeze, lay the uncooked gnocchi on a parchment-lined baking sheet and open freeze until solid, then transfer to an airtight freezer container. Cook from frozen, as above, for 3-5 minutes or until the gnocchi float to the surface.

STATISTICS PER SERVING

Energy 532kcals/2222kJ

Protein 14.5g

Fat 22g
Saturated fat 14g

Carbohydrate 65g

Sugar 1.5g

Fibre 5g

Salt 1.1g

BAKED POLENTA GNOCCHI WITH MUSHROOMS AND PARMESAN

SERVES 4   **PREP** 20 MINS   **COOK** 40 MINS

Earthy flavours just right for colder days. If you're making for kids try cutting out the gnocchi with shaped cutters.

GREAT FOR KiDS

200g (7oz) instant polenta or fine cornmeal
salt and freshly ground black pepper
80g (2¾oz) Parmesan cheese, finely grated, plus extra for topping
3 tbsp olive oil

500g (1lb 2oz) chestnut mushrooms, sliced
2 tsp dried chilli flakes
2 tbsp gluten-free plain flour
600ml (1 pint) milk
rocket salad, to serve

NUTRiENT BOOST
High in B vitamins, 4 tablespoons cooked mushrooms count as 1 of 5-a-day.

STATISTICS PER SERVING

Energy 492kcals/2055kJ

Protein 21g

Fat 23g
Saturated fat 9g

Carbohydrate 47g
Sugar 7g

Fibre 3g

Salt 0.7g

1 Tip the polenta into a medium pan and pour over about 800ml (1½ pints) water. Season with salt and pepper and heat gently, stirring frequently. Simmer for 5–10 minutes until thickened, or as per pack instructions, then stir through the Parmesan.

2 Use a drizzle of the oil to grease a shallow roasting tin, spoon in the polenta, spread to a thickness of about 1cm (½in), and leave to cool. When cooled, cut into bite-sized pieces and lift with a spatula to separate. Leave in the tin and set aside. Preheat the oven to 190°C (375°F/Gas 5).

3 Heat the remaining oil in a medium pan, add the mushrooms and chilli flakes, and season to taste. Cook on a low-medium heat for 5–6 minutes, then remove from the heat and stir in the flour and a little milk. Return to the heat and slowly pour in the remaining milk, stirring constantly. Cook for 5 minutes and season again. Pour the mixture over the gnocchi pieces, sprinkle over the Parmesan, and bake in the oven for 20 minutes until golden. Serve with a lightly dressed rocket salad.

VARIATION
Slices of roasted butternut squash make a tasty addition to this dish.

BANH XEO

SERVES 4 **PREP** 10 MINS **COOK** 50 MINS

These "sizzling cakes" from Vietnam are incredibly light, savoury pancakes made with rice flour and flavoured with turmeric and coconut.

100g (3½oz) rice flour
1 egg, lightly beaten
125ml (4fl oz) coconut cream
½ tsp ground turmeric
salt and freshly ground black pepper
3 spring onions, greens only,
   finely sliced

sunflower or vegetable oil, for frying
3 carrots, very finely diced
splash of gluten-free nam pla
   (fish sauce)
handful of beansprouts

1 Place the flour, egg, coconut cream, turmeric, and salt and pepper in a bowl and whisk until combined. Whisk in about 150ml (5fl oz) water until the mixture is the consistency of batter, then stir in the spring onions.

2 Heat 1 tablespoon oil in a small frying pan, add the carrots, season, and add the nam pla. Cook on a medium heat for 5 minutes until softened. Remove and set aside.

3 Wipe out the pan and add a little more oil to fry each pancake. Ladle a small amount of the batter into the pan and tilt so it coats evenly. Cook for 3 minutes until the base is cooked and the pancake is beginning to cook through. Then add a spoonful of the carrots and some beansprouts to one edge, fold the pancake over the filling, creating a half-moon shape, and cook for a further 1–2 minutes. Then carefully turn over and cook the other side for 1–2 minutes; don't let the filling fall out. Repeat until all the batter and filling has been used up.

COOK'S TIPS

Make sure you use coconut cream and not creamed coconut, which is too thick. You can sometimes buy banh xeo powder (to make an authentic batter with no egg) from Asian stores.

STATISTICS PER SERVING

Energy 305kcals/1268kJ

Protein 6g

Fat 19g
Saturated fat 10g

Carbohydrate 27g

Sugar 8g

Fibre 3.5g

Salt 0.8g

● ○ ○   CALORIES

● ● ○   SATURATED FAT

● ○ ○   SALT

CHARGRILLED POLENTA WITH SUMAC-ROASTED TOMATOES

SERVES 4   **PREP** 10 MINS   **COOK** 40 MINS

Polenta is elevated to new heights in this dish packed with added flavour and served with juicy vine tomatoes.

about 40 baby vine tomatoes
1 tbsp olive oil
2 tsp sumac (see page 126)
2 tbsp capers
wild rocket salad, lightly dressed,
    to serve

For the polenta
125g (4½oz) instant polenta or
    fine cornmeal
25g (scant 1oz) butter

large handful of freshly grated
    Parmesan cheese
pinch of dried chilli flakes
salt and freshly ground black pepper
olive oil, to coat

SPECIAL EQUIPMENT 18cm (7in) square
    tin, at least 2.5cm (1in) deep, or
    similar-sized serving dish, lined
    with parchment; griddle pan

1 Preheat the oven to 200°C (400°F/Gas 6). Cook the instant polenta mix as per pack instructions, adding it to the water in a steady stream and stirring as it simmers. Cook for 10 minutes, then beat in the butter, Parmesan, and chilli flakes, and season well with salt and pepper. Spoon into the prepared tin or serving dish, and set aside to cool.

2 Add the tomatoes to a roasting tin and pour over the oil to cover, then sprinkle with the sumac and season to taste. Roast in the oven for 15–20 minutes or until just beginning to char, then add the capers for the last 5 minutes of cooking. Remove and set aside.

3 Remove the polenta from the tin and cut into 8 triangles or stamp out circles, then coat the pieces lightly with the oil. Heat a griddle pan until hot and add the polenta pieces a few at a time. Cook for 2–3 minutes on each side until char lines appear. Serve topped with the tomatoes and capers and a lightly dressed wild rocket salad.

STATISTICS PER SERVING

Energy 304kcals/1267kJ

Protein 8g

Fat 18g
Saturated fat 6.5g

Carbohydrate 26g
Sugar 4.5g

Fibre 3g

Salt 0.9g

SICHUAN CRISPY BEAN CURD

SERVES 4   **PREP** 15 MINS   **COOK** 20 MINS

Hot and spicy and incredibly simple to make, this recipe relies on good-quality bean curd – buy it from an Asian store where you'll often find it's home-made.

GUIDELINES PER SERVING

◑○○ CALORIES

◑○○ SATURATED FAT

◑○○ SALT

300g (10oz) firm bean curd or tofu, cut into 1cm (½in) squares
3 tbsp sunflower or vegetable oil, or more if needed
½ tsp ground Sichuan pepper
3 tomatoes, cut in half lengthways, then each half into 4 wedges
5cm (2in) piece of fresh root ginger, peeled and finely sliced

pinch of soft light brown sugar
2 tbsp tamari (gluten-free soy sauce)
1 tbsp rice vinegar
bunch of spring onions, cut into 5cm (2in) lengths
cooked basmati rice, to serve

SPECIAL EQUIPMENT wok or large, deep non-stick frying pan

1 Toss the bean curd with a drizzle of the oil and the Sichuan pepper. Heat the remaining oil in a wok on a medium-high heat, add the bean curd, and fry for 2 minutes until golden, then turn and cook the other side for the same amount of time.

2 Add the tomatoes and ginger and stir-fry for 2 minutes, trying not to break up the bean curd.

3 Add the sugar and stir-fry until caramelized, add the tamari and vinegar, and cook for a further 2–3 minutes. Stir through the spring onions and serve hot with rice.

COOK'S TIP
Make sure you drain and press the curd before using: it needs to be really dry before frying to ensure it crisps nicely.

STATISTICS PER SERVING

Energy 174kcals/725kJ

Protein 9g

Fat 13g
Saturated fat 2g

Carbohydrate 6g
Sugar 5g

Fibre 1.5g

Salt 1.4g

● ● ○ CALORIES

● ● ● SATURATED FAT

● ○ ○ SALT

STUFFED BUTTERNUT SQUASH

SERVES 4　**PREP** 15 MINS　**COOK** 1¼ HOURS

A vibrantly coloured autumnal dish that would work just as well with pumpkin. You could use Cheddar, Parmesan, or goat's cheese instead of the Gruyère.

GREAT FOR KIDS

2 medium, or 4 small, butternut squash, halved lengthways and deseeded
1 tbsp olive oil, plus extra for greasing
225g (8oz) Gruyère cheese, grated

For the fruit and nut mix
100g (3½oz) hazelnuts, toasted and roughly chopped

75g (2½oz) dried cranberries, roughly chopped
small handful of flat-leaf parsley, finely chopped
pinch of dried chilli flakes
salt and freshly ground black pepper
wild rocket salad, to serve

NUTRIENT BOOST
Butternut squash is exceptionally rich in vitamin B6.

1 Preheat the oven to 190°C (375°F/Gas 5). Brush 2 baking sheets with oil. With a sharp knife, score a crisscross pattern on the flesh of each butternut squash half and brush with the oil. Sit the squash on the greased baking sheets, flesh-side down, and roast for about 1 hour until the flesh begins to soften. Now scoop out most of the flesh, leaving a thin layer still attached to the skins, and reserve the hollowed squash halves.

2 Place the flesh in a bowl and mash with a fork. Add all the fruit and nut mix ingredients to the mashed squash and mix well. Divide the mixture between the squash skins.

3 Sprinkle over the cheese and return the squash halves to the oven. Bake for a further 10–15 minutes until the cheese is bubbling. Serve the squash with a lightly dressed wild rocket salad.

STATISTICS PER SERVING

Energy 555kcals/2320kJ

Protein 23g

Fat 38g
Saturated fat 14g

Carbohydrate 31g
Sugar 18g

Fibre 11g

Salt 1g

⬤◯◯ CALORIES

⬤◯◯ SATURATED FAT

⬤◯◯ SALT

CHINESE PUMPKIN FRITTERS

SERVES 4 **PREP** 15 MINS **COOK** 40 MINS
PLUS CHILLING

These crisp, bite-sized fritters, fried in a gluten-free beer batter, make a light supper accompanied by rice.

500g (1lb 2oz) pumpkin or butternut
  squash, peeled and grated
5cm (2in) piece of fresh root ginger,
  peeled and grated
½ tsp turmeric
1 red chilli, deseeded and finely
  chopped
1 tbsp rice flour, plus extra for dusting
salt and freshly ground black pepper
vegetable oil, for deep frying
tamari (gluten-free soy sauce) and rice
  to serve

For the batter
100ml (3½fl oz) gluten-free beer
50g (1¾oz) rice flour
50g (1¾oz) gram (chickpea) flour
50ml (1¾fl oz) carbonated water

SPECIAL EQUIPMENT wok or large,
  deep, non-stick frying pan

1 Put the pumpkin in a colander or steamer basket and sit it over a pan of simmering water, covered, for 10–15 minutes until the pumpkin is tender. Remove, leave to cool slightly, then squeeze out any excess water. Place in a bowl and mix in the ginger, turmeric, chilli, and rice flour and season to taste.

2 Dust your hands with the extra rice flour, then take a tablespoonful of the pumpkin mixture and shape it into a ball. Repeat to make 19 more round balls. Chill them in the fridge on a lightly floured baking tray while you make the batter. Place all the batter ingredients in a bowl and season. Stir until combined, but still lumpy. If the batter is too thin, add more of the flours in equal amounts.

3 Pour the oil to a depth of 5cm (2in) into the wok and heat on a medium-high heat until hot. Don't leave the wok or pan unattended, take off the heat when not using, and keep a fire blanket nearby in case of fire. Dip the pumpkin balls into the batter one at a time, making sure they are well coated. Fry them in the hot oil, about 5 at a time, cooking each side for 2–3 minutes until golden and crisp. Remove and sit on kitchen paper to drain. Serve with a small bowl of tamari and some rice.

STATISTICS PER SERVING

Energy 180kcals/755kJ

Protein 5g

Fat 7.5g
Saturated fat 2.5g

Carbohydrate 22.5g
Sugar 2.5

Fibre 5g

Salt trace

MUSHROOM POT WITH FETA AND HERB TOPPING

GUIDELINES PER SERVING

● ○ ○ CALORIES

● ● ○ SATURATED FAT

● ● ○ SALT

SERVES 4 **PREP** 15 MINS **COOK** 50 MINS **FREEZE** 3 MONTHS WITHOUT TOPPING

A hearty vegetarian stew made with meaty mushrooms for a rich depth of flavour. Try baking individual portions if you have some mini ovenproof casserole dishes.

2 tbsp olive oil
1 red onion, finely chopped
2 garlic cloves, finely chopped
2 tsp dried oregano
1 tsp paprika
grated zest of ½ lemon
salt and freshly ground black pepper
2 green peppers, halved, deseeded, and sliced
200g (7oz) chestnut mushrooms, halved and quartered
200g (7oz) baby button mushrooms

1 small glass of dry white wine
450ml (15fl oz) hot gluten-free vegetable stock (see page 115)

For the topping
150g (5½oz) feta cheese, crumbled
2 eggs
handful of flat-leaf parsley, finely chopped

SPECIAL EQUIPMENT large flameproof casserole or lidded ovenproof pan

1 Heat the oil in the flameproof casserole, add the onion, and cook for 2–3 minutes on a low heat. Stir through the garlic, oregano, paprika, lemon zest, and some seasoning and cook for a further 1–2 minutes.

2 Add the peppers and cook on a low heat for 5 minutes or until beginning to soften, then add the mushrooms and cook for 5 minutes. Increase the heat, add the wine, and bubble for 1 minute. Add the stock and bring to the boil. Partly cover and cook on a low-medium heat for 20 minutes; it should begin to thicken slightly. If it is too thin, uncover, turn up the heat a little, and cook for 3–4 minutes more. Preheat the oven to 180°C (350°F/Gas 4).

3 To make the topping, mix together the feta, eggs, half the parsley, and a little seasoning; you may not need much salt as feta is already salty. Pour this over the mushroom mixture and bake in the oven for 15–20 minutes until the egg has set and the top is golden. Remove and sprinkle with the remaining parsley to serve.

STATISTICS PER SERVING

Energy 259kcals/1076kJ

Protein 13g

Fat 18g
Saturated fat 7g

Carbohydrate 8g
Sugar 7g

Fibre 3.5g

Salt 1.5g

BREAD AND PIZZA

● ● ○ CALORIES

● ○ ○ SATURATED FAT

● ○ ○ SALT

BROWN BREAD

MAKES 12 SLICES   **PREP** 20 MINS   **COOK** 35-40 MINS   **FREEZE** 3 MONTHS
PLUS RISING

A spongy and moist gluten-free loaf that rises well and has a good colour and flavour. This dough can also be used to make a tasty, seeded loaf (see Variation).

GREAT FOR KIDS

oil, for greasing
450g (1lb) gluten-free brown bread
  flour blend (see page 38), plus
  extra for dusting
2 tsp fast-action dried yeast
½ tsp salt
2 tbsp black treacle

1 egg
2 tbsp vegetable oil
1 tsp vinegar
beaten egg, for brushing

SPECIAL EQUIPMENT 450g (1lb) loaf tin

1 Lightly oil the tin. Sift the flour into a large bowl and add the yeast and salt. Measure 300ml (10fl oz) lukewarm water into a jug and add the treacle, egg, vegetable oil, and vinegar. Whisk together with a fork.

2 Make a well in the centre of the dry ingredients, add the wet ingredients, and mix well to form a dough. Turn onto a lightly floured surface and knead for about 5 minutes until smooth.

3 Shape the dough into a rectangle the same size as the tin and place in the prepared tin. Cover loosely with oiled cling film and leave in a warm place to rise for 1 hour or until doubled in size.

4 Preheat the oven to 200°C (400°F/Gas 6). Brush the top of the loaf with the beaten egg and bake in the oven for 35–40 minutes or until it is risen and golden brown. Remove from the oven and allow to cool for 5 minutes in the tin, then turn out and cool on a wire rack.

Energy	222kcals/941kJ
Protein	8g
Fat	5g
Saturated fat	2g
Carbohydrate	36g
Sugar	3.5g
Fibre	7g
Salt	0.3g

VARIATION

Seeded loaf Simply sprinkle a mix of seeds (poppy, pumpkin, and sunflower are all good) into the oiled tin before adding the dough. Once risen, finish with a final flourish of more seeds after brushing with egg.

SEEDED BROWN ROLLS

MAKES 12　　**PREP** 15 MINS　　**COOK** 15–20 MINS　　**FREEZE** 3 MONTHS
PLUS RISING

Golden-coloured and studded with crunchy seeds, these flavoursome rolls are a sure-fire success.

2 tbsp vegetable oil, plus extra
　for greasing
6 tbsp mixed seeds (see Cook's tip)
350g (12oz) gluten-free brown bread
　flour blend (see page 38), plus extra
　for dusting

100g (3½oz) buckwheat flour
2 tsp fast-action dried yeast
1 tsp xanthan gum
½ tsp salt
2 tbsp black treacle
2 eggs

1 Lightly oil 2 baking sheets and sprinkle over 1 tablespoon of the seeds. Sift the flours into a large bowl, add the yeast, xanthan, and salt. Measure 300ml (10fl oz) lukewarm water into a jug, then add the treacle, 1 egg, and the vegetable oil. Whisk together with a fork.

2 Make a well in the centre of the dry ingredients, add 4 tablespoons of the seeds, then gradually add the wet mixture until a soft, workable dough is formed. Turn onto a lightly floured surface and knead for about 5 minutes until smooth. Divide the dough into 12 balls. Place on the prepared sheets, cover loosely with oiled cling film, and leave in a warm place for about 1 hour or until doubled in size.

3 Preheat the oven to 200°C (400°F/Gas 6). Beat the remaining egg. Brush the rolls all over with the egg and sprinkle on the remaining seeds. Bake for 15–20 minutes or until the rolls are risen and golden brown. Remove from the oven and cool for 5 minutes on the sheets, then transfer to a wire rack to cool completely.

COOK'S TIP

Vary the seeds according to preference: pumpkin, caraway, and sesame work particularly well with the flavour of the bread. Alternatively, bags of pre-mixed seeds are often cheaper than buying separately.

STATISTICS PER ROLL

Energy 200kcals/844kJ

Protein 7.5g

Fat 7g
Saturated fat 1g

Carbohydrate 26g

Sugar 2g

Fibre 4g

Salt 0.2g

SOFT WHITE ROLLS

MAKES 8   **PREP** 20 MINS   **COOK** 15-20 MINS   **FREEZE** 3 MONTHS
PLUS RISING

These rolls are great for breakfast baps, sandwiches, and burger buns.

GUIDELINES PER SERVING

CALORIES

SATURATED FAT

SALT

450g (1lb) gluten-free white bread flour blend (see page 38), plus extra for dusting
2 tsp fast-action dried yeast
1 tsp xanthan gum
½ tsp salt

300ml (10fl oz) milk, plus extra for glazing
2 tbsp caster sugar
1 egg
2 tbsp vegetable oil, plus extra for greasing

1 Lightly flour 2 baking sheets. Sift the flour, yeast, xanthan, and salt into a large bowl. Heat the milk in a small pan until lukewarm, then add the sugar, egg, and oil and whisk together with a fork.

2 Make a well in the centre of the dry ingredients, pour in the wet ingredients, and mix until you have a soft, workable dough. Turn the dough out onto a lightly floured surface and knead for about 5 minutes until smooth.

3 Divide the dough into 8 balls. Place well apart on the prepared baking sheets and flatten each slightly. Cover loosely with oiled cling film and leave in a warm place for about 1 hour or until doubled in size.

4 Preheat the oven to 200°C (400°F/Gas 6). Brush the rolls all over with milk and dust with a little flour. Cover the rolls with a roasting tin turned upside down (see Cook's tip) and bake for 15–20 minutes or until the rolls are risen. Remove from the oven and cool for 5 minutes on the sheets, then transfer to a wire rack to cool completely.

COOK'S TIP
Baking the rolls under a roasting tin makes them crisp on the outside and soft on the inside.

STATISTICS PER ROLL

Energy 271kcals/1147kJ

Protein 8g

Fat 6g
Saturated fat 1.5g

Carbohydrate 47g
Sugar 6g

Fibre 2.5g

Salt 0.4g

BRIOCHE ROLLS

MAKES 12   **PREP** 15 MINS   **COOK** 20–25 MINS   **FREEZE** 3 MONTHS
PLUS RISING

Brioche needs a long rising time. If you prefer, start it the night before and leave it out somewhere cool – you can then have warm brioche for breakfast!

300ml (10fl oz) milk
200g (7oz) unsalted butter, softened
2 tbsp caster sugar
4 eggs
450g (1lb) gluten-free white bread
  flour blend (see page 38)
2 tsp fast-action dried yeast

2 tsp xanthan gum
1 tsp salt
oil, for greasing

SPECIAL EQUIPMENT 12 brioche moulds
  or a 12-hole deep muffin tin

1 Warm the milk in a small pan, stir in the butter and sugar until the butter melts and the sugar is dissolved, then take off the heat. Lightly beat 3 eggs in a small bowl or jug.

2 Sift the flour, yeast, xanthan, and salt into a large bowl, make a well in the centre, and add the milk mixture and beaten egg. Mix well to a sticky dough, similar to cake mixture. Cover with oiled cling film, then leave to rise in a warm place for at least 3 hours (or a cool place overnight) until it doubles in size.

3 Preheat the oven to 200°C (400°F/Gas 6). Grease the brioche moulds or the muffin tin and beat the remaining egg. Divide the dough into 12 lumps about the size of small oranges. Pass each lump back and forth between the palms of your hands to make rough balls and drop them into the holes; wet your hands if the dough is particularly sticky. Brush with the beaten egg.

4 Bake for 20–25 minutes or until golden and risen. Cool in the tin for 5 minutes before serving warm.

STATISTICS PER ROLL

Energy 308kcals/1296kJ

Protein 7g

Fat 18g
Saturated fat 10g

Carbohydrate 31g
Sugar 4g

Fibre 1.5g

Salt 0.5g

FOCACCIA

SERVES 6   PREP 15 MINS   COOK 30-35 MINS   FREEZE 3 MONTHS
             PLUS RISING

GUIDELINES PER SERVING

CALORIES
SATURATED FAT
SALT

This versatile Italian loaf, richly flavoured with olive oil, should be crisp on top with a light, airy crumb.

450g (1lb) gluten-free white bread flour blend (see page 38), plus extra for dusting
2 tsp xanthan gum
2 tsp fast-action dried yeast
2 tsp caster sugar
1 tsp salt

6 tbsp olive oil, plus extra for greasing
few sprigs of rosemary
coarse sea salt, to sprinkle

SPECIAL EQUIPMENT 25 x 16cm (10 x 6in) rectangular tin

1 Sift the flour, xanthan, yeast, sugar, and salt into a large bowl. Add 300ml (10fl oz) lukewarm water and 3 tablespoons oil to the flour, and mix to a slightly sticky, soft dough using a round-bladed knife. Transfer to a lightly floured surface and knead for 10 minutes until smooth and elastic. Return to the bowl, cover with oiled cling film, and leave in a warm place for about 1 hour or until doubled in size.

2 Lightly grease the tin. Tip the dough out onto a floured surface, knead lightly, and roll out to roughly the same size as the tin. Lift the dough into the tin and push it into the corners. Cover with oiled cling film and leave to rise in a warm place for 30 minutes or until doubled again in size.

3 Preheat the oven to 200°C (400°F/Gas 6). Firmly press the surface of the dough with your fingertips to give a dimpled effect. Scatter the rosemary, drizzle over the remaining olive oil, and sprinkle over the sea salt. Bake for 30–35 minutes or until the top is pale golden.

VARIATIONS

Red onion and feta Finely slice a small red onion, scatter over the top of the dough instead of the rosemary, along with 115g (4oz) crumbled feta cheese.
Olive and anchovy Roughly chop 140g (5oz) pitted green and black olives and scatter over the dough with 60g (2oz) chopped anchovy fillets. Drizzle with the oil and scatter over a few fresh or dried oregano leaves instead of the rosemary.

STATISTICS PER SERVING

Energy 361kcals/1522kJ

Protein 7g

Fat 12g
Saturated fat 2g

Carbohydrate 56g
Sugar 3g

Fibre 3g

Salt 0.9g

● ● ○ CALORIES

● ● ● SATURATED FAT

● ● ○ SALT

PIZZA MARGHERITA

GREAT FOR KiDS

SERVES 4　**PREP** 20 MINS　**COOK** 20-25 MINS
PLUS RISING

Add different toppings to this basic recipe: wilted spinach and ricotta; sliced mushrooms and Parma ham; pepperoni and chilli, sprinkled with rocket after baking.

oil, for greasing
450g (1lb) gluten-free white
　bread flour blend (see page 38),
　plus extra for dusting
1 tsp xanthan gum
2 tsp fast-action dried yeast
2 tsp caster sugar
1 tsp salt
1 egg
2 tbsp olive oil, plus extra to drizzle
300g (10oz) mozzarella cheese,
　drained and torn into pieces

a few black olives
basil leaves

For the tomato sauce
2 tbsp olive oil
1 small onion, finely chopped
2 garlic cloves, crushed
400g can cherry tomatoes
1 tbsp tomato purée
1 tsp dried oregano
pinch of sugar
salt and freshly ground black pepper

1 Lightly oil 2 baking sheets. Sift the flour, xanthan, yeast, sugar, and salt into a large bowl. Combine 300ml (10fl oz) warm water, the egg, and 2 tablespoons oil in a jug and whisk with a fork. Make a well in the centre of the dry ingredients, add the wet ingredients, and mix well to form a dough. Turn the dough out onto a floured surface and knead for 5 minutes until smooth. Return the dough to a lightly oiled bowl and cover loosely with oiled cling film. Leave in a warm place to rise until doubled in size, about 1 hour.

2 For the tomato sauce, heat the oil in a medium pan, add the onion, and sauté over a medium heat for 5 minutes. Stir in the garlic and cook for 1 minute. Add the remaining ingredients and simmer, uncovered, for 10 minutes. Set aside.

3 Preheat the oven to 230°C (450°F/Gas 8). Knock back the dough, divide into 2 balls and roll each out to a large circle. Place on the baking sheets. Divide the sauce, mozzarella, and olives between the pizza bases. Season with black pepper and drizzle over a little oil. Bake for 10 minutes or until golden. Scatter the basil over each pizza and serve.

STATISTICS PER SERVING

Energy 759kcals/3190kJ

Protein 28g

Fat 32g
Saturated fat 13g

Carbohydrate 89g
Sugar 9g

Fibre 6g

Salt 1.9g

CALZONE

MAKES 6   **PREP** 30 MINS   **COOK** 20-25 MINS
PLUS RISING

These folded pizzas are traditionally made without tomato sauce, relying instead on a combination of cheeses and pesto for a moist filling.

450g (1lb) gluten-free white bread flour blend (see page 38), plus extra for dusting
1 tsp xanthan gum
2 tsp fast-action dried yeast
2 tsp caster sugar
salt and freshly ground black pepper
1 egg, plus 1 egg, beaten, to glaze

2 tbsp olive oil, plus extra for greasing
6 tsp gluten-free pesto (shop-bought or see page 137)
1 red onion, finely sliced
125g (4½oz) mozzarella ball, diced
60g (2oz) Dolcelatte or Gorgonzola cheese, crumbled
6 slices of prosciutto ham

GREAT FOR KIDS

STATISTICS PER CALZONE

Energy 473kcals/1989kJ

Protein 19g

Fat 18g
Saturated fat 7g

Carbohydrate 57.5g
Sugar 3.5g

Fibre 3.5g

Salt 1g

1 Sift together the flour, xanthan, yeast, sugar, and 1 teaspoon salt in a large bowl. Mix 300ml (10fl oz) lukewarm water with the whole egg and oil, pour into the flour mixture, and use a round-bladed knife to mix to a slightly sticky, soft dough. Tip it out onto a floured surface and knead for 5 minutes until smooth and elastic. Return to the bowl, cover with oiled cling film, and leave in a warm place for about 1 hour or until doubled in size.

2 Preheat the oven to 220°C (425°F/Gas 7). Divide the mixture into 6 and, on a floured surface, roll each into a 20cm (8in) round. Divide between 2 large, lightly oiled baking sheets. Spread 1 teaspoon pesto on one half of each round. Scatter over some onion, the cheeses, ham, and season with black pepper. Brush the outside edge of the circle with the beaten egg and fold. Pinch and twist the edges to seal and make a steam hole on top. Brush with more egg and lightly dust with flour. Repeat for all 6 rounds. Bake for 20–25 minutes or until golden and puffy. Serve hot with salad.

VARIATIONS

Brie and bacon Scatter over 140g (5oz) sliced brie with sliced, cooked, smoked bacon rashers and a few sliced green olives.
Spicy pepper and salami Scatter over 125g (4½oz) sliced mozzarella, a sliced red pepper, 75g (2½oz) salami, and a sprinkle of dried chilli flakes.

SOCCA

MAKES 6   PREP 10 MINS   COOK 20 MINS
PLUS RESTING

These crispy, nutty pancakes made with chickpea flour are served as street food in the south of France.

140g (5oz) chickpea (gram) flour
2 tsp ground cumin
½ tsp salt

3 tbsp olive oil, plus extra to serve
sea salt flakes, to serve

1 Mix together the flour, cumin, and salt in a large bowl, make a well in the centre, add 300ml (10fl oz) water, then use a hand whisk to beat until smooth. Pour into a jug and leave to stand for at least 10 minutes for the batter to thicken.

2 Preheat the grill and line a baking sheet with baking parchment. Heat a little of the oil in a large, non-stick frying pan and, when hot, pour in enough of the batter to cover the bottom of the pan, tilting the pan to cover it quickly. Cook over a medium heat until the base is golden.

3 Transfer the socca to the lined baking sheet and pop under the hot grill. Cook for a further 2–3 minutes until the top is lightly charred. Transfer to a board. Repeat using the remaining oil and batter to make 5 more pancakes.

4 To serve, sprinkle the pancakes with sea salt flakes and a drizzle of olive oil, then roughly chop into bite-sized pieces. Heap onto a platter and serve as an appetizer with drinks.

COOK'S TIP
These are finished off under the grill to speed up the process, but if you prefer, simply turn over the pancakes and cook the other side in the pan until golden brown. They should become crisp and almost charred at the edges.

STATISTICS PER SOCCA

Energy 139kcals/581kJ

Protein 5g

Fat 9g
Saturated fat 1g

Carbohydrate 11g
Sugar 0.5g

Fibre 3.5g

Salt 0.4g

● ● ● CALORIES

● ● ● SATURATED FAT

● ● ○ SALT

GARLIC BREAD

MAKES 12 SLICES   **PREP** 35 MINS
PLUS RISING   **COOK** 1 HOUR 5 MINS   **FREEZE** 3 MONTHS
UNBUTTERED LOAF

For variety, try adding a few chopped tarragon leaves, a pinch of dried chilli flakes, or some grated Cheddar cheese.

GREAT FOR KIDS

450g (1lb) gluten-free white bread
  flour blend (see page 38), plus extra
  for dusting
2 tsp fast-action dried yeast
1 tbsp caster sugar
1 tsp xanthan gum
salt and freshly ground black pepper
1 egg, plus 1 egg, beaten, to glaze

2 tbsp vegetable oil
2–3 garlic cloves, crushed or
  finely chopped
175g (6oz) unsalted butter,
  softened, plus extra for greasing
2 tbsp finely chopped flat-leaf parsley
1 tbsp dried oregano

1 Lightly grease a baking sheet. Sift together the flour, yeast, sugar, xanthan, and salt in a large bowl. In a jug, whisk together 300ml (10fl oz) lukewarm water, the whole egg, and oil. Make a well in the centre of the dry ingredients, add the wet ingredients, and mix until it comes together in a ball. Transfer to a lightly floured surface and knead for 5–6 minutes until smooth and springy to the touch. Shape a fat sausage 15cm (6in) long, place on the baking sheet, and make several slashes across the top. Cover with oiled cling film and leave in a warm place for 1 hour or until doubled in size.

2 Preheat the oven to 220°C (425°F/Gas 7). Add a little salt to the beaten egg and brush over the loaf. Bake for 35–40 minutes or until risen, golden brown, and crusty. The loaf should make a hollow sound when tapped from below. Remove from the oven and cool completely on a wire rack.

3 Reduce the heat to 200°C (400°F/Gas 6). For the garlic butter, in a bowl mix the garlic, butter, parsley, oregano, a little salt, and plenty of pepper. Beat well. Make diagonal slices in the loaf, about 3cm (1¼in) apart. Don't slice all the way through. Place on a piece of foil large enough to wrap the loaf and spread the garlic butter on both sides of each slice. Lightly press together. Wrap tightly in the foil and seal, making the seam on the top.

4 Place on a baking sheet and bake for 10 minutes. Loosely unwrap the foil and bake for 6–8 minutes more or until the bread is crusty. Serve right away.

STATISTICS PER SLICE

Energy 274kcals/1155kJ

Protein 5g

Fat 16g
Saturated fat 8.5g

Carbohydrate 24g
Sugar 2g

Fibre 1.5g

Salt 0.5g

CHEESE AND ONION BREAD

MAKES 8 SLICES   **PREP** 30 MINS   **COOK** 30 MINS   **FREEZE** 3 MONTHS
PLUS RISING

A great loaf to serve with soup. The onions are caramelized before adding to the dough for a sweeter flavour.

15g (½oz) butter
3 tbsp olive oil, plus extra for greasing
3 large onions, finely sliced
4 tsp caster sugar
salt and freshly ground black pepper
450g (1lb) gluten-free white bread
  flour blend (see page 38), plus extra
  for dusting

2 tsp xanthan gum
2 tsp fast-action dried yeast
2 tsp mustard powder
115g (4oz) mature Cheddar cheese,
  coarsely grated
1 egg, plus 1 egg, beaten, to glaze

1 Melt the butter and 1 tablespoon oil in a large frying pan, add the onions, and fry over a medium heat for 6 minutes until just golden. Reduce the heat, add 2 teaspoons sugar and a pinch of salt, then cook the onions for a further 5–10 minutes or until soft and caramelized. Allow to cool.

2 Sift together the flour, xanthan, yeast, mustard, the remaining sugar, and 1 teaspoon salt in a large bowl, add a good grinding of pepper, and stir in two-thirds of the onions and cheese. Mix 250ml (8fl oz) lukewarm water with the whole egg and remaining oil, then pour into the flour mixture. Use a round-bladed knife to mix to a slightly sticky, soft dough, tip it out onto a lightly floured surface, and knead for 5 minutes until smooth and elastic. Shape the dough into a 16cm (6½in) round, place on a lightly oiled baking sheet, and cover loosely with oiled cling film. Leave in a warm place for 1 hour or until doubled in size.

3 Preheat the oven to 220°C (425°F/Gas 7). Add a good pinch of salt to the beaten egg and brush over the loaf. Sprinkle over the remaining onions and cheese and bake for 30 minutes until golden and crusty. Cool and then slice.

VARIATION
Omit the caramelized onion and use 5 sliced spring onions instead. They add a lovely green colour.

STATISTICS PER SLICE

Energy 350kcals/1463kJ

Protein 11g

Fat 13g
Saturated fat 5g

Carbohydrate 46g
Sugar 5g

Fibre 3g

Salt 0.9g

⬤⬤◯ CALORIES

⬤⬤◯ SATURATED FAT

⬤⬤◯ SALT

CARAWAY SEED BREAD

MAKES 12 SLICES   **PREP** 20 MINS   **COOK** 40-50 MINS   **FREEZE** 1 MONTH
PLUS RISING

This crunchy, crusty loaf, peppered with caraway seeds, is particularly good served with cured meats and cheese.

oil, for greasing
450g (1lb) gluten-free white
  bread flour blend (see page 38)
2 tsp fast-action dried yeast
2 tsp salt
2 tbsp light soft brown sugar
2 tsp caraway seeds

300ml (10fl oz) milk
2 eggs
2 tbsp vegetable oil
1 tsp balsamic vinegar
2 tsp caster sugar

SPECIAL EQUIPMENT 900g (2lb) loaf tin

1 Lightly oil the loaf tin. Sift the flour, yeast, and 1 teaspoon salt into a large bowl. Stir in the sugar and 1 teaspoon of the caraway seeds. Heat the milk until lukewarm (see Cook's tip). Add one of the eggs, the oil, and vinegar to the milk, and whisk with a fork. Make a well in the centre of the dry ingredients, add the wet ingredients, and mix well to form a dough. Knead on a lightly floured surface for 5 minutes, until smooth.

2 Shape the dough into a fat roll and transfer to the tin. Use a sharp knife to make diagonal slashes across the dough. Cover loosely with oiled cling film and leave in a warm place to rise for 1 hour or until doubled in size.

3 Preheat the oven to 220°C (425°F/Gas 7). To glaze, beat together the remaining egg, salt, and caster sugar, generously brush it over the loaf, and sprinkle the remaining caraway seeds. Bake for 35–40 minutes or until the loaf is risen and golden brown. Remove from the tin and bake for a further 5–10 minutes to crisp the crust. Remove from the oven and cool on a wire rack.

STATISTICS PER SLICE

Energy 190kcals/802kJ

Protein 6g

Fat 4.5g
Saturated fat 1g

Carbohydrate 31.5g
Sugar 5g

Fibre 1.6g

Salt 0.7g

COOK'S TIP
The ideal temperature for yeast to work is 35°C (95°F). Temperatures above 60°C (140°F) will kill the yeast, so it's important the milk is heated until warm but not hot to the touch.

● ● ● CALORIES

● ● ○ SATURATED FAT

● ● ○ SALT

SUN-DRIED TOMATO BREAD

MAKES 8 SLICES   **PREP** 20 MINS   **COOK** 30 MINS   **FREEZE** 3 MONTHS
PLUS RISING

Colourful and packed with intense Mediterranean flavours, this bloomer-style loaf is perfect for summer.

85g (3oz) sun-dried tomatoes in oil, drained, retaining the oil
450g (1lb) gluten-free white bread flour blend (see page 38), plus extra for dusting
2 tsp xanthan gum
2 tsp fast-action dried yeast
1 tsp caster sugar

salt and freshly ground black pepper
1 tsp dried oregano
30g (1oz) freshly grated Parmesan cheese
2 tbsp tomato purée
3 tbsp olive oil, drained from the sun-dried tomatoes
1 egg, plus 1 egg, beaten, to glaze

1 Roughly chop the sun-dried tomatoes. Sift together the flour, xanthan, yeast, sugar, and 1 teaspoon salt in a large bowl, add a good grinding of black pepper, then stir in the oregano, tomatoes, and two-thirds of the cheese.

2 Mix 250ml (8fl oz) lukewarm water with the tomato purée and oil, pour into the flour mix with the whole egg, and use a round-bladed knife to mix to a slightly sticky, soft dough. Tip the dough out onto a lightly floured surface and knead for 5 minutes until smooth and elastic. Shape into a 23cm (9in) long fat loaf shape. Use a sharp knife to make diagonal slashes across the top. Place on a floured baking sheet and cover loosely with oiled cling film. Leave in a warm place for 1 hour or until doubled in size.

3 Preheat the oven to 220°C (425°F/Gas 7). Add a good pinch of salt to the beaten egg and brush all over the loaf. Sprinkle with the remaining Parmesan and bake for 30 minutes or until golden and crusty. Cool slightly before slicing.

STATISTICS PER SLICE

Energy 305kcals/1284kJ

Protein 9g

Fat 10g

Saturated fat 1.9g

Carbohydrate 42g

Sugar 2g

Fibre 2.5g

Salt 0.6g

VARIATION

Roast pepper bread Use an equal drained weight of roasted peppers in oil instead of the sun-dried tomatoes.

SPICED LAMB FLATBREAD

MAKES 6　**PREP** 20 MINS　**COOK** 20-25 MINS
PLUS RISING

A street food supper – in Turkey, these are served garnished with a sprinkling of flat-leaf parsley and a squeeze of lemon.

GUIDELINES PER SERVING

CALORIES

SATURATED FAT

SALT

450g (1lb) gluten-free white bread flour blend (see page 38), plus extra for dusting
3 tsp fast-action dried yeast
2 tsp xanthan gum
1 tsp salt
1 tsp caster sugar
3 tbsp olive oil
2 tsp ground cumin

½–1 tsp chilli powder
1 red pepper, deseeded and roughly chopped
1 red onion, roughly chopped
1 garlic clove
handful of flat-leaf parsley, plus extra to garnish
175g (6oz) lamb mince
lemon and salad, to serve

1 Sift the flour, yeast, xanthan, salt, and sugar into a large bowl. Pour 325ml (11fl oz) lukewarm water and 2 tablespoons oil into the flour, mix to a slightly sticky, soft dough, and knead on a lightly floured surface for 5 minutes until smooth and elastic. Divide into 6 balls, place on oiled baking sheets, and cover with clean damp tea towels. Set aside in a warm place.

2 Preheat the oven to 200°C (400°F/Gas 6). For the topping, whizz together the spices, pepper, onion, garlic, and parsley in a food processor until finely chopped. Strain and discard the juice. Transfer to a bowl, add 1 tablespoon oil and the lamb mince, and season.

3 Roll out the dough balls into thin, flat ovals and place on oiled baking sheets. Spread a thin layer of the lamb mixture over each oval, leaving a thin border clear around the edges. Bake for 20–25 minutes or until the bread is crisp and the topping is cooked. Top with parsley and a squeeze of lemon, fold in half lengthways, and serve with salad for a light supper.

VARIATIONS

Chicken Instead of the lamb, mince an equal weight of chicken with the vegetables.
Vegetarian Omit the lamb and add 1 roughly chopped aubergine to the food processor. Strain out excess liquid and stir through 1 tablespoon gluten-free tahini.

STATISTICS PER FLATBREAD

Energy 371kcals/1565kJ

Protein 13g

Fat 9.5g
Saturated fat 2.4g

Carbohydrate 58g
Sugar 4g

Fibre 4g

Salt 0.8g

CALORIES

SATURATED FAT

SALT

GREAT FOR KIDS

PITTA BREAD

MAKES 8   **PREP** 15 MINS   **COOK** 10-15 MINS   **FREEZE** 3 MONTHS
PLUS RISING

These are pale and soft when baked, and take on a slight golden hue when reheated. Cooling them wrapped in a damp tea towel gives them their soft texture.

450g (1lb) gluten-free white bread
  flour blend (see page 38), plus extra
  for dusting
3 tsp fast-action dried yeast
2 tsp xanthan gum

1 tsp salt
1 tsp caster sugar
2 tbsp olive oil, plus extra for greasing
  hummus and dips (see page 188),
  to serve (optional)

1 Sift together the flour, yeast, xanthan, salt, and sugar in a large bowl. Mix 350ml (12fl oz) lukewarm water with the oil, pour into the flour mix, and use a round-bladed knife to mix to a slightly sticky, soft dough.

2 Tip the dough out onto a lightly floured surface and knead for 5 minutes until smooth and elastic. Divide the dough into 8 balls. Place the balls on 2 large oiled baking sheets and cover loosely with oiled cling film. Leave in a warm place for 10 minutes.

3 On a lightly floured surface, roll out each ball into a flat oval, then return to the oiled baking sheets, cover with a damp tea towel, and leave in a warm place for 20 minutes or until puffy.

4 Preheat the oven to 220°C (425°F/Gas 7). Bake for 10–15 minutes or until pale golden and puffed up. Remove from the oven, wrap the pittas in a damp tea towel on a wire rack and leave until cold. To serve, pop under a hot grill or in a toaster until warm. Serve with hummus and dips or split the pittas and add a filling of your choice.

COOK'S TIPS

Make these with gluten-free brown bread flour blend (see page 38), if preferred, adding a little more water if required. You can freeze the cold pittas in a plastic bag; thaw before toasting to warm through.

STATISTICS PER PITTA

Energy 217kcals/917kJ

Protein 5g

Fat 3.5g
Saturated fat 0.5g

Carbohydrate 41g
Sugar 1g

Fibre 2.5g

Salt 0.5g

TORTILLA

GREAT FOR KiDS

MAKES 6   **PREP** 20 MINS   **COOK** 20-30 MINS

These Mexican flatbreads are simple to make and cooked on the hob. Serve them with a choice of delicious fillings.

115g (4oz) gluten-free plain flour, plus
  extra for dusting
85g (3oz) fine cornmeal or polenta
2 tsp xanthan gum
1 tsp salt

1 tsp gluten-free baking powder
15g (½oz) vegetable shortening,
  lard, or butter, cubed
ready-made salsa, guacamole,
  or soured cream, to taste

1 Sift together the flour, cornmeal, xanthan, salt, and baking powder in a bowl, and rub in the fat. Stir in 150ml (5fl oz) lukewarm water and mix to a soft dough. Knead on a floured surface for 2–3 minutes until smooth and elastic. Leave for 20 minutes in a bowl covered with oiled cling film. Divide into 6 balls. Roll out each ball between 2 pieces of baking parchment to a thin, flat round, about 20cm (8in) in diameter. Dust with flour.

2 Heat a large, heavy frying pan, add a tortilla, and cook for 5–6 minutes, turning once, until speckled with brown spots. Keep warm in a dry tea towel. Cook the remainder in the same way. Prepare a filling of your choice (see below). Divide the mixture between the tortillas, adding a spoonful of salsa, guacamole, or soured cream to taste. Roll up and serve.

CHOOSE YOUR FILLING

Spicy chicken filling Heat 2 tablespoons vegetable oil in a large, heavy frying pan. Add 4 thinly sliced chicken breasts and sauté for 10 minutes. Add 1 red pepper, cut into strips, 1 sliced red onion, and 1 crushed garlic clove. Sauté for 6-8 minutes. Add 1 teaspoon each of ground cumin, ground coriander, paprika, and ½ teaspoon dried chilli flakes. Cook for 30 seconds and remove. Stir through the juice of 1 lime and some chopped fresh coriander.

Mixed pepper filling Substitute the chicken with 3 mixed colour peppers, cut into strips, and 115g (4oz) baby sweetcorn, halved lengthways. Add the sweetcorn with the garlic after the peppers and onions have cooked, and sauté for 1 minute, before adding the spices.

STATISTICS PER TORTILLA

Energy 141kcals/592kJ

Protein 3g

Fat 3g
Saturated fat 1g

Carbohydrate 24g
Sugar 0.5g

Fibre 1g

Salt 0.9g

MASALA DOSA

SERVES 6   **PREP** 20 MINS   **COOK** 40-50 MINS   **FREEZE** 1 MONTH
PLUS SOAKING

These spicy vegan pancakes, made from ground lentils and rice, are traditionally served for breakfast in southern India.

175g (6oz) basmati rice
60g (2oz) urad dal
1 tsp fenugreek seeds
salt
vegetable oil, for frying

For the potato filling
2 tbsp vegetable oil
1 onion, finely chopped
1 green chilli, deseeded and chopped
1 garlic clove, finely chopped
2.5cm (1in) piece of fresh root ginger, grated

2 tsp black mustard seeds
¼ tsp turmeric
6 dried curry leaves
450g (1lb) potatoes, cubed
zest and juice of ½ lemon
2 tbsp finely chopped fresh coriander

For the dipping sauce
30g (1oz) fresh coriander
1 small tomato
½ green chilli, deseeded
juice of 1 lemon
½ tsp caster sugar

1 Place the rice, dal, and fenugreek seeds in a large bowl, cover with cold water, and soak for 6–8 hours or overnight. Drain and coarsely grind in a food processor with a pinch of salt. Add 300ml (10fl oz) cold water and process to a smooth batter the consistency of thin cream.

2 For the spicy potato filling, heat the oil in a medium pan and fry the onion for 4 minutes or until soft. Add the chilli, garlic, ginger, mustard seeds, turmeric, and curry leaves and cook for 30 seconds or until the mustard seeds start to pop. Add the potatoes, lemon zest and juice, a good pinch of salt, and 250ml (8fl oz) water. Bring to the boil, cover, and simmer for 15–20 minutes until tender. Remove the lid and simmer until soft and breaking up. Stir in the coriander and keep warm. For the sauce, place all the ingredients with a pinch of salt in a food processor and whizz to a rough paste.

3 Heat 1 teaspoon oil in a small frying pan. Cover the pan with a ladleful of batter and cook over medium heat for 2–3 minutes. Flip and cook for another 1–2 minutes. Keep warm. Repeat to make 5 pancakes. Divide the potato filling between the pancakes, fold over, and serve with the sauce.

STATISTICS PER SERVING

Energy 250kcals/1049kJ

Protein 6.5g

Fat 6g
Saturated fat 0.7g

Carbohydrate 40g
Sugar 2.3g

Fibre 3g

Salt 0.3g

○○○ CALORIES

○○○ SATURATED FAT

○○○ SALT

NAAN BREAD

SERVES 8   **PREP** 15 MINS   **COOK** 15-30 MINS   **FREEZE** 3 MONTHS

Using fizzy lemonade in a bread recipe sounds strange, but it really does work. The naan puff up to give a wonderfully soft-textured bread – and they don't taste of lemonade at all!

250g (9oz) gluten-free plain flour, plus extra for dusting
2 tsp xanthan gum
2 tsp gluten-free baking powder
1 tsp salt

1–2 tsp black onion (nigella) seeds (optional)
175ml (6fl oz) clear sparkling lemonade
30g (1oz) butter, melted

1 Sift together the flour, xanthan, baking powder, and salt in a large bowl. Stir through the black onion seeds (if using), pour the lemonade into the mixture, and mix with a round-bladed knife to a slightly sticky, soft dough.

2 Tip the dough out onto a lightly floured surface and knead for 5 minutes until smooth and elastic. Transfer to a bowl, cover with a damp tea towel, and leave for 10 minutes. Divide the mixture into 4 pieces. Roll out each ball into a flat teardrop-shaped oval.

3 Heat a heavy frying pan, brush one side of each naan with the melted butter, and cook butter-side down in the pan for 3–4 minutes, or until the base is golden. Brush the top with butter, then turn over and cook for a further 3–4 minutes or until puffed up and golden. Transfer to a tea towel while you cook the remainder in the same way. Serve warm.

STATISTICS PER SERVING

Energy 142kcals/597kJ

Protein 3g

Fat 3.5g
Saturated fat 2g

Carbohydrate 24g
Sugar 1.75g

Fibre 1.25g

Salt 0.95g

VARIATIONS

Garlic and coriander Once cooked on both sides, scatter a little chopped garlic and a small handful of chopped fresh coriander leaves over the top, flip over, and cook for 30 seconds or until the garlic is golden.
Peshwari Mix 2 tablespoons desiccated coconut with 1 teaspoon sugar. Once cooked on both sides, brush the top with more butter, scatter over the coconut, flip over, and cook for 30-45 seconds or until the coconut is toasted.

CORNBREAD WITH OLIVES

SERVES 12   **PREP** 10 MINS   **COOK** 30-35 MINS   **FREEZE** 3 MONTHS

Cornbread is served in the United States alongside spicy stews and fried chicken – it's great for mopping up juices. If making for kids, omit the olives.

326g can sweetcorn, drained and
 juice reserved
225g (8oz) fine cornmeal or polenta
115g (4oz) gluten-free plain flour
60g (2oz) caster sugar
1 tbsp gluten-free baking powder
1 tsp xanthan gum
½ tsp salt
120ml (4fl oz) milk

2 eggs, beaten
60g (2oz) butter, melted, plus
 extra for greasing
115g (4oz) pimento-stuffed green
 olives, halved

SPECIAL EQUIPMENT 20cm (8in) round
 cake tin

GREAT FOR KIDS

1 Preheat the oven to 200°C (400°F/Gas 6). Grease the tin and line the base with baking parchment. Add half the sweetcorn to a large jug, then blitz with a stick blender until creamed or transfer to a food processor. Sift together the cornmeal, flour, sugar, baking powder, xanthan, and salt in a large bowl.

2 Beat the milk and eggs together, add to the dry ingredients along with the butter, creamed sweetcorn, and the remaining whole kernels, and beat together until just mixed.

3 Spoon the mixture into the cake tin, level the surface, and scatter over the olives. Bake for 30–35 minutes or until risen and golden. Leave to cool in the tin for 5 minutes. Run a knife around the edge of the loaf and turn out from the tin. Cool slightly on a wire rack, then serve warm in wedges.

COOK'S TIPS
If you like a bit of heat, add a couple of chopped chillies to the mixture. If freezing, leave to cool completely, then pack into a plastic bag and freeze for up to 3 months. Reheat for 10 minutes in a hot oven after defrosting.

STATISTICS PER SERVING

Energy 288kcals/1201kJ

Protein 5g

Fat 16g
Saturated fat 4.5g

Carbohydrate 30g
Sugar 7g

Fibre 1.5g

Salt 0.8g

WALNUT AND THYME DAMPER

MAKES 8   **PREP** 20 MINS   **COOK** 10-15 MINS   **FREEZE** 3 MONTHS

A real campfire recipe: get the kids to make these, winding strips of dough around sticks they've collected.

GREAT FOR KiDS

225g (8oz) gluten-free plain flour
2 tsp xanthan gum
1 tsp gluten-free baking powder
1 tsp salt
30g (1oz) walnuts, finely chopped
2 tsp thyme leaves
garlic butter (see page 226), to serve

SPECIAL EQUIPMENT 8 clean wooden sticks or skewers, soaked in cold water for 30 minutes

1 Preheat the grill to medium (if using). Sift together the flour, xanthan, baking powder, and salt into a bowl, then stir in the walnuts and thyme. Gradually add 175ml (6fl oz) water and mix to form a soft dough.

2 Divide the dough into 8 balls and roll each between your fingers to make a slim sausage about 28cm (11in) long. Wrap around the soaked sticks.

3 Cook these held over the flames of a fire, or under a medium grill on an oiled baking sheet, for 10–15 minutes until crisp, turning occasionally. Serve with garlic butter.

NUTRiENT BOOST

The essential fats in walnuts can help reduce the risk of heart disease.

VARIATION

Skip the walnuts and thyme and carry on as above. Once cooked, serve with butter and strawberry jam – Brownie-camp style!

STATISTICS PER DAMPER

Energy 123kcals/518kJ

Protein 3g

Fat 3g
Saturated fat 0.3g

Carbohydrate 21g
Sugar 0.5g

Fibre 1.5g

Salt 0.6g

« Walnuts
Like most nuts, walnuts contain plenty of oil and can quickly turn rancid. Always check any packets that look like they've been hanging around in the cupboard for a while.

OATEN BROWN SODA BREAD

⬤⬤◯ CALORIES

⬤⬤◯ SATURATED FAT

⬤⬤◯ SALT

MAKES 8 WEDGES   **PREP** 10 MINS   **COOK** 40–45 MINS

Soda bread is quick to make and bake as it doesn't require the long rising time of a yeast dough.

oil or butter, for greasing
350g (12oz) gluten-free brown bread flour blend (see page 38), plus extra for dusting
2 tsp xanthan gum
1½ tsp gluten-free bicarbonate of soda
1½ tsp gluten-free cream of tartar
1 tsp salt

60g (2oz) rolled oats, plus extra to sprinkle
400ml (14fl oz) buttermilk, plus extra to glaze
2 tbsp black treacle

SPECIAL EQUIPMENT 25cm (10in) deep, round cake tin

1 Preheat the oven to 220°C (425°F/Gas 7). Lightly grease a baking sheet.

2 Sift together the flour, xanthan, soda, cream of tartar, and salt in a large bowl. Stir in the oats. Make a well in the centre of the dry ingredients, add the buttermilk and treacle, and mix to form a soft dough using a round-bladed knife. Lightly knead on a floured surface until just smooth.

3 Shape the dough into a 15cm (6in) round and place on the baking sheet. Use a knife to score the loaf into 8 wedges across the top, brush over a little more buttermilk, and sprinkle lightly with a few more oats.

4 Place the cake tin over the top of the soda bread and bake near the top of the oven for 30 minutes. Remove the tin and brown for 15–20 minutes until the top is crusty. Remove from the oven and transfer to a wire rack to cool for 10 minutes before slicing into wedges to serve.

COOK'S TIPS
Cooking the loaf under a cake tin helps it rise and keeps the centre moist. It is best eaten while still fresh and warm, as it goes stale quicker than yeast bread.

STATISTICS PER WEDGE

Energy 194kcals/825 kJ

Protein 8g

Fat 2g
Saturated fat 0.3g

Carbohydrate 36g
Sugar 6g

Fibre 6g

Salt 1.1g

● ● ● CALORIES

● ● ● SATURATED FAT

● ● ○ SALT

PUMPKIN BREAD WREATH

SERVES 12   **PREP** 25 MINS   **COOK** 1 HOUR 5 MINS-1¼ HOURS
PLUS RISING

Gently spiced, this lovely moist bread makes an impressive centrepiece for a party, especially around Hallowe'en.

GREAT FOR KIDS

vegetable oil, for greasing
500g (1lb 2oz) pumpkin or butternut
   squash, peeled, deseeded, and cut
   into 5cm (2in) cubes, or 400g (14oz)
   canned pumpkin purée
2 tbsp olive oil
salt and freshly ground black pepper
675g (1½lb) gluten-free white bread
   flour blend (see page 38),
   plus extra for dusting
2 tsp xanthan gum

1 tbsp fast-action dried yeast
2½ tsp salt
1 tsp ground cinnamon
1 tsp ground ginger
½ tsp ground cloves
60g (2oz) light soft brown sugar
30g (1oz) butter
200ml (7fl oz) milk
2 large eggs
1 tsp caster sugar
2 tbsp pumpkin seeds

1 Oil a large baking sheet. Place the butternut cubes in a roasting tin and drizzle over the olive oil, 3 tablespoons water, and seasoning. Cover with foil and roast for 30–35 minutes or until tender. Transfer to a food processor and whizz until smooth. Spread in the roasting tin and leave until cold.

2 Sift the flour, xanthan, yeast, 1½ teaspoons salt, and the spices into a large bowl and stir in the brown sugar. Melt the butter in a pan, add the milk and heat to lukewarm, then add 1 egg and beat with a fork. Pour the wet mixture over the dry ingredients, add the squash, and mix to form a dough. Knead the dough on a lightly floured surface for 5 minutes until smooth. Roll it into 12 even-sized balls. Place 9 of these in a circle on a large, oiled baking sheet and 3 in the centre to make a wreath. Cover with oiled cling film and leave in a warm place for 1 hour or until doubled in size.

3 Preheat the oven to 200°C (400°F/Gas 6). Beat the remaining egg, caster sugar, and 1 teaspoon salt, and brush over the rolls. Scatter over the pumpkin seeds and bake for 35–40 minutes until golden brown. Cool for 30 minutes. Serve the bread warm on a large board, so guests can break off the rolls.

STATISTICS PER SERVING

Energy 304kcals/1283kJ

Protein 8g

Fat 8g
Saturated fat 2.5g

Carbohydrate 50g
Sugar 9g

Fibre 3.5g

Salt 0.9g

SAVOURY TARTS AND PIES

FENNEL AND GRUYÈRE TART

SERVES 6   **PREP** 20 MINS   **COOK** 40 MINS
PLUS CHILLING

The light aniseed flavour of fennel and sweet, tangy
Gruyère make a winning combination in this recipe.

400g (14oz) gluten-free shortcrust
pastry (see pages 44–5)
gluten-free plain flour, for dusting

For the filling
3 tbsp olive oil
1 onion, sliced
1 large fennel bulb, trimmed,
quartered, and sliced

salt and freshly ground black pepper
½ tsp freshly grated nutmeg
4 eggs
300ml (10fl oz) double cream
100g (3½oz) Gruyère cheese, grated
salad leaves, to serve

SPECIAL EQUIPMENT 23cm (9in) round,
3cm (1¼in) deep, fluted tart tin

1 Preheat the oven to 200°C (400°F/Gas 6). For the filling, heat the oil in a
frying pan, add the onion, and fry on a medium heat for 2–3 minutes. Add
the fennel and sauté for 6–8 minutes, stirring occasionally, until golden.
Season with salt, pepper, and nutmeg and set aside. Beat the eggs and
cream together in a jug.

2 Roll out the pastry on a lightly floured surface to a thickness of 5mm (¼in).
Lift it over the tin and press into the base and sides. (Gluten-free pastry is
delicate, so if you get a few cracks, "glue" them with a little water.) Trim the
edges. Prick the base with a fork, line with baking parchment and fill with
baking beans, and bake for 15 minutes. Remove the beans and paper, then
return to the oven for another 5 minutes to crisp up.

3 Scatter the onions and fennel over the base and sprinkle the cheese.
Pour the egg and cream mixture into the pastry case. Return the tart to the
oven. Reduce the temperature to 180°C (350°F/Gas 4) and bake for 20–25
minutes or until the filling is set and golden brown. Serve warm or cold
with salad leaves.

STATISTICS PER SLICE

Energy 698kcals/2886kJ

Protein 14g

Fat 58g
Saturated fat 31g

Carbohydrate 31g
Sugar 2.5g

Fibre 1g

Salt 1.2g

RED PEPPER AND CHILLI TART

GUIDELINES PER SERVING

● ● ○ CALORIES

● ● ● SATURATED FAT

● ● ○ SALT

SERVES 6   **PREP** 25-30 MINS   **COOK** 1¼-1½ HOURS   **FREEZE** 1 MONTH

These hot flavours are tempered with cool sheep's cheese.
Swap the cheese for your favourite – blue, Brie, or feta.

400g (14oz) gluten-free shortcrust
  pastry (see pages 44–5)
gluten-free plain flour, for dusting

For the filling
3 red peppers
2 red chillies
2 tbsp olive oil
1 red onion, finely chopped
salt and freshly ground black pepper

leaves from a few sprigs of thyme
150g (5½oz) soft sheep's
  cheese, crumbled
150ml (5fl oz) double cream
2 eggs
2 garlic cloves, grated

SPECIAL EQUIPMENT 20.5cm (8in)
  round, loose-bottomed tart tin

1 Preheat the oven to 200°C (400°F/Gas 6). For the filling, sit the peppers
and chillies on a baking sheet and coat with half the oil. Cook in the oven
for 30–40 minutes until the skins begin to char. Transfer the peppers to a
plastic bag to cool. Chop and deseed the chillies. When the peppers are
cool, remove the skins and seeds, roughly chop, and add to the chillies.

2 Carefully roll out the pastry on a lightly floured surface to a thickness
of 5mm (¼in). Lift it over the tin and press into the base and sides. Prick
the base with a fork, line with baking parchment and fill with baking beans,
and bake for 15 minutes. Remove the beans and paper and return to the
oven for another 5 minutes to crisp up. Reduce the oven temperature to
180°C (350°F/Gas 4).

3 Heat the remaining oil in a frying pan, add the onion, and cook for
6–8 minutes on a medium-low heat until softened. Season to taste, then
stir through half the thyme. Leave to cool a little, then transfer to the pastry
case. Add the peppers and chillies, spreading them out evenly, and tuck in
the cheese so it covers all the tart. Mix together the cream and egg and
season. Add the remaining thyme and the garlic and stir well. Pour the
mixture over the tart evenly, sit the tin on a baking sheet, and bake for
20–25 minutes or until the top is set and golden. Remove and leave to cool
before releasing from the tin.

STATISTICS PER SLICE

Energy 597kcals/2481kJ

Protein 13g

Fat 45g
Saturated fat 20g

Carbohydrate 35g
Sugar 6.5g

Fibre 4g

Salt 1.1g

⬤⬤◯ CALORIES

⬤⬤⬤ SATURATED FAT

⬤◯◯ SALT

GOAT'S CHEESE TARTLETS

MAKES 6　　**PREP** 30 MINS
PLUS CHILLING　　**COOK** 25–35 MINS

Sweet prunes pair well with goat's cheese and the tartlets can be served with sun-dried tomato bread (see page 230).

GREAT FOR KIDS

100g (3½oz) butter, cubed, plus extra for greasing
225g (8oz) gluten-free plain flour, plus extra for dusting
pinch of salt
1 tsp xanthan gum
1 tbsp olive oil
1 large red onion, finely sliced
leaves from a few sprigs of thyme

225g (8oz) semi-hard, mild goat's cheese, finely cubed
125g (4½oz) pitted soft prunes, chopped
freshly ground black pepper

SPECIAL EQUIPMENT 6 x 9cm (3½in) round, 2.5cm (1in) deep, tart tins

1 Preheat the oven to 200°C (400°F/Gas 6). Grease the tins with butter. Mix the flour, salt, and xanthan in a bowl. Rub the butter in with your fingertips until it forms crumbs. Gradually add 1–2 tablespoons cold water until the mixture binds to form a dough. Briefly knead the dough on a lightly floured surface until smooth, wrap in cling film, and chill for 10 minutes.

2 Cut the pastry dough into 6 even pieces. Roll out each piece between 2 pieces of cling film and cut 6 x 12cm (5in) rounds. Lift the pastry into the tart tins, pushing it into the base and sides. If it tears, patch it up. Trim the top, prick the bases with a fork, and line each with baking parchment and fill with baking beans. Bake for 10–15 minutes or until the edges turn pale golden. Remove the beans and paper, and set the cases aside.

3 For the filling, heat the oil in a small pan, add the onion and thyme, and cook on a medium heat for 5 minutes until the onion begins to soften and turn transparent. Reduce the heat and cook for a further 5 minutes, to sweeten them a little, then spoon them into the pastry cases.

4 Mix the goat's cheese and prunes and season with pepper. Divide between the cases and bake for 15–20 minutes or until the mixture is bubbling and the pastry is golden brown. Remove and serve warm.

STATISTICS PER TARTLET

Energy　435kcals/1818kJ

Protein　12g

Fat　26g

Saturated fat　16g

Carbohydrate　36g

Sugar　10g

Fibre　4g

Salt　1g

● ○ ○ CALORIES

● ● ● SATURATED FAT

● ○ ○ SALT

GOAT'S CHEESE AND RED ONION PASTRY SLICES

SERVES 8   **PREP** 20 MINS   **COOK** 40 MINS   **FREEZE** 1 MONTH

Sweet onion partnered with goat's cheese works perfectly on this very easy, free-form tart.

400g (14oz) gluten-free rough puff
  pastry (see pages 46–7)
gluten-free plain flour, for dusting

For the topping
2 tbsp olive oil
3 large red onions, finely chopped

salt and freshly ground black pepper
leaves from a few sprigs of rosemary,
  finely chopped
5 anchovies, roughly chopped
225g (8oz) goat's cheese, crumbled
handful of pine nuts (optional)

1 Preheat the oven to 200°C (400°F/Gas 6). Roll out the pastry on a lightly floured surface to a rectangle as large as you can get the pastry to go without tearing. Place it on a baking sheet, prick with a fork all over, and bake in the oven for 15–20 minutes until puffed and golden. Remove and set aside.

2 While the pastry is baking, heat the oil in a large, heavy frying pan, add the onion, and season with salt and pepper. Cook on a low heat for 10 minutes, stir in the rosemary and anchovies, and cook for a further 10–15 minutes until soft and sweetened.

3 Spread the onions all over the pastry base, leaving a 2.5cm (1in) border, then top with the goat's cheese and pine nuts (if using). Bake in the oven for 10–15 minutes or until the cheese has melted. Leave to cool for 10 minutes, then cut into slices to serve. Delicious served with home-made chutney.

STATISTICS PER SLICE

Energy 342kcals/1425kJ

Protein 10g

Fat 24g
Saturated fat 11g

Carbohydrate 22g
Sugar 4g

Fibre 1g

Salt 1g

« Red onion
The red and crimson flesh of a red onion is milder than brown and white onions and cooks to a caramel sweetness, the perfect foil to tangy goat's cheese.

WILD MUSHROOM AND TALEGGIO TART

SERVES 6   **PREP** 20 MINS   **COOK** 50 MINS   **FREEZE** 1 MONTH

GUIDELINES PER SERVING

CALORIES

SATURATED FAT

SALT

An earthy, robust tart that is good for entertaining, served with roasted new potatoes and a lightly dressed watercress and orange salad.

400g (14oz) gluten-free shortcrust pastry (see pages 44–5)
gluten-free plain flour, for dusting

For the filling
2 tbsp olive oil
150g (5¹/₂oz) mixed wild or exotic mushrooms, larger ones sliced
150g (5¹/₂oz) chestnut mushrooms, roughly chopped
25g (scant 1oz) dried porcini mushrooms, soaked in boiling water for 30 minutes and drained
3 garlic cloves, finely chopped

50g (1³/₄oz) hazelnuts, toasted and roughly chopped
salt and freshly ground black pepper
handful of flat-leaf parsley, finely chopped
3 tbsp double cream
1 egg, lightly beaten
200g (7oz) Taleggio cheese, sliced
pinch of paprika

SPECIAL EQUIPMENT 35 x 12cm (14 x 5in) rectangular, loose-bottomed tart tin, 2.5cm (1in) deep

1 Preheat the oven to 200°C (400°F/Gas 6). Roll out the pastry on a lightly floured surface to a thickness of 5mm (¹/₄in). Line the tin with the pastry, patching up any holes. Trim to neaten. Prick the base with a fork, line with baking parchment and fill with baking beans, and bake in the oven for 15 minutes or until the edges start turning golden. Remove the beans and paper and return to the oven for 5 minutes to crisp up.

2 Meanwhile, for the filling, heat the oil in a large frying pan, add all the mushrooms, and cook on a medium-high heat for 10 minutes. Stir through the garlic and nuts and season to taste.

3 Transfer the mixture to a large bowl and toss with the parsley, cream, and egg. Spoon the mixture into the tart case and top with the cheese. Sprinkle with paprika and bake for 15–20 minutes until golden and set. Remove and leave for at least 10 minutes before releasing from the tin.

STATISTICS PER SLICE

Energy 567kcals/2358kJ

Protein 15g

Fat 43g
Saturated fat 16g

Carbohydrate 30g
Sugar 1g

Fibre 3g

Salt 1.2g

● ● ○ CALORIES

● ● ● SATURATED FAT

● ● ○ SALT

GREAT FOR KiDS

SOUTHWEST CORN AND JALAPEÑO TART

SERVES 6   **PREP** 20 MINS   **COOK** 45 MINS–1 HOUR   **FREEZE** 1 MONTH

The mix of sweet and hot flavours in this colourful tart are characteristic of the American Southwest.

400g (14oz) gluten-free shortcrust pastry (see pages 44–6)
gluten-free plain flour, for dusting
2 tbsp olive oil
bunch of spring onions, finely chopped
pinch of cayenne pepper or paprika (optional)
1 large red pepper, halved, deseeded, and finely chopped
400g can sweetcorn, drained

salt and freshly ground black pepper
150ml (5fl oz) double cream
1 egg, beaten
1–2 tbsp sliced green jalapeño chillies, from a jar
60g (2oz) Monterey Jack or Cheddar cheese, sliced or grated

SPECIAL EQUIPMENT 18cm (7in) round, loose-bottomed, straight-sided tart tin

1 Preheat the oven to 200°C (400°F/Gas 6). Roll out the pastry on a lightly floured surface to a thickness of 5mm (¼in). Line the tin with the pastry, letting it overlap, then trim the surplus. Prick the base with a fork, line with baking parchment, and fill with baking beans. Bake for 15 minutes. Remove the beans and paper, and return to the oven for 5 minutes to crisp up. Reduce the oven temperature to 180°C (350°F/Gas 4).

2 Meanwhile, heat the oil in a large pan, add the spring onions, and cook on a low heat for 2 minutes. Stir in the cayenne or paprika (if using) and add the pepper. Cook for 5 more minutes, add the sweetcorn, and season to taste.

3 Remove from the heat and leave to cool. Stir in the cream and egg to coat. Spoon the mixture into the pastry case and top with the jalapeños and cheese. Bake for 20–30 minutes or until set and golden. Remove and leave to cool for 10 minutes. Slice and serve with a tomato and avocado salad.

VARIATIONS
Children will love a corn pie minus the hot jalapeños and cayenne. You can also add cooked chicken to the mix and top with pastry for a pie rather than a tart.

STATISTICS PER SLICE

Energy 590kcals/2454kJ

Protein 10g

Fat 41g
Saturated fat 17g

Carbohydrate 45g
Sugar 8g

Fibre 3.5g

Salt 1.2g

SMOKED SAUSAGE TART

SERVES 4-6   **PREP** 25-30 MINS   **COOK** 50 MINS   **FREEZE** 1 MONTH

Layered with sausage, leeks, and spinach, this tart will make a meal in one for lunch or a picnic pie.

400g (14oz) gluten-free shortcrust pastry (see pages 44–5)
gluten-free plain flour, for dusting
2 tbsp olive oil
3 leeks, sliced
leaves from a few sprigs of thyme
2 garlic cloves, finely chopped
salt and freshly ground black pepper

250g spinach leaves
120g (4½oz) gluten-free smoked sausage, sliced (see Cook's tip)
6 tbsp crème fraîche
2 eggs

SPECIAL EQUIPMENT 20.5cm (8in) round, loose-bottomed tart tin

1 Preheat the oven to 200°C (400°F/Gas 6). Roll out the pastry on a lightly floured surface to a thickness of 5mm (¼in). Line the tin with the pastry, patching up any holes and pricking with a fork. Trim to neaten, then line with baking parchment and fill with baking beans. Bake for 15 minutes, then remove the beans and paper and return to the oven for another 5 minutes to crisp up.

2 Heat the oil in a large frying pan, add the leeks, and cook gently on a low heat for 5–8 minutes. Add the thyme and garlic, season to taste with salt and pepper, and cook for 2 more minutes. Set aside and leave to cool. Reduce the oven temperature to 180°C (350°F/Gas 4).

3 Cook the spinach by placing the leaves in a colander in the sink and pouring over a kettle of boiling water. Leave to drain and cool slightly, then squeeze out the excess water. Spoon the leek mixture over the tart case along with the spinach and layer with the sausage. Mix the crème fraîche and eggs and pour over the tart so it covers evenly. Season again with pepper if you prefer, then bake in the oven for 15–20 minutes until set and golden. Leave to cool for 10 minutes before releasing from the tin. Slice to serve.

COOK'S TIP
Smoked sausage is available from Polish delis.

STATISTICS PER SLICE

Energy 484kcals/2017kJ

Protein 11g

Fat 35g
Saturated fat 13g

Carbohydrate 32g
Sugar 3g

Fibre 4g

Salt 1.1g

QUICHE LORRAINE

SERVES 6   **PREP** 20 MINS   **COOK** 1 HOUR

A timeless classic that never fails to please. You can add fresh chopped tomatoes into the mix, but do keep this tart simple.

400g (14oz) gluten-free shortcrust
   pastry (see pages 44–5)
gluten-free plain flour, for dusting

For the filling
1 tbsp olive oil
1 onion, finely chopped
salt and freshly ground black pepper
200g (7oz) bacon or pancetta, cubed

200g (7oz) Cheddar cheese, grated
250ml (9fl oz) double cream
3 eggs, lightly beaten
50g (1¾oz) Gruyère cheese, grated

SPECIAL EQUIPMENT 20.5cm (8in)
   round, loose-bottomed tart tin,
   at least 4.5cm (1¾in) deep

1 Preheat the oven to 200°C (400°F/Gas 6). Roll out the pastry on a lightly floured surface to a thickness of 5mm (¼in). Line the tin with the pastry, patching up any holes, then neaten and trim the edges. Prick the base with a fork, line with baking parchment and fill with baking beans, then bake in the oven for 15 minutes. Remove the beans and paper and return to the oven for another 5 minutes to crisp up. Set aside. Reduce the oven temperature to 180°C (350°F/Gas 4).

2 Meanwhile, heat the oil in a frying pan, add the onion, and cook for 6–8 minutes or until beginning to soften. Season to taste with salt and pepper, then transfer to a bowl and set aside to cool. Add the bacon or pancetta to the pan and cook on a medium heat for 5–8 minutes until golden. Set aside.

3 Sprinkle the onion over the base of the pastry case. Add the bacon or pancetta, draining off any excess fat, then add the Cheddar, mixing it up a little. Mix the cream and eggs together and season. Pour the mixture into the case and sprinkle over the Gruyère cheese. Cook for 25–30 minutes until the top is dark golden and the quiche is set. Leave to cool slightly in the tin to set more, then serve warm.

STATISTICS PER SLICE

Energy 838kcals/3478kJ

Protein 25g

Fat 68g
Saturated fat 32g

Carbohydrate 31g
Sugar 2g

Fibre 2g

Salt 2.6g

SHALLOT TARTE TATIN

SERVES 4   **PREP** 20 MINS   **COOK** 1 HOUR

Shallots are caramelized and topped with pastry in this surprisingly easy, and impressive, savoury tarte Tatin.

GUIDELINES PER SERVING

⬤⬤◯ CALORIES

⬤⬤⬤ SATURATED FAT

⬤⬤◯ SALT

1 tbsp olive oil, plus extra if needed
about 20 shallots, peeled
salt and freshly ground black pepper
drizzle of thick balsamic vinegar
leaves from a few sprigs of thyme
400g (14oz) gluten-free shortcrust
  pastry (see pages 44–5)

gluten-free plain flour, for dusting
1 egg, lightly beaten, to glaze
mixed leaf salad, to serve

SPECIAL EQUIPMENT small, deep,
  non-stick ovenproof frying pan

1 Preheat the oven to 200°C (400°F/Gas 6). Heat the oil in the ovenproof frying pan and arrange the shallots to fill the pan. Season with salt and pepper and cook on a medium heat for 5 minutes or until light golden. Reduce the heat and cook for 20–30 minutes until the shallots begin to caramelize, adding more oil if needed and turning them halfway through cooking. Drizzle with the vinegar and cook for a further 2–3 minutes, then sprinkle over the thyme.

2 Roll out the pastry on a lightly floured surface to a thickness of 3–5mm (⅛–¼in). Cut out a circle the same size as the top of the pan and discard any surplus pastry. Sit the circle over the shallots and tuck the edges in neatly.

3 Brush all over with the beaten egg. Bake in the oven for 20–30 minutes until the pastry is cooked and golden all over, then remove from the oven; be careful, the handle will be extremely hot. Leave to stand for 2–3 minutes, then invert onto a plate. Slice and serve with a mixed leaf salad.

VARIATION
You can also make this with gluten-free rough puff pastry (see pages 46–7).

STATISTICS PER SLICE

Energy 527kcals/2203kJ

Protein 9.5g

Fat 33g
Saturated fat 10g

Carbohydrate 48g
Sugar 6g

Fibre 5g

Salt 1.1g

SPICY PEPPER EMPANADAS

SERVES 5   **PREP** 30 MINS   **COOK** 30 MINS   **FREEZE** 1 MONTH UNCOOKED

A variety of savoury or sweet fillings – pumpkin and cheese to mixed berries – work well in this South American snack.

GREAT FOR KiDS

1 tbsp olive oil
1 large onion, sliced
salt and freshly ground black pepper
1 red pepper, deseeded and chopped
2 garlic cloves, finely chopped
3 red or green jalapeños, chopped
2 tbsp dry sherry
300g can chickpeas, drained
2 tbsp finely chopped fresh coriander

2 tbsp finely chopped flat-leaf parsley
100g (3½oz) butter
juice of 1 lemon
225g (8oz) gluten-free plain flour, plus extra for dusting
1 tsp paprika
sunflower oil, for frying

SPECIAL EQUIPMENT food processor

1 For the filling, heat the oil in a medium pan, add the onion, and season. Cook on a low heat for 2–3 minutes until soft. Add the red pepper, garlic, and jalapeños, and cook for 10 minutes or until the pepper starts to soften Add the sherry to the pan, raise the heat, and cook for 2 minutes. Tip in the chickpeas, coriander, and parsley, and stir. Season to taste. Transfer to a food processor and pulse to break it up, but not mince it.

2 To make the pastry, melt the butter in a pan, add the lemon juice and 100ml (3½fl oz) water. Combine the flour, 1 teaspoon salt, and paprika in a mixing bowl. Add the melted butter liquid and mix to a thick paste. Knead gently for 2 minutes. Leave to rest for 2–3 minutes at room temperature.

3 To form the empanadas, roll the pastry out on a floured surface to about 3mm (⅛in) thick, adding more flour if needed. Cut out 10 rounds, 10cm (4in) in diameter. Spoon a generous amount of filling onto one half of each round, wet around the edges with water, fold over, and seal with a pinch.

4 Pour sunflower oil into a small, deep-sided frying pan, to a depth of 1cm (½in), and heat to medium. Add 3 empanadas at a time and cook for 2–3 minutes on each side until golden. Transfer to a plate lined with kitchen paper. Serve hot or warm.

STATISTICS PER SERVING

Energy 424kcals/1774kJ

Protein 8g

Fat 24g
Saturated fat 12g

Carbohydrate 42g
Sugar 4g

Fibre 3g

Salt 1.2g

LAMB MASALA PASTIES

MAKES 8   **PREP** 30 MINS   **COOK** 1 HOUR 20 MINS   **FREEZE** 1 MONTH

These pasties can be made with either puff or shortcrust pastry. You can also add peas or broad beans to the filling.

2 tbsp cashew nuts
5cm (2in) piece of fresh root ginger, peeled and roughly chopped
1 tsp coriander seeds, crushed
½ tsp cumin seeds
1 tsp turmeric
1 tbsp garam masala
1–2 green chillies, deseeded and finely chopped
salt and freshly ground black pepper
1 tbsp olive oil, plus extra if needed
1 onion, chopped
300g (10oz) lamb shoulder, cut into bite-sized pieces

4 tomatoes, skinned and roughly chopped
1 tbsp tomato purée
handful of fresh coriander leaves, finely chopped (optional)
600g (1lb 5oz) gluten-free rough puff pastry (see pages 46–7, scaling up quantities by one half)
gluten-free plain flour, for dusting
1 egg, lightly beaten, to glaze
1 tbsp black onion (nigella) seeds, to top (optional)

1 Preheat the oven to 200°C (400°F/Gas 6). Place the first 7 ingredients, up to and including the chillies, in a food processor and whizz to a paste. Season well and set aside. Heat the oil in a large, deep frying pan, add the onion, and cook on a low heat for 3–4 minutes, then push to one side of the pan. Season the lamb and add to the pan, increasing the heat a little; add a drop of oil if needed. Cook for 6–8 minutes or until the lamb is sealed.

2 Add the spice paste, tomatoes, and purée, and stir. Pour in 150–200ml (5–7fl oz) hot water to just cover and simmer for 30 minutes or until the meat is tender. Top up with more water if needed; the sauce should have a thick consistency. Taste, season, and stir in the coriander (if using). Set aside.

3 Roll out the pastry on a lightly floured surface to a thickness of 5mm (¼in). Cut eight 15cm (6in) circles and wet the edges. Divide the lamb between the circles of pastry, spooning it onto one side. Fold the pastry over to make a half-moon and sit them on a lightly oiled baking sheet. Brush with the beaten egg and sprinkle with onion seeds (if using). Bake for 30–40 minutes or until golden. Remove and leave to cool a little before serving.

STATISTICS PER PASTY

Energy 396kcals/1655kJ

Protein 14g

Fat 25g

Saturated fat 10g

Carbohydrate 29g

Sugar 3.5g

Fibre 1g

Salt 0.7g

CHEESE AND ASPARAGUS TURNOVERS

MAKES 9   **PREP** 20 MINS   **COOK** 20-25 MINS

These flaky, crumbly parcels are perfect for a light lunch or picnic on a sunny summer's day.

salt and freshly ground black pepper
100g (3½oz) asparagus spears, cut
  into 1cm (½in) lengths
50g (1¾oz) mature Cheddar
  cheese, grated
3 tbsp snipped fresh chives

400g (14oz) gluten-free rough puff
  pastry (see pages 46–7)
gluten-free plain flour, for dusting
1 egg, beaten, to glaze
ground paprika, for dusting
salad leaves, to serve

1 Bring a small pan of salted water to the boil and blanch the asparagus tips for 2 minutes. Drain and refresh in cold water. Drain again and cool. Mix the asparagus with the cheese, chives, and plenty of black pepper. Set aside.

2 Carefully roll out the pastry on a lightly floured surface to form a 30cm (12in) square, 5mm (¼in) in thickness. Trim the edges, then cut out 9 equal squares. Brush the edges of each square with water. Divide the asparagus filling between the squares, heaping it over one diagonal half of each. Fold the pastry over the filling and pinch the edges together to seal. Use a knife to flute and crimp the edges together.

3 Place the triangles well apart on a large baking sheet. Make a steam hole on top of each, then glaze with beaten egg and dust with paprika. Bake for 20–25 minutes or until golden and risen. Serve warm or cold with salad leaves.

VARIATION

Vary the cheese and herbs if you like – goat's cheese and mint would taste great with the asparagus.

NUTRIENT BOOST

Asparagus is a source of folic acid, vital for women planning a pregnancy.

STATISTICS PER TURNOVER

Energy 200kcals/840kJ

Protein 5g

Fat 13g
Saturated fat 6.5g

Carbohydrate 15.5g

Sugar 0.8g

Fibre 0.3g

Salt 0.5g

CALORIES

SATURATED FAT

SALT

SPANAKOPITA

SERVES 6   **PREP** 20 MINS   **COOK** 1 HOUR

Rolling out gluten-free pastry thin enough for filo is difficult for the home cook. This version works just as well with thin shortcrust and saves you the Herculean challenge!

1 tbsp olive oil
½ onion, very finely chopped
salt and freshly ground black pepper
1kg (2¼lb) spinach
250g (9oz) feta cheese, crumbled
pinch of freshly grated nutmeg
handful of dill, finely chopped
3 eggs

400g (14oz) gluten-free shortcrust
  pastry (see pages 44–5)
gluten-free plain flour, for dusting
1 egg, beaten, to glaze
tomato salad, to serve

SPECIAL EQUIPMENT 20.5cm (8in) square,
  4cm (1½in) deep baking dish or tin

1 Preheat the oven to 200°C (400°F/Gas 6). Heat the oil in a large frying pan, add the onion, and cook for 2–3 minutes. Season to taste. In a separate large pan, cook the spinach in 4 batches of 250g (9oz) each on a low heat for 4–5 minutes until it wilts. Remove and set aside.

2 In a bowl, stir together the feta, nutmeg, and dill, and season to taste with more black pepper. Add the eggs and combine. Squeeze any excess water from the spinach, then add this and the onion to the feta mixture and mix.

3 Halve the pastry and roll out each piece as thinly as possible on a lightly floured surface, or between sheets of cling film, if easier. Cut a square the size of the base of the dish or tin, use it to line the dish, trim any surplus, and neaten the edges. Spoon a little of the mixture into the bottom of the dish and add a layer of pastry, patching up any holes. Spoon the rest of the mixture on top and finish with a layer of pastry. Brush with the beaten egg to cover and bake in the oven for 30–40 minutes until golden. Cool for 15 minutes before slicing into 6 rectangles and serving with a tomato salad.

STATISTICS PER SLICE

Energy 524kcals/2182kJ

Protein 20g

Fat 35g

Saturated fat 13g

Carbohydrate 33g

Sugar 4g

Fibre 6.5g

Salt 2.9g

VARIATIONS
Add some toasted pine nuts to the spinach mix or a pinch of cayenne pepper for a little heat. For a lighter dish, substitute half the feta with ricotta.

SMOKED SALMON AND CREAM CHEESE PICNIC PIES

MAKES 12   **PREP** 30 MINS   **COOK** 40 MINS

Baked in a muffin tray, these delightful little pies are perfect for a summer picnic or buffet lunch.

600g (1lb 5oz) gluten-free shortcrust pastry (see pages 44-5, scaling up quantities by one half)
gluten-free plain flour, for dusting
oil, for greasing
300g (10oz) cream cheese
3-4 tbsp crème fraîche
300g (10oz) smoked salmon slices, chopped, or use trimmings
handful of dill, finely chopped

1-2 tbsp green jalapeño chillies from a jar, chopped (optional)
salt and freshly ground black pepper
1 egg, beaten

SPECIAL EQUIPMENT 12-hole 3cm (1¼in) deep non-stick muffin tray, 10cm (4in) and 7.5cm (3in) metal round cutters

1 Preheat the oven to 190°C (375°F/Gas 5). Roll out two-thirds of the pastry on a lightly floured surface to a thickness of 5mm (¼in). Using the larger cutter, cut out 12 circles and use them to line the lightly oiled muffin tin, patching up any holes. You will have to keep gathering and re-rolling. Put in the fridge while you mix the filling.

2 In a bowl, mix together the cream cheese, crème fraîche, smoked salmon, dill, jalapeños (if using), and season well with salt and pepper.

3 Roll out the remaining pastry as before and cut out the tops using the smaller cutter. Remove the muffin tray from the fridge and divide the mixture between the pastry cases. Wet the rims of the pastry cases with water, cover with the tops, and pinch the edges to secure. Make a steam hole in each one and brush with the beaten egg. Bake in the oven for 30–40 minutes until golden, then remove and leave to cool completely before turning each one out of the tray.

STATISTICS PER PIE

Energy	392kcals/1632kJ
Protein	11g
Fat	29g
Saturated fat	13g
Carbohydrate	22g
Sugar	0.5g
Fibre	1.5g
Salt	1.9g

● ● ○ CALORIES

● ● ● SATURATED FAT

● ● ○ SALT

CHICKEN AND PARSLEY POT PIES

SERVES 4 **PREP** 20 MINS **COOK** 25-30 MINS **FREEZE** 1 MONTH
PLUS CHILLING

These pies are great to make after a roast chicken dinner or to use up leftover ham, and can also be prepared ahead and stored in the fridge overnight before glazing and baking.

GREAT FOR KiDS

150g (5½oz) frozen broad beans, or 400g can sweetcorn, drained
50g (1¾oz) butter
1 onion, finely chopped
salt and freshly ground black pepper
50g (1¾oz) gluten-free plain flour, plus extra for dusting
450ml (15fl oz) milk
1 tsp Dijon mustard
300g (10oz) cooked chicken, cut into chunky bite-sized pieces
150g (5½oz) gluten-free cooked ham, cubed

3 tbsp finely chopped curly or flat-leaf parsley
1 tbsp finely chopped marjoram leaves (optional)
300g (10oz) gluten-free rough puff pastry or shortcrust pastry (see pages 45–7)
1 egg, beaten
boiled potatoes and carrots, to serve

SPECIAL EQUIPMENT
4 x 300ml (10fl oz) or 1 x 1.2 litre (2 pint) pudding basins

1 Preheat the oven to 200°C (400°F/Gas 6). Place the broad beans in a bowl and pour over boiling water. Leave for 5–8 minutes, drain, and set aside.

2 Melt the butter in a large pan over a low heat, add the onion, season, and cook for 5–7 minutes until soft and transparent. Remove from the heat and stir in the flour. Pour in a little milk, stir, put back on a low heat, and gradually add the rest of the milk, stirring as you go. You may need to switch to a balloon whisk for a lump-free sauce. Bring to the boil, then reduce to a simmer. Cook for 2–3 minutes, remove from the heat, and stir in the mustard, chicken, ham, herbs, and broad beans. Season and set aside.

3 Roll out the pastry on a lightly floured surface. Cut out 4 small lids or 1 large lid 4cm (1½in) larger than the basins. Set aside. Spoon the filling into the basins and wet the edges. Drape the lids and press to secure. Make a hole in the top of each pie. Brush with half the beaten egg and chill for 20 minutes, then brush with the remaining egg and bake for 25–30 minutes until golden; cooking a large pie may take a little longer. Remove and serve.

STATISTICS PER SERVING

Energy 703kcals/2942kJ

Protein 43g

Fat 39g
Saturated fat 19g

Carbohydrate 46g
Sugar 9g

Fibre 4g

Salt 2.3g

● ○ ○ CALORIES

● ● ● SATURATED FAT

● ○ ○ SALT

SQUASH AND CIDER COBBLER

SERVES 6 **PREP** 20 MINS **COOK** 1 HOUR

Autumnal vegetables are simmered in cider and topped with herby dough – great for a Hallowe'en supper.

1 butternut squash, halved, deseeded, peeled, and cut into bite-sized cubes
2 tbsp olive oil
pinch of freshly grated nutmeg
few sage leaves, roughly chopped
salt and freshly ground black pepper
1 onion, finely chopped
2 garlic cloves, finely chopped
2 leeks, sliced
400g can chopped tomatoes
300ml (10fl oz) dry cider

225g (8oz) gluten-free plain flour
3 tsp gluten-free baking powder
100g (3½oz) cold butter, cubed
few sprigs of rosemary, finely chopped
75ml (2½fl oz) buttermilk
200g (7oz) Savoy cabbage, cored and roughly chopped
jacket potatoes, to serve (optional)

SPECIAL EQUIPMENT large flameproof casserole or lidded ovenproof pan

1 Preheat the oven to 200°C (400°F/Gas 6). Put the squash in a roasting tin, add half the oil, and toss to coat thoroughly. Add the nutmeg and sage, season well, and toss again. Roast for 15 minutes, then remove and set aside.

2 Heat the remaining oil in the casserole or pan, add the onion, and cook for 2–3 minutes. Season, stir in the garlic and leeks, and cook on a low heat for 2 more minutes. Add the tomatoes and cider, then add 400ml (14fl oz) hot water, or enough to cover the vegetables. Bring to the boil, reduce to a simmer, and stir through the squash. Simmer gently for 5–10 minutes.

3 For the cobbler topping, place the flour, baking powder, and a pinch of salt in a bowl and mix. Rub in the butter with your fingertips until it forms crumbs and stir in the rosemary. Add the buttermilk, a little at a time, until it forms a soft dough. Alternatively, make the topping in a food processor, adding the buttermilk a little at a time and pulsing until the dough forms.

4 Stir the cabbage into the simmering vegetables, then tear large lumps of the dough, flatten slightly, and sit on top of the vegetables. Bake for in the oven for 25–30 minutes or until golden and bubbling. Cover loosely with foil if it starts to brown too much. Serve alone or with jacket potatoes.

STATISTICS PER SERVING

Energy 389kcals/1632kJ

Protein 8g

Fat 19g
Saturated fat 9g

Carbohydrate 45g
Sugar 12.5g

Fibre 7.5g

Salt 1.3g

CORNMEAL CRUST CHILLI PIE

SERVES 4   **PREP** 20 MINS   **COOK** 1 HOUR

A hot and spicy mince mixture topped with golden cornmeal pastry.

125g (4½oz) gluten-free plain flour, plus extra for dusting
100g (3½oz) fine cornmeal or polenta
pinch of salt
2 tsp xanthan gum
100g (3½oz) cold butter, cubed
1 egg yolk
1 tbsp olive oil
500g (1lb 2oz) beef mince
1 onion, finely chopped
salt and freshly ground black pepper
1 green chilli, deseeded and finely chopped

1 red pepper, deseeded and finely chopped
340g can sweetcorn, drained
pinch of cayenne pepper (optional)
75ml (2½fl oz) gluten-free beer
75ml (2½fl oz) hot gluten-free vegetable stock (see page 115)
3 tomatoes, deseeded and chopped

SPECIAL EQUIPMENT 26cm (10in) round, deep pie dish

1 For the pastry, mix the flour, cornmeal, salt, and xanthan, then rub in the butter with your fingertips to form crumbs. Add the yolk and 1 tablespoon water and mix until it forms a dough. Wrap in cling film and set aside.

2 For the filling, heat the oil in a large frying pan, add the beef mince, and cook on a medium heat for 5–6 minutes, stirring until the meat is no longer pink. Remove from the pan, leaving the fat behind, and set aside. Add the onion to the pan, season, and cook on a low heat for 2–3 minutes. Stir in the chilli and cook for 1 more minute, then add the pepper and cook for 5 minutes until it softens. Return the beef mince to the pan, add the sweetcorn and cayenne (if using), and stir. Increase the heat, add the beer, and bubble for 2–3 minutes, then add the stock and simmer, uncovered, over a medium heat for 10–15 minutes; the mixture shouldn't be too runny. Stir in the tomatoes, season to taste, spoon into the pie dish, and set aside.

3 Preheat the oven to 200°C (400°F/Gas 6). Roll out the pastry on a lightly floured surface, wet the ridge of the pie dish, and drape the pastry over the top. Press the edges to seal and trim. Make a steam hole and bake for 30 minutes, or until pale golden. Serve on its own or with steamed carrots.

STATISTICS PER SERVING

Energy 801kcals/3342kJ

Protein 34g

Fat 44g
Saturated fat 22g

Carbohydrate 62g
Sugar 12g

Fibre 5g

Salt 1.4g

PORK PIE

SERVES 6   **PREP** 20 MINS   **COOK** 1¼HOURS   **FREEZE** 1 MONTH
PLUS CHILLING

A great British classic with a unique pastry. It's best to handle the pastry while it's hot and pliable.

500g (1lb 2oz) pork shoulder, cubed
100g (3½oz) unsmoked back
  bacon, diced
1 tsp dried sage
½ tsp ground mace
¼ tsp ground allspice
salt and freshly ground black pepper
oil, for greasing

500g (1lb 2oz) gluten-free hot water
  crust pastry (see page 47)
1 egg
pickles and salad, to serve

SPECIAL EQUIPMENT 20cm (8in) round
  springform cake tin

1 For the filling, place the pork, bacon, sage, mace, allspice, and seasoning in a food processor. Pulse until the meat is finely chopped. Chill.

2 Preheat the oven to 200°C (400°F/Gas 6) and put a baking tray in to heat up. Lightly grease the base and sides of the tin. Roll out two-thirds of the pastry between 2 sheets of baking parchment to a 30cm (12in) wide circle. Press it into the base and sides of the tin – there should be 2cm (¾in) of pastry standing up taller than the tin. Trim any excess pastry.

3 Spoon in the filling, compacting it down. Roll out the remaining pastry between the baking parchment sheets and cut to make a 20cm (8in) lid. Place on top of the filling. Beat the egg with a pinch of salt and brush over the pie. Bend the 2cm (¾in) of pastry down and over the lid. Roll and turn over to form a seal, crimp with a knife, and make a steam hole in the centre. Brush with the egg, place on the hot baking tray, and bake for 40 minutes.

4 Remove the pie and cool slightly. Loosen the sides with a round-bladed knife and remove the sides of the tin. Reduce the oven temperature to 190°C (375°F/Gas 5). Place the pie back on the tray and glaze the sides with the beaten egg. Bake for 30–35 minutes. Remove, cool, and chill. Cut into wedges and serve with pickles and a crisp salad.

STATISTICS PER SERVING

Energy 518kcals/2171 kJ

Protein 28g

Fat 26g
Saturated fat 10g

Carbohydrate 42g
Sugar 1.3g

Fibre 2.7g

Salt 1.7g

● ● ● CALORIES

● ● ● SATURATED FAT

● ○ ○ SALT

GALA LOAF PIE

SERVES 8   **PREP** 40 MINS   **COOK** 2 HOURS

A great pie to make ahead of a picnic. Serve with a dollop of English mustard or some home-made chutney.

750g (1lb 10oz) gluten-free hot water crust pastry (see page 47, doubling quantities)
gluten-free plain flour, for dusting
250g (9oz) gluten-free pork sausages, skins removed
175g (6oz) pork tenderloin, diced
350g (12oz) gluten-free cooked ham, diced
1 onion, finely chopped
1 tsp paprika

¼ tsp ground allspice
¼ tsp cayenne pepper
bunch of flat-leaf parsley, finely chopped
salt and freshly ground black pepper
2 eggs, lightly beaten
4 hard-boiled eggs, peeled
½ x 7g sachet of gelatine

SPECIAL EQUIPMENT long, shallow 900g (2lb) non-stick loaf tin

1 Preheat the oven to 200°C (400°F/Gas 6). Set aside one-third of the pastry for the lid. Roll out the remaining pastry on a lightly floured surface.Use it to line the tin with an overhang, patching up any holes. Line with baking parchment, fill with baking beans, and bake for 15 minutes. Remove the beans and paper and return to the oven for 5 minutes to crisp up.

2 In a large bowl, use your fingers to mix the sausagemeat, pork, ham, onion, parsley, and spices together until well combined, then season. Add half the beaten egg and mix again. Spoon half the mixture into the tin and pack it down evenly. Sit the hard-boiled eggs lengthways down the middle. Spoon over the remaining mixture and press so it's tightly packed.

3 Roll out the remaining pastry to make the lid. Brush the sides of the pastry case with beaten egg, sit the lid on top, pinch to secure, and trim. Brush the lid with the remaining egg. Make a fairly large steam hole in the centre. Bake for 30 minutes, then reduce the temperature to 170°C (340°F/Gas 3½) and cook for 1½ hours. Cover with foil if it starts to brown. Remove and leave to cool slightly. Now, mix the gelatine with 300ml (10fl oz) water and pour the mixture through the steam hole. Leave to cool for another 20 minutes, loosen the edges with a round-bladed knife, and cool completely before removing from the tin.

STATISTICS PER SERVING

Energy 642kcals/2684kJ

Protein 28g

Fat 39g
Saturated fat 12g

Carbohydrate 44g
Sugar 2.5g

Fibre 2.6g

Salt 0.3g

GAME PIE

SERVES 6　　**PREP** 30 MINS　　**COOK** 1 HOUR 40 MINS

This rich, comforting pie will keep the cold out on a crisp winter's day. Serve with spiced, slow-cooked red cabbage.

GUIDELINES PER SERVING

● ● ○ CALORIES

● ● ● SATURATED FAT

● ● ○ SALT

1-2 tbsp olive oil
125g (4½oz) bacon, chopped
900g (2lb) mixed game meat, cut into
　chunky bite-sized pieces
salt and freshly ground black pepper
1 onion, finely chopped
3 celery sticks, finely chopped
200ml (7fl oz) red wine
few sprigs of rosemary
1 bay leaf
450ml (15fl oz) hot gluten-free
　vegetable stock (see page 115)

25g (scant 1oz) butter
250g (9oz) chestnut mushrooms,
　roughly chopped
400g (14oz) gluten-free shortcrust
　pastry (see pages 44–5)
gluten-free plain flour, for dusting
1 egg, lightly beaten, to glaze
mashed potato, red cabbage, and
　gluten-free gravy, to serve

SPECIAL EQUIPMENT large pie dish

1 Preheat the oven to 190°C (375°F/Gas 5). Heat the oil in a large frying pan, add the bacon, and fry on a medium-high heat for 5–6 minutes until golden, then remove the meat and set aside. Season the game meat, add to the pan in batches, and cook until browned all over, adding more oil if needed. Remove the meat and set aside. Now add the onion and celery to the pan and cook on a medium heat for 5–6 minutes until beginning to soften. Then increase the heat, add the wine, and bubble for 2–3 minutes. Add the rosemary and bay leaf and pour over the stock. Return the meat to the pan and simmer gently for 40 minutes or until tender. Season to taste and remove the bay leaf and rosemary sprigs.

2 Heat the butter in a frying pan, add the mushrooms, and cook on a medium-high heat for 5–6 minutes until golden, then stir them into the meat mixture. Spoon the pie filling into the pie dish.

3 Roll out the pastry on a lightly floured surface to a thickness of 5mm (¼in). Wet the rim of the pie dish with water, top with the pastry, trim away any excess, and pinch to secure. Make a couple of steam holes in the top, brush with the egg, and bake in the oven for 40 minutes or until golden. Serve with mashed potato, red cabbage, and gluten-free gravy.

STATISTICS PER SERVING

Energy 618kcals/2585kJ

Protein 43g

Fat 33g
Saturated fat 12g

Carbohydrate 31g
Sugar 2g

Fibre 3g

Salt 1.9g

SWEET TARTS
AND PIES

LEMON TART

SERVES 8   **PREP** 30 MINS   **COOK** 1 HOUR 10 MINS

Take care to ensure there are no holes in the pastry case or all that delicious lemon cream filling may leak out.

400g (14oz) gluten-free shortcrust
  pastry (see pages 44–5)
gluten-free plain flour, for dusting
icing sugar, for dusting

For the filling
5 eggs
200g (7oz) caster sugar

250ml (9fl oz) double cream
125ml (4fl oz) lemon juice
  and grated zest of 4 lemons

SPECIAL EQUIPMENT 20.5cm (8in)
  round loose-bottomed tart tin

1 Preheat the oven to 200°C (400°F/Gas 6). Roll out the pastry on a lightly floured surface to a thickness of 5mm (¼in). Line the tin with the pastry, patching up any holes. Trim any surplus and neaten. Prick the base with a fork. Line with baking parchment and fill with baking beans, and bake in the oven for 15 minutes. Remove the beans and paper, and return to the oven for 5 minutes to crisp up. Set aside to cool.

2 While the tart is baking, prepare the filling. Place the eggs in a bowl and whisk gently. Add the sugar and mix well, then pour in the cream and the lemon juice and stir. Strain the mixture through a nylon sieve so it is smooth, then stir through the lemon zest. Reduce the oven temperature to 150°C (300°F/Gas 2).

3 Sit the tin on a baking sheet, then carefully pour the lemon mixture into the pastry case to fill. You can put it in the oven, pull out the shelf a little, and top up to save any spills. Bake in the oven for 50 minutes or until the filling is just starting to set; it will continue to set once out of the oven. Remove and leave to cool completely. To serve, dust with icing sugar.

VARIATION

Orange tart Substitute the lemon for the zest of 2 oranges and 125ml (4fl oz) fresh orange juice, then dust dark cocoa powder over the cooked tart to serve.

STATISTICS PER SLICE

Energy 535kcals/2232kJ

Protein 8g

Fat 35g
Saturated fat 16g

Carbohydrate 47g
Sugar 26g

Fibre 1.5g

Salt 0.7g

STRAWBERRY TARTS

GUIDELINES PER SERVING

●●● CALORIES

●●● SATURATED FAT

●●○ SALT

MAKES 6   PREP 35 MINS   COOK 20-25 MINS
PLUS CHILLING

This recipe for easy crème pâtissière tarts can be adapted by topping with whatever fruit is in season.

225g (8oz) gluten-free plain flour,
  plus extra for dusting
1 tsp xanthan gum
2 tbsp icing sugar
pinch of salt
100g (3½oz) butter, cubed
zest and juice of 1 lemon
1 egg, beaten, plus 3 egg yolks
60g (2oz) caster sugar

20g (¾oz) cornflour
300ml (10fl oz) milk
150ml (5fl oz) double cream
½ tsp vanilla extract
400g (14oz) ripe strawberries, hulled
  and sliced or halved

SPECIAL EQUIPMENT 6 x 12cm (5in)
  loose-bottomed fluted tart tins

1 Pulse the first 5 ingredients and the lemon zest in a food processor until the mixture resembles breadcrumbs. Add the whole beaten egg and 3 tablespoons lemon juice and pulse until a ball of dough forms. Lightly knead it on a floured surface, wrap in cling film, and chill for 10 minutes.

2 Preheat the oven to 200°C (400°F/Gas 6). Cut the pastry into 4 pieces and roll each out to a thickness of 5mm (¼in), then line 4 tins with the pastry. Re-roll the trimmings and line the other 2 tins in the same way. Prick the base of each with a fork. Line each tin with baking parchment and fill with baking beans, and bake in the oven for 15 minutes. Remove the paper and beans and bake for 5 minutes more to crisp up. Set aside to cool.

3 For the crème pâtissière, beat the egg yolks, caster sugar, and cornflour with a splash of milk to form a smooth paste. Heat the remaining milk to just below boiling in a small pan, pour onto the cornflour mix, stirring, then return to the rinsed-out pan. Bring to the boil, stirring continuously, and cook for 1 minute. Spoon into a bowl, place damp baking parchment directly on the surface to prevent skin from forming and cool completely. Once cool, whip the double cream until soft peaks form. Fold into the crème pâtissière with the vanilla. To serve, spoon the crème pâtissière into each tart case. Arrange the strawberries on top and serve.

STATISTICS PER TART

Energy 542kcals/2255kJ

Protein 7g

Fat 34g
Saturated fat 19g

Carbohydrate 52g
Sugar 22g

Fibre 1g

Salt 1g

APRICOT FRANGIPANE TART

SERVES 10   **PREP** 20 MINS   **COOK** 25-35 MINS

An impressive dessert of crisp buttery pastry filled with a sweet almond paste and topped with apricots.

250g (9oz) gluten-free shortcrust pastry (see pages 44-5)
gluten-free plain flour, for dusting

For the filling
200g (7oz) butter
200g (7oz) caster sugar
1 tsp vanilla extract

5 egg yolks
200g (7oz) ground almonds
4-5 ripe apricots, halved and stoned
crème fraîche, to serve

SPECIAL EQUIPMENT 25cm (10in) round, loose-bottomed tart tin

1 Preheat the oven to 200°C (400°F/Gas 6). Roll the pastry out on a lightly floured surface to a 35cm (14in) circle, about 3mm (⅛in) thick. Place it into the base of the tin, with the edges overlapping, patching up any tears in the pastry. Ease it into the corners and sides of the tin, and trim the edges. Prick the base with a fork, line with baking parchment, and fill with baking beans. Bake for 15 minutes or until the edges begin to turn golden. Remove from the oven, take out the beans and paper, and return to the oven for 5 more minutes. Set aside. Reduce the oven temperature to 180°C (350°F/Gas 4).

2 To make the filling, beat the butter in a large bowl with an electric whisk for 2 minutes. Add the sugar and beat until pale and creamy. Add the vanilla extract and mix. Now add the egg yolks, one at a time, and beat gently until they are all incorporated. Gently stir through the ground almonds.

3 Pour the filling into the pastry case and arrange the apricots, cut side down, in the mixture, pressing them in slightly so they fit snugly. Bake for 25–35 minutes or until the mixture is cooked and golden. Leave to cool and serve at room temperature with crème fraîche.

VARIATIONS
Try other seasonal fruits like peaches, blackberries, or stoned cherries. For a sweeter tart, spread the pastry base with strawberry or raspberry jam before filling.

STATISTICS PER SLICE

Energy 499kcals/2079kJ

Protein 7.5g

Fat 37.4g
Saturated fat 14g

Carbohydrate 33g
Sugar 25g

Fibre 1g

Salt 0.6g

AUTUMN FRUIT GALETTES

MAKES 8   **PREP** 30 MINS   **COOK** 25–30 MINS
PLUS CHILLING

Top these delicious puff pastries with whatever seasonal fruit you fancy; apricots work particularly well too.

125g (4½oz) gluten-free marzipan
1 pear
2 tbsp lemon juice
400g (14oz) gluten-free rough puff
  pastry (see pages 46–7)

gluten-free plain flour, for dusting
2 plums, quartered and stoned
caster sugar, for sprinkling
15g (½oz) flaked almonds
milk, to glaze

1 To prepare the filling, coarsely grate the marzipan. Peel, quarter, core, and thinly slice the pear, then toss in a little lemon juice.

2 Preheat the oven to 220°C (425°F/Gas 7). Roll out the pastry on a lightly floured surface to a rectangle 5mm (¼in) thick and about 35 x 30cm (14 x 12in). Trim the edges and then cut into 8 equal rectangles. Place well apart on a baking sheet (see Cook's tip).

3 Leaving a 1cm (½in) border all around the edges, scatter a little marzipan in the centre of each tart, top half with the pear slices and the others with plum quarters. Brush with the remaining lemon juice, then sprinkle with caster sugar and almonds. Brush the pastry edges with milk and bake for 25–30 minutes or until the pastry is golden and puffy around the edges.

STATISTICS PER GALETTE

Energy 225kcals/945kJ

Protein 3.5g

Fat 12g
Saturated fat 4.5g

Carbohydrate 26g
Sugar 14g

Fibre 0.8g

Salt 0.3g

COOK'S TIP

For a professional finish, "knock up" the edges of the pastry by holding a sharp knife horizontally against the cut edge and gently tapping all the way around.

« Choosing a pear
Use a sweet dessert pear for this recipe, but try to pick one that's slightly underripe, as these are better for baking.

ITALIAN-STYLE PLUM TART

GUIDELINES PER SERVING

● ● ● CALORIES

● ● ● SATURATED FAT

● ● ○ SALT

SERVES 8   **PREP** 30 MINS   **COOK** 1 HOUR 10 MINS

Fruit and nuts combined with mascarpone make this a really stunning tart. Swap the plums for pears and hazelnuts for almonds, if you like.

400g (14oz) gluten-free shortcrust
  pastry (see pages 44–5)
gluten-free plain flour, for dusting
125g (4½oz) mascarpone cheese
50g (1¾oz) caster sugar
1 egg
1 tbsp amaretto liqueur or 1 tsp
  almond extract (optional)
1 tbsp rice flour

few drops of milk or double cream,
  as needed
4 plums, halved and stoned
50g (1¾oz) hazelnuts, roughly chopped
1 tbsp sugar, for dusting
1 tbsp apricot jam, to glaze

SPECIAL EQUIPMENT 20.5cm (8in)
  round, loose-bottomed tart tin

1 Preheat the oven to 200°C (400°F/Gas 6). Roll out the pastry on a lightly floured surface to a thickness of 5mm (¼in). Line the tin with the pastry, patching up any holes, and trim. Line with baking parchment and fill with baking beans, then bake for 15 minutes. Remove the beans and paper and return to the oven for 5 minutes to crisp up. Remove the tart case from the oven and reduce the temperature to 170°C (340°F/Gas 3½).

2 For the filling, place the mascarpone, sugar, egg, liqueur or almond extract (if using), and flour in a bowl, and beat gently to combine. If it is too stiff, add a few drops of milk or double cream to loosen it; it should have a spreadable consistency. Spoon into the pastry case and smooth the surface.

3 Arrange the plums on top, cut-side down, pushing them in a little. Sprinkle over the hazelnuts and sugar and bake for 40–50 minutes until set. Cover loosely with foil if it starts to colour too much. Remove from the oven, heat the apricot jam, and brush over the plums. Leave to cool for 10–15 minutes before releasing it from the tin. Serve warm or at room temperature.

STATISTICS PER SLICE

Energy 399kcals/1670kJ

Protein 5.5g

Fat 25.5g
Saturated fat 10g

Carbohydrate 36g
Sugar 13g

Fibre 2.5g

Salt 0.6g

● ● ● CALORIES

● ● ○ SATURATED FAT

● ● ○ SALT

CHERRY LATTICE PIE

SERVES 6   **PREP** 30 MINS   **COOK** 1 HOUR

Sweet plump cherries encased in crisp gluten-free pastry with an impressive looking lattice crust.

900g (2lb) cherries, stoned
juice of ½ lemon
1 vanilla pod, split lengthways
100g (3½oz) caster sugar, plus extra
  for sprinkling
1 tbsp cornflour
400g (14oz) gluten-free shortcrust
  pastry (see pages 44–5)

gluten-free plain flour, for dusting
1 egg, beaten, to glaze
cream or gluten-free ice cream
  (see page 299), to serve

SPECIAL EQUIPMENT 20.5cm (8in)
  round pie tin

1 Preheat the oven to 190°C (375°F/Gas 5). Toss the cherries with the lemon juice and add them to a pan along with the vanilla pod. Sprinkle in the sugar and simmer gently on a low heat, stirring occasionally, until it dissolves. Continue to simmer on a low heat until the cherries begin to soften. Mix the cornflour with a little water until it forms a paste, stir it into the cherry mixture, and cook for 5–8 minutes or until the mixture begins to thicken. Remove and set aside to cool completely.

2 Roll out two-thirds of the pastry on a lightly floured surface to a thickness of 5mm (¼in). Use it to line the tin, draping the pastry over the edge, and trim the pastry to neaten. Remove the vanilla pod from the cherries and spoon them into the case.

3 Roll out the remaining pastry and cut 8 long strips to lay over the pie; each strip should be about 1cm (½in) wide and 5mm (¼in) thick. Wet the edges of the pastry with water, drape 4 strips one way, and 4 the other way for a crisscross lattice effect. Press around the edges to secure and trim off any excess. Brush the pastry with the beaten egg and sprinkle the lattice top with the sugar.

4 Bake in the preheated oven for 40–45 minutes, covering loosely with foil if the pastry starts to burn. Remove and leave to cool in the tin for 15 minutes. Slice and serve warm with cream or ice cream.

STATISTICS PER SLICE

Energy 470kcals/1967kJ

Protein 6g

Fat 20g

Saturated fat 6g

Carbohydrate 65g

Sugar 35g

Fibre 3.5g

Salt 0.7g

PUMPKIN TART

GREAT FOR KiDS

SERVES 8   **PREP** 20 MINS   **COOK** 1½ HOURS

If serving this American classic at a Hallowe'en party,
you could make smaller individual tarts and drizzle them
with dark chocolate.

GUIDELINES PER SERVING

●●● CALORIES

●●○ SATURATED FAT

●●○ SALT

400g (14oz) gluten-free shortcrust
  pastry (see pages 44–5)
gluten-free plain flour, for dusting
pinch of ground cinnamon
cream, to serve (optional)

For the filling
1 small pumpkin or 1 medium
  butternut squash, peeled, halved,
  deseeded, and roughly chopped

drizzle of sunflower oil
200ml (7fl oz) evaporated milk
200g (7oz) caster sugar
2 eggs
2 tsp mixed spice

SPECIAL EQUIPMENT 20.5cm (8in)
  round, loose-bottomed tart tin

1 Preheat the oven to 200°C (400°F/Gas 6). Put the pumpkin or squash in
a large roasting tin and toss with the oil, using your hands to coat. Roast for
25 minutes or until soft, then remove and transfer to a food processor and
whizz until puréed. Transfer to a bowl and leave to cool. Drain the purée in
a sieve if it looks a little watery.

2 Roll out the pastry on a lightly floured surface to a thickness of 5mm (¼in),
then line the tin with it, patching up any holes. Trim away excess pastry
and prick the base all over with a fork. Line with baking parchment and fill
with baking beans, and bake in the oven for 15 minutes. Remove the beans
and paper, then return to the oven for another 5 minutes to crisp up.

3 In another bowl or large jug, mix together the milk, sugar, eggs, and
mixed spice, then pour into the pumpkin or squash purée and stir well to
combine. Pour the mixture into the pastry case and smooth the top, then
sprinkle over the cinnamon and bake in the oven for 40–50 minutes until
set. If it starts to colour too much, cover loosely with foil. Leave to cool
and continue to set in the tin before releasing, then serve at room
temperature with a trickle of cream, if you like.

STATISTICS PER SLICE

Energy 404kcals/1695kJ

Protein 7g

Fat 20g
Saturated fat 6.5g

Carbohydrate 49g
Sugar 28g

Fibre 2g

Salt 0.7g

⬤⬤⬤ CALORIES

⬤⬤⬤ SATURATED FAT

⬤⬤◯ SALT

CHOCOLATE MOCHA TART

SERVES 8   **PREP** 20 MINS   **COOK** 40 MINS

A chocolate tart for grown ups! This version uses coffee-flavoured chocolate, but you could vary it with different flavours or chocolate with nuts to add texture.

400g (14oz) gluten-free shortcrust pastry (see pages 44–5)
gluten-free plain flour, for dusting
icing sugar or dark cocoa powder, to dust
crème fraîche, to serve

For the filling
100g (3½oz) dark chocolate (at least 70% cocoa solids), broken into pieces

100g (3½oz) coffee-flavoured dark chocolate (at least 70% cocoa solids), broken into even pieces
100g (3½oz) butter
3 eggs
75g (2½oz) caster sugar

SPECIAL EQUIPMENT 12 x 35cm (5 x 14in) rectangular loose-bottomed tart tin

1 Preheat the oven to 200°C (400°F/Gas 6). Roll out the pastry on a lightly floured surface to a thickness of 5mm (¼in). Line the tin with the pastry, patching up any holes, and trim away excess pastry. Prick the base all over with a fork. Line with baking parchment and fill with baking beans, and bake for 15 minutes. Remove the beans and paper and return to the oven for 5 minutes to crisp up. Remove the tart case from the oven and reduce the temperature to 170°C (340°F/Gas 3½).

2 For the filling, add the chocolate and butter to a heatproof bowl, sit it over a pan of barely simmering water, and stir occasionally until melted. Remove and leave to cool. In another bowl, whisk together the eggs and sugar with an electric whisk for 5 minutes or until thick and creamy.

3 Fold the cooled chocolate mixture into the egg mixture until combined, then pour it into the pastry case. Bake in the oven for 15–20 minutes until set and the top just forms a crust; it should still be slightly wobbly. Remove from the oven and leave to cool completely before releasing from the tin; it will continue to set. Dust with icing sugar or dark cocoa powder, slice, and serve with crème fraîche.

STATISTICS PER SLICE

Energy 516kcals/2152kJ

Protein 7g

Fat 34g
Saturated fat 16g

Carbohydrate 46g
Sugar 24g

Fibre 2g

Salt 0.8g

TREACLE TART

SERVES 8   **PREP** 30 MINS   **COOK** 55 MINS–1 HOUR
PLUS CHILLING

Made with sweet shortcrust pastry, this very English of tarts is a great family favourite.

225g (8oz) gluten-free plain flour,
  plus extra for dusting
2 tbsp icing sugar
1 tsp xanthan gum
100g (3½oz) butter, cubed
pinch of salt
2 eggs, beaten
cream, to serve

For the filling
400g (14oz) golden syrup
200g (7oz) gluten-free white bread,
  crusts removed

2 eggs, beaten
zest and juice of ½ lemon
½ tsp ground ginger

SPECIAL EQUIPMENT
23cm (9in) round, loose-bottomed
  tart tin

1 Preheat the oven to 200°C (400°F/Gas 6). Pulse the flour, icing sugar, xanthan, butter, and salt in a food processor until the mix forms crumbs. Add 1 egg and 1 tablespoon cold water and continue to pulse until the mixture forms a ball of dough. Briefly knead it on a lightly floured surface until smooth, then wrap in cling film and chill for 10 minutes.

2 Gently roll out the pastry on a lightly floured surface, place it over the tin, and push it into the base and sides. Trim the edges. Prick the base with a fork, line with baking parchment and fill with baking beans, and bake in the oven for 15 minutes. Remove the beans and paper, brush with the remaining egg, and bake for a further 5 minutes.

3 Reduce the oven temperature to 180°C (350°F/Gas 4). For the filling, warm the syrup in a small pan. Place the bread in a food processor and whizz to make fine breadcrumbs. In a large bowl, beat the eggs, lemon zest and juice, and ginger. Add the breadcrumbs and syrup and beat again. Pour the mixture into the pastry case and bake for 35–40 minutes or until the filling is golden and set. Serve warm or cold with cream.

STATISTICS PER SLICE

Energy 455kcals/1912kJ

Protein 7g

Fat 14.5g
Saturated fat 7.5g

Carbohydrate 73g
Sugar 42g

Fibre 0.5g

Salt 1.4g

⬤⬤⬤ CALORIES

⬤⬤◯ SATURATED FAT

⬤◯◯ SALT

BLACKBERRY AND APPLE PIE

SERVES 6   **PREP** 15 MINS   **COOK** 40–50 MINS   **FREEZE** 3 MONTHS
PLUS CHILLING

A classic pie using late summer fruits. Omit the spices and serve with gluten-free ice cream to make this perfect for kids.

GREAT FOR KiDS

450g (1lb) gluten-free shortcrust
  pastry (see pages 44–5)
gluten-free plain flour, for dusting
1 egg, lightly beaten
1 tbsp caster sugar

For the filling
3 cooking apples, peeled, cored,
  and sliced
1 star anise

1 vanilla pod, split lengthways
pinch of freshly grated nutmeg
100g (3½oz) demerara sugar
250g (9oz) blackberries
zest of ½ lemon or ½ orange

SPECIAL EQUIPMENT
18cm (7in) round pie dish

1 Set aside one-third of the pastry for the lid. On a lightly floured surface, roll out the remaining pastry into a circle large enough to line the pie dish and overlap the sides. Chill in the fridge while you prepare the filling.

2 Place the apple slices in a pan with 6 tablespoons cold water, add the star anise, vanilla pod, nutmeg, and half the sugar, and cook over a very gentle heat for 10–15 minutes until the apples begin to soften. Remove from the heat and set aside for 20 minutes to allow the flavours to infuse.

3 Sprinkle the pastry base with the remaining sugar. Remove the vanilla pod, star anise, and any excess liquid from the apples. Arrange the apple slices over the pastry, then add the blackberries and lemon or orange zest.

4 Wet the edges of the pastry with a little water. Roll out the pastry for the lid and drape, pressing the edges to seal. Trim the edges and slash the top a couple of times. Brush with half the egg and chill for 20 minutes.

5 Preheat the oven to 200°C (400°F/Gas 6). Brush the pie with the remaining egg and sprinkle with caster sugar. Bake for 40–50 minutes until golden. If it starts to brown too much, cover the top with a little foil, as you need the underside of the pastry to cook. Leave to cool slightly and serve warm.

STATISTICS PER SLICE

Energy 323kcals/1362kJ

Protein 4.5g

Fat 13g
Saturated fat 4g

Carbohydrate 47g
Sugar 30g

Fibre 5g

Salt 0.5g

⬤⬤◯ CALORIES

⬤◯◯ SATURATED FAT

⬤◯◯ SALT

MINCE PIES

MAKES 18   **PREP** 30 MINS   **COOK** 20–30 MINS
PLUS SOAKING

GREAT FOR KiDS

Mincemeat often contains gluten from the suet, but this easy home-made recipe does without. At other times of year, substitute the mincemeat with jam to make jam tarts.

400g (14oz) gluten-free shortcrust
  pastry (see pages 44–5)
gluten-free plain flour, for dusting
1 egg, beaten, to glaze
icing sugar, for sprinkling
clotted cream, to serve

For the mincemeat
500g (1lb 2oz) mixed dried fruits,
  such as sultanas, currants, and raisins
pinch of freshly grated nutmeg
2 tsp mixed spice

50g (1¾oz) soft prunes, finely chopped
450g (1lb) cooking apples, peeled,
  cored, and grated
grated zest and juice of 1 lemon
grated zest and juice of 1 orange
125g (4½oz) caster sugar
125g (4½oz) soft brown sugar
2 tbsp dessert wine

SPECIAL EQUIPMENT 2 x 12-hole patty
  tins, 6cm (2½in) round metal cutter,
  star cutter

1 For the mincemeat, put all the ingredients in a large bowl and stir, then cover and leave to soak overnight. Preheat the oven to 190°C (375°F/Gas 5). Roll out the pastry on a lightly floured surface to a thickness of 3mm (⅛in). Cut out 18 rounds, re-rolling if needed, and neatly tuck them into the tins.

2 Fill each case with about 1½ teaspoons mincemeat; don't overfill or it will spill out during cooking. Re-roll the remaining pastry, cut out 18 star shapes, and sit them on top of each pie. Brush with the egg and bake for 20–30 minutes until golden. Remove and leave to cool for 10 minutes, then release the pies from the tins. Serve warm or cold with a sprinkling of icing sugar and a dollop of clotted cream.

COOK'S TIPS

For full pie lids, cut out the pastry using a 4–5cm (1½–2in) round cutter. Wet the edges to seal, then make a steam hole in each lid. There will be plenty of mincemeat left over. Store in a sterilized, sealed jar for up to 6 months.

STATISTICS PER PIE

Energy 250kcals/1053kJ

Protein 2.5g

Fat 7g

Saturated fat 2g

Carbohydrate 44g

Sugar 36g

Fibre 2g

Salt 0.3g

TARTE TATIN

SERVES 8   **PREP** 20 MINS   **COOK** 30–35 MINS
PLUS CHILLING

GUIDELINES PER SERVING

⬤⬤⬤ CALORIES

⬤◯◯ SATURATED FAT

⬤◯◯ SALT

An impressive dessert for a dinner party, this can be prepared ahead and baked when needed. Choose apples with a good flavour – Cox, Braeburn, and Jazz all work well.

225g (8oz) gluten-free plain flour,
  plus extra for dusting
1 tsp xanthan gum
pinch of salt
3 tbsp caster sugar
140g (5oz) cold unsalted butter, cubed
1 egg

For the filling
60g (2oz) unsalted butter
115g (4oz) caster sugar
450g (1lb) dessert apples

SPECIAL EQUIPMENT 23cm (9in) round, springform cake tin or Tatin tin

1 Sift the flour, xanthan, and salt into a large bowl, then stir in the sugar. Add the butter and mix with your fingertips until fine crumbs form; alternatively, mix in a food processor. Add the egg and mix it in with a round-bladed knife until it starts to form a dough, then bring it together into a ball with your hands. Wrap with cling film and refrigerate.

2 For the filling, melt the butter in a small, heavy frying pan, add the sugar along with 6 tablespoons water, and stir over a medium heat until the sugar dissolves, then cook until caramelized and golden. Pour into the tin and swirl to coat the bottom. Peel, core, and quarter the apples, then cut each quarter into 3 slices. Pack the apples tightly into the cake tin, leaving no gaps.

3 On a lightly floured surface, or between 2 pieces of baking parchment, roll out the pastry to a round slightly larger than the tin and to a thickness of 5mm (¼in). Place on top of the apples and tuck the pastry under at the edges of the tin. Prick with a fork and chill for 10 minutes.

4 Preheat the oven to 200°C (400°F/Gas 6). Bake the tart on a baking sheet for 30–35 minutes until it is golden. Remove from the oven. Place a large plate on top of the tin, invert it, and leave to stand for about 1 minute before carefully removing the tin.

STATISTICS PER SERVING

Energy   401kcals/1692kJ

Protein   4g

Fat   22g
Saturated fat   4g

Carbohydrate   47g

Sugar   27g

Fibre   3g

Salt   0.3g

DESSERTS, CAKES, AND OTHER SWEET TREATS

⬤⬤⬤ CALORIES

⬤◯◯ SATURATED FAT

⬤◯◯ SALT

GREAT FOR KIDS

APPLE FRITTERS AND CUSTARD

SERVES 4   **PREP** 20 MINS   **COOK** 50 MINS–1 HOUR

Custard is easier to make at home than you might think and is the perfect partner to these fruity fritters.

4 dessert apples, each cored and
  sliced into 4-5 rings
vegetable oil, for frying

For the custard
200ml (7fl oz) milk, or half milk and
  half double cream
1 vanilla pod, halved lengthways
3 egg yolks
1 tbsp caster sugar

For the batter
150g (5½oz) rice flour
1 tbsp cornflour
pinch of ground cinnamon, plus extra
60g (2oz) caster sugar, plus extra
150ml (5fl oz) milk, or more if needed

SPECIAL EQUIPMENT deep-fat fryer
  or large pan

1 For the custard, pour the milk, or milk and cream, into a pan, add the vanilla pod, and leave to infuse for 20 minutes. In a large bowl, beat the egg yolks and sugar together. Gently heat the milk and vanilla to near boiling point. Remove from the heat, discard the vanilla pod, and pour over the egg mixture, whisking as you go. Return the mixture to the pan and heat gently over a low heat, stirring constantly, for 10–20 minutes until the custard begins to thicken and coats the back of a wooden spoon; do not allow it to boil or it will turn lumpy and split. If need be, pass the prepared custard through a fine metal sieve, so it's smooth and lump-free. Set aside.

2 For the fritters, put the dry batter ingredients in a bowl and whisk in the milk until it has the consistency of double cream; you may not need it all.

3 Heat the oil in a large pan or deep-fat fryer to 190°C (375°F), if using a thermometer, or until hot enough to crisp a piece of bread, and maintain this temperature. Do not leave the pan or fryer unattended, switch off when not using, and keep a damp tea towel nearby in case of fire. Dip the apple slices into the batter to coat, add to the oil a couple at a time, and fry for 2–3 minutes until golden. Remove and transfer to kitchen paper. Keep the finished fritters warm while you fry the remaining slices. Sprinkle the fritters with extra sugar and cinnamon. Gently reheat the custard and serve with the fritters.

STATISTICS PER SERVING

Energy 441kcals/1851kJ

Protein 8g

Fat 14g
Saturated fat 4g

Carbohydrate 68g

Sugar 38g

Fibre 4g

Salt 0.15g

BLACK CHERRY CLAFOUTIS

SERVES 4   **PREP** 20 MINS   **COOK** 30 MINS

This simple French dessert is nothing more than fruit and batter, baked until golden, but it tastes divine.

500g (1lb 2oz) cherries, stoned
grated zest of 1 orange
1 tbsp kirsch or cherry brandy
  (optional)
150g (5½oz) caster sugar

2 eggs
150ml (5fl oz) double cream
50g (1¾oz) rice flour
1 tbsp ground almonds
icing sugar, for dusting

1 Preheat the oven to 180°C (350°F/Gas 4). Put the cherries, orange zest, kirsch (if using), and half the sugar in a frying pan and cook on a very low heat for 5 minutes to dissolve the sugar and soften the cherries just a little. Then transfer it all to a baking dish.

2 For the batter, put the eggs and the remaining sugar in a bowl and whisk until creamy, then mix in the cream, rice flour, and almonds. Pour over the cherries to cover, then bake in the oven for 20–30 minutes until the batter is puffed and golden. Remove from the oven, dust with icing sugar, and serve with cream and a further drizzle of kirsch or cherry brandy, if you like.

VARIATIONS
You could use frozen forest fruits or berries if cherries are not available, or try fresh apricots or peaches.

Stoning cherries »
If you don't own a cherry stoner, take a clean metal paper clip and unfold it so that it looks like an "S". Press the larger end of the paper clip into the stalk end of the cherry until you feel the stone, twist it round, and the stone should pull out easily.

STATISTICS PER SERVING

Energy 514kcals/2152kJ

Protein 7g

Fat 26g
Saturated fat 14g

Carbohydrate 60g
Sugar 52g

Fibre 2g

Salt 0.1g

RASPBERRY AND WHITE CHOCOLATE TRIFLE

SERVES 6   **PREP** 20 MINS
PLUS COOLING

Tart raspberries contrast well with sweet white chocolate, and a trickle of cassis liqueur transforms this dessert into an indulgent, special occasion trifle.

200g (7oz) white chocolate, broken into even-sized pieces, plus extra for grating to decorate
175g (6oz) gluten-free sponge (see page 40) or amaretti biscuits (see page 339), crumbled
juice of 1–2 oranges

2 tbsp cassis (optional)
300ml (10fl oz) double cream, lightly whipped, or mascarpone cheese
300g (10oz) raspberries
50g (1¾oz) flaked almonds, lightly toasted

1 Put the chocolate in a heatproof bowl over a pan of barely simmering water and stir occasionally until melted. Remove the bowl from the pan and leave to cool slightly.

2 Place the crumbled sponge or biscuits in the base of a glass serving dish. Pour over just enough orange juice to wet the sponge, then add half the cassis (if using). Set aside for the sponge or biscuits to absorb the juice.

3 Mix the melted chocolate with half the whipped cream or mascarpone and stir well to combine. Mix the remaining cassis with the raspberries. Reserve some raspberries for decoration. Spoon half the cream mixture into the dish and top with half the raspberry mixture. Repeat the layers to use the remaining cream and raspberry mixture. Top with the leftover cream and dot with the reserved raspberries, then sprinkle over the almonds and grated white chocolate. Chill before serving.

COOK'S TIP

A variety of bases can be used for the trifle - try gluten-free brownies, biscuits, or fruit cake for a heavier version - and try stewed fruits for a winter pudding.

STATISTICS PER SERVING

Energy 644kcals/2676kJ

Protein 8g

Fat 50g
Saturated fat 25g

Carbohydrate 39g
Sugar 33g

Fibre 2g

Salt 0.4g

SUMMER FRUIT COBBLER

SERVES 8   **PREP** 20 MINS   **COOK** 35–40 MINS

You can vary the fruit in this dessert, but keep a similar ratio of soft berries to firmer fruit, such as peaches or pears, so that the cobbler topping has a firm base to rise on.

225g (8oz) gluten-free self-raising
  flour, plus extra for dusting
2 tsp gluten-free baking powder
1 tsp xanthan gum
pinch of salt
60g (2oz) caster sugar
60g (2oz) cold unsalted butter, cubed
200ml (7fl oz) buttermilk, or half milk
  and half natural yogurt
1 egg, beaten
2 tsp demerara sugar
single cream, to serve

For the filling
450g (1lb) ripe peaches or nectarines
60g (2oz) caster sugar
2 tbsp cornflour
200g (7oz) raspberries
200g (7oz) blueberries

SPECIAL EQUIPMENT 5cm (2in)
  round fluted metal cutter and
  1.4 litre (2½ pint) oval pie dish

1 Preheat the oven to 200°C (400°F/Gas 6). If using peaches, soak them in boiling water for 1 minute, drain, and peel. Halve the peaches or nectarines, remove the stones, and slice. Mix the caster sugar and cornflour in the pie dish. Add the sliced peaches or nectarines and the berries and toss until evenly coated. Tossing the fruit in the cornflour and sugar mixture makes a lovely sauce. Spread the fruit out in an even layer.

2 For the topping, sift the flour, baking powder, xanthan, and salt into a large bowl and stir in the sugar. Add the butter and rub it in with your fingertips, or pulse in a food processor until it resembles fine breadcrumbs. Stir in the buttermilk, or half milk and half natural yogurt, and mix using a round-bladed knife to make a soft dough. Knead briefly.

3 On a lightly floured surface, roll out the dough to a thickness of 2cm (¾in). Using the cutter, cut out 12 circles, re-rolling the dough as necessary. Lay the circles on top of the fruit, overlapping them slightly. Brush with the egg and sprinkle over the demerara sugar. Bake on a baking tray, near the top of the oven, for 35–40 minutes or until the cobbler is risen and golden brown on top and the fruit is bubbling. Serve warm with single cream.

STATISTICS PER SERVING

Energy 286kcals/1211kJ

Protein 6g

Fat 8g
Saturated fat 4g

Carbohydrate 46g
Sugar 25g

Fibre 3.5g

Salt 0.9g

FRUIT CRUMBLE

GUIDELINES PER SERVING

● ● ● CALORIES

● ● ● SATURATED FAT

● ○ ○ SALT

SERVES 6   **PREP** 20 MINS   **COOK** 35 MINS   **FREEZE** 3 MONTHS

A real family favourite. You can swap the fruit to suit the seasons or mix and match the toppings.

400g (14oz) rhubarb, trimmed and
 chopped into 5cm (2in) pieces
zest of 1 orange and juice of 2
400g (14oz) strawberries, quartered
125g (4½oz) cold butter, cubed

200g (7oz) gluten-free plain flour
125g (4½oz) demerara sugar
handful of flaked almonds
gluten-free custard or ice cream
 (see pages 286 or 299), to serve

1 Preheat the oven to 180°C (350°F/Gas 4). Put the rhubarb and the orange zest and juice in a shallow pan and simmer gently for 8–10 minutes until the rhubarb softens. If it needs more liquid, add a little water. Transfer to a shallow ovenproof dish and mix in the strawberries.

2 In a bowl, rub the butter into the flour with your fingertips until crumbs form, or pulse in a food processor. Stir through the sugar. Tip the topping over the fruit to cover and scatter with the almonds. Bake in the oven for 25 minutes until golden. Serve with gluten-free custard or ice cream.

VARIATIONS

Apple and cranberry Peel, core, and slice 2 large cooking apples. Simmer for 4-5 minutes with the juice of ½ lemon, 3 tablespoons water, and 3 tablespoons light soft brown sugar, until just soft. Transfer to an ovenproof dish and scatter over 200g (7oz) fresh or 100g (3½oz) dried cranberries. Sprinkle 3 tablespoons brown sugar and a pinch of cinnamon. Top with the crumble topping and bake as above.
Pear and blackberry Slice 3 sweet pears and simmer for 3-5 minutes with the juice of ½ lemon, 2 tablespoons water, and ½ vanilla pod, sliced lengthways, until just soft. Transfer to an ovenproof dish, add 300g (10oz) blackberries and 1-2 tablespoons demerara sugar, and combine. Add a topping and bake as above.
Almond topping Replace the plain flour with 100g (3½oz) rice flour and 150g (5½oz) ground almonds, and continue as above. Great with pear and blackberries.
Quinoa topping Replace the plain flour with 50g (1¾oz) rice flour and 100g (3½oz) quinoa flakes. Process with 75g (2½oz) roughly chopped mixed nuts until combined. Add 50g (1¾oz) butter and pulse until it resembles breadcrumbs, then add 125g (4½oz) demerara sugar and pulse a few more times.

STATISTICS PER SERVING

Energy 404kcals/1696kJ

Protein 5.5g

Fat 20g
Saturated fat 11g

Carbohydrate 51g
Sugar 28g

Fibre 3.5g

Salt 0.3g

● ● ● CALORIES

● ● ● SATURATED FAT

● ○ ○ SALT

CHINESE-STYLE DUMPLINGS

SERVES 4   **PREP** 20 MINS   **COOK** 28 MINS

These simple doughnut-like sweet dumplings are flavoured with cinnamon and stem ginger.

300g (10oz) gluten-free plain flour
½ tsp salt
3 tsp gluten-free baking powder
½ tsp ground cinnamon
50g (1¾oz) cold unsalted butter, cubed
3 balls of preserved stem ginger, finely chopped

100ml (3½fl oz) milk
1 egg
1 litre (1¾ pints) sunflower oil, for frying
caster sugar, for sprinkling

SPECIAL EQUIPMENT deep-fat fryer or large pan

1 Sift the flour, salt, baking powder, and cinnamon into a bowl, then add the butter, rubbing it in with your fingertips until the mixture forms fine crumbs. Stir through the ginger, then beat the milk and egg together and add to the mixture, stirring until you get a smooth dough.

2 Divide and roll the dough into 20 balls, then make a thumb indentation on each one. Heat the oil in the fryer or pan until hot, but not too hot or the dumplings will burn quickly. The pan or fryer should not be more than one-third full. Do not leave the pan or fryer unattended, switch off when not using, and keep a fire blanket nearby in case of fire.

3 Carefully add the dough balls into the pan or fryer, 3 at a time, and deep-fry at a low sizzle for 4 minutes, turning them halfway through cooking so they turn golden all over. Remove and drain on kitchen paper. Repeat until all the dumplings are cooked. Tip the caster sugar out onto a plate and roll the dumplings in it. Serve piled high in bowls.

COOK'S TIP

These dumplings are very delicate. The key is to have the oil at the correct temperature; too hot and they burn, too cold and the inside doesn't cook.

STATISTICS PER SERVING

Energy 680kcals/2835kJ

Protein 10g

Fat 40g
Saturated fat 10g

Carbohydrate 65g
Sugar 12.5g

Fibre 3g

Salt 0.75g

PASSION FRUIT AND LEMON SOUFFLÉS

GUIDELINES PER SERVING

●●○ CALORIES

●●○ SATURATED FAT

●○○ SALT

MAKES 6 **PREP** 15 MINS **COOK** 12–15 MINS

This is a really easy version of a sweet soufflé that relies on good-quality lemon curd.

30g (1oz) unsalted butter, melted
115g (4oz) caster sugar, plus
  6 tsp for sprinkling
4 passion fruit
4 tbsp gluten-free lemon curd

4 eggs, separated
icing sugar, for sprinkling

SPECIAL EQUIPMENT 6 x 150ml (5fl oz)
  ramekin dishes

1 Preheat the oven to 200°C (400°F/Gas 6). Grease the ramekin dishes generously with the butter, then dust each with 1 teaspoon caster sugar. Put them in the fridge while you prepare the soufflé mixture.

2 Scoop the seeds from the passion fruit and strain through a nylon sieve set over a bowl, to collect the juice and remove the pips. Stir the juice into the lemon curd along with the egg yolks.

3 Whisk the egg whites in a grease-free bowl (see Cook's tip) using an electric whisk until stiff peaks form. Add the caster sugar and whisk until the mixture is stiff and shiny. Stir a heaped tablespoonful of the egg whites into the curd mixture to loosen it. Gently fold the remaining egg whites into the mixture; do this slowly and gently so you don't knock out the air.

4 Divide the mixture between the ramekins, tap them on the work surface so that the mixture settles inside, then wipe a clean finger around the inside edge of each dish; this helps the soufflés rise evenly. Bake for 12–15 minutes or until well-risen and golden tinged. Remove from the oven, transfer each ramekin to a plate, and sprinkle with icing sugar before serving.

COOK'S TIP
When whisking the egg whites, ensure that the bowl is really clean or you just won't get the volume you need.

STATISTICS PER SOUFFLÉ

Energy 229kcals/964kJ

Protein 5g

Fat 9g
Saturated fat 4g

Carbohydrate 32g
Sugar 30g

Fibre 0.4g

Salt 0.2g

● ● ● CALORIES

● ● ● SATURATED FAT

● ○ ○ SALT

GREAT FOR KIDS

CHOCOLATE TAPIOCA PUDDING

SERVES 6   **PREP** 5 MINS   **COOK** 25 MINS

An old-fashioned pudding that takes you back to your childhood, but one that's given a more grown-up twist by using dark chocolate.

1 litre (1¾ pints) milk
100g (3½oz) tapioca
1–2 tbsp dark cocoa powder
2 egg yolks
125g (4½oz) sugar
pinch of salt

pinch of freshly grated nutmeg
2–3 tbsp double cream, to serve (optional)
25g (scant 1oz) dark chocolate, grated, to top

1 Put the milk in a pan, tip in the tapioca and cocoa powder, stir, and warm gently on a low heat. In a bowl, mix together the egg yolks, sugar, and salt. Pour a little of the warmed milk mixture into the egg and stir to combine, then pour it all back into the pan.

2 Bring to the boil, stirring constantly, then reduce the heat to medium-low. Simmer gently for 20 minutes, stirring frequently, until the tapioca is cooked. Top up with more milk if it's too thick. Add the nutmeg and serve with a swirl of cream mixed through (if using), and top with grated chocolate.

COOK'S TIP
Children will love this, though they may prefer the sweeter flavour of drinking chocolate to the dark cocoa powder, and milk chocolate grated on top.

VARIATION
Make this without the cocoa powder and chocolate, and stir through jam to serve.

STATISTICS PER SERVING

Energy 326kcals/1370kJ

Protein 7g

Fat 13g
Saturated fat 7g

Carbohydrate 45g
Sugar 30g

Fibre 0.6g

Salt 0.6g

CHOCOLATE FONDANTS

MAKES 6   **PREP** 20 MINS   **COOK** 10 MINS   **FREEZE** 3 MONTHS
UNCOOKED

Lightly cooked cake on the outside with an oozy, runny centre, chocolate fondants are far easier to make than their reputation implies – just don't over-cook them.

140g (5oz) butter, plus extra
  for greasing
cocoa powder, for dusting
140g (5oz) dark chocolate (at least
  70% cocoa solids)
4 eggs and 3 egg yolks
85g (3oz) caster sugar

3 tbsp gluten-free plain flour
cream or gluten-free ice cream (see
  page 299), to serve

SPECIAL EQUIPMENT 6 x 175ml (6fl oz)
  dariole moulds or ramekins

1 Preheat the oven to 200°C (400°F/Gas 6). Generously grease the moulds with butter, then dust with cocoa powder. Melt the butter and chocolate together in a large heatproof bowl set over a pan of gently simmering water. Once melted, remove from the heat.

2 Using an electric whisk, beat together the eggs, egg yolks, and sugar until pale and thick; the mixture should leave a trail when the whisk is lifted.

3 Pour the egg mixture into the melted chocolate and sift the flour on top. Gently fold everything together using a large metal spoon. Divide the mixture evenly between the moulds and chill until required.

4 Place the moulds on a baking sheet and bake for 10 minutes. Remove from the oven and leave to rest for 1 minute. Holding the moulds with a heatproof cloth, run a knife around the edges of each pudding, and invert onto a plate. Serve with cream or gluten-free ice cream.

COOK'S TIPS
Make these up to 3 days ahead: simply cover the tops with cling film and refrigerate until ready to bake. You can also freeze and bake straight from frozen by adding 4 minutes to the cooking time.

STATISTICS PER FONDANT

Energy 471kcals/1962kJ

Protein 8g

Fat 34g
Saturated fat 18g

Carbohydrate 33g
Sugar 28g

Fibre 1g

Salt 0.6g

CHOCOLATE CHEESECAKE

SERVES 8   **PREP** 20 MINS   **COOK** 35-40 MINS
PLUS COOLING

A gooey mixture of dark chocolate and mascarpone baked on a crumbly base of almond or ginger biscuits.

85g (3oz) butter, plus
  extra for greasing
175g (6oz) gluten-free ginger
  or amaretti biscuits (see pages
  338 or 339), crushed
150g (5½oz) dark chocolate
  (70% cocoa solids), broken
  into even-sized pieces
2 eggs, separated

pinch of salt
400g (14oz) mascarpone cheese
zest and juice of 1 orange
115g (4oz) caster sugar
2 tbsp cornflour
double cream, to serve

SPECIAL EQUIPMENT
20cm (8in) round springform cake tin

1 Preheat the oven to 180°C (350°F/Gas 4). Grease the tin and line with baking parchment. Gently melt the butter in a pan, remove from the heat, and stir in the crushed biscuits. Press the buttery biscuit mixture into the base and edges of the tin, using the back of a wooden spoon to smooth it out. Leave to cool then chill in the fridge.

2 Meanwhile, put the chocolate in a heatproof bowl set over a pan of barely simmering water and stir occasionally until melted. Remove the bowl from the pan and leave the chocolate to cool slightly.

3 Place the egg whites and salt in a bowl and whisk until stiff. Set aside.

4 Place the mascarpone, melted chocolate, orange zest and juice, caster sugar, and egg yolks in a large bowl and beat gently with an electric whisk to combine. Fold in the cornflour and then the egg whites.

5 Pour the mixture over the biscuit base and spread it until even and smooth. Bake for 35–40 minutes or until firm to the touch. Switch off the heat and leave the cheesecake to cool inside the oven; this helps prevent cracking. Once cool, remove from the oven and set aside until completely cold, then release the sides and ease from the tin. Serve with a drizzle of double cream.

STATISTICS PER SLICE

Energy 598kcals/2501kJ

Protein 7g

Fat 43g

Saturated fat 23.5g

Carbohydrate 41g

Sugar 41g

Fibre 0.6g

Salt 0.4g

● ● ● CALORIES

● ● ● SATURATED FAT

● ○ ○ SALT

PROFITEROLES

SERVES 4   **PREP** 20 MINS   **COOK** 20-25 MINS   **FREEZE** 3 MONTHS

Crisp choux pastry buns filled with cream and drizzled with dark chocolate – or use white chocolate as a variation.

85g (3oz) gluten-free white bread
  flour blend (see page 38)
½ tsp xanthan gum
pinch of salt
85g (3oz) butter, plus extra for greasing
2 tbsp caster sugar
4 eggs, beaten

115g (4oz) chocolate (at least 70%
  cocoa solids)
400ml (14fl oz) double cream
2 tbsp golden syrup

SPECIAL EQUIPMENT piping bag fitted
  with a 2cm (¾in) plain nozzle

1 Preheat the oven to 200°C (400°F/Gas 6). Sift together the flour, xanthan, and salt into a bowl. Place 60g (2oz) of the butter in a pan with 150ml (5fl oz) water and the sugar, bring to the boil, quickly add the flour, and beat until the mixture forms a ball and comes away from the sides of the pan. Remove from the heat and cool for 5 minutes.

2 Gradually add the eggs to the mix, whisking between additions with an electric whisk until smooth and glossy. Spoon it into the piping bag (see Cook's tips), then pipe 3cm (1¼in) rounds, spaced well apart, on 2 greased baking sheets. Bake for 15–20 minutes until risen. Remove and cut each ball in half. Bake again for 5 minutes to crisp the insides. Leave to cool.

3 For the sauce, break the chocolate into a small pan, add 150ml (5fl oz) cream, the syrup, remaining butter, and 4 tablespoons water. Cook over a gentle heat, stirring until the chocolate melts and a smooth shiny sauce forms. Whip the remaining cream until it forms soft peaks. Fill each bun with a heaped teaspoon of whipped cream, transfer the buns to a serving plate, and drizzle over the warm chocolate sauce. Serve immediately.

COOK'S TIPS
Stand the piping bag in a tall glass or jug to make it easier to fill. Store the unfilled profiteroles in an airtight container for up to 2 days, simply re-crisp in a hot oven. Or you can freeze the filled buns and they will thaw in 1 hour.

STATISTICS PER SERVING

Energy 681kcals/2824kJ

Protein 8.5g

Fat 58g

Saturated fat 34g

Carbohydrate 31g

Sugar 22g

Fibre 1.2g

Salt 0.6g

BROWN BREAD ICE CREAM

SERVES 6   **PREP** 30 MINS   **COOK** 25 MINS   **FREEZE** 3 MONTHS
PLUS INFUSING
AND FREEZING

In this slightly retro dessert, the toasted bread tastes like toffee. Kids will love this with sliced banana or chocolate.

250ml (9fl oz) whole milk
250ml (9fl oz) double cream
1 vanilla pod, split lengthways
75g (2½oz) gluten-free brown
   breadcrumbs (see page 38)

75g (2½oz) dark soft brown sugar
5 egg yolks
50g (1¾oz) caster sugar

SPECIAL EQUIPMENT food processor

1 To make the custard for the ice cream, put the milk, cream, and vanilla in a large pan and bring just to the boil. Remove and leave for 30 minutes to cool and for the vanilla to infuse. Then discard the vanilla pod.

2 Preheat the oven to 200°C (400°F/Gas 6). Spread the breadcrumbs out on a large roasting tin or baking sheet and toast for 10 minutes until just turning pale golden. Add the sugar, toss together, and bake for 5 more minutes. Remove and leave to cool, then tip into a food processor and pulse once or twice to break up the bigger lumps.

3 In a bowl, whisk together the egg yolks and caster sugar until creamy. Pour in the infused milk and whisk to combine. Pour the custard into the cleaned-out pan and simmer gently over a very low heat for 10–15 minutes, stirring, until it begins to thicken. Stir constantly and do not let it boil or it may split and turn lumpy. Pour the custard through a nylon sieve into a large bowl so it is smooth. Cover the custard with baking parchment so that the paper touches the surface to prevent a skin forming. Cool completely.

4 Pour the mixture into a freezer-proof container and freeze for 2 hours. Remove, place in a food processor, and pulse until creamy. Add the breadcrumb mixture and pulse once more to combine. Put back in the freezer and repeat once the ice cream has frozen, pulsing it again in the food processor. If using an ice cream maker, you can skip this step: simply add the mixture and leave until frozen.

GUIDELINES PER SERVING

● ● ● CALORIES

● ● ● SATURATED FAT

● ○ ○ SALT

GREAT FOR KiDS

STATISTICS PER SERVING

Energy 407kcals/1697kJ

Protein 6g

Fat 29g
Saturated fat 16g

Carbohydrate 31g

Sugar 23g

Fibre 0.4g

Salt 0.3g

● ● ○ CALORIES

● ○ ○ SATURATED FAT

● ○ ○ SALT

SUMMER PUDDING

GREAT FOR KiDS

SERVES 6　　**PREP** 25 MINS　　**COOK** 5 MINS
PLUS CHILLING

This traditional fruit dessert is useful for using up leftover gluten-free bread as it works better than fresh. Children will love it too and it's a great way to get them eating fruit.

1.25kg (2¾lb) frozen mixed berries, or a mixture of fresh summer berries and currants that are in season, reserving a few for decoration

2-3 tbsp caster sugar, or more if the fruit is tart

8-10 slices of gluten-free white bread
pouring cream, to serve

SPECIAL EQUIPMENT 900 ml (1½ pint) pudding bowl

1 Place the fruit in a large pan with the sugar and 3 tablespoons water. Simmer gently on a low heat for 3–5 minutes, then set aside until cool; you need to bring out the juices from the fruit to colour the bread. Drain the fruit with a slotted spoon and transfer to another bowl. Reserve the juice.

2 Remove the crusts from the bread, reserve 1 slice for the base of the bowl (what will be the top of the pudding), and cut each of the remaining slices into 3 even fingers. Line the pudding bowl with cling film, leaving plenty of overlap. Cut a circle for the base from the reserved slice, dip into the juice, and sit it at the bottom of the bowl. Line the bowl with bread fingers, first dipping them into the juice, and overlapping them slightly, so there are no gaps and they follow the shape of the bowl.

3 Spoon the fruit into the bowl. Dip the remaining bread fingers into the juice and top the pudding, ensuring that it's completely covered. Press them down to secure. Pull the cling film over to cover the top, then sit a plate on top and use a can to weigh it down. Chill in the fridge overnight.

4 If you have any leftover juice, you could make a sauce by simmering it in a small pan over medium heat until slightly thickened. Transfer to a jug and chill with the pudding. To serve, invert the pudding onto a plate and peel away the cling film. Decorate with the reserved berries and serve with the fruit sauce or pouring cream.

NUTRiENT BOOST
Frozen berries are rich in vitamin C and a good option when fresh aren't in season.

STATISTICS PER SERVING

Energy 178kcals/756kJ

Protein 6g

Fat 1g
Saturated fat 0.2g

Carbohydrate 31g
Sugar 19g

Fibre 5.5g

Salt 0.5g

STICKY TOFFEE PUDDINGS

GUIDELINES PER SERVING

⬤⬤⬤ CALORIES

⬤⬤⬤ SATURATED FAT

⬤⬤◯ SALT

SERVES 6 **PREP** 20–25 MINS **COOK** 1–1¼ HOURS **FREEZE** 3 MONTHS

Deliciously moreish, these little puddings can also be made into a big one. Simply spoon the mixture into a 1.2 litre (2 pint) pudding basin and steam for an extra 20 minutes.

vegetable oil, for greasing
175g (6oz) butter, softened
175g (6oz) dark soft brown sugar
3 eggs
115g (4oz) gluten-free self-raising flour
1 tsp xanthan gum
60g (2oz) ground almonds
60g (2oz) fudge pieces
3 tbsp milk

For the sauce
450ml (15fl oz) milk
3 tbsp cornflour
4 tbsp dark soft brown sugar
1 tsp vanilla extract

SPECIAL EQUIPMENT 6 x 175ml (6fl oz) dariole moulds or ramekins

1 Preheat the oven to 180°C (350°F/Gas 4). Oil the moulds and place a disc of baking parchment in the base of each. Cream together the butter and sugar with an electric whisk, until fluffy. Add the eggs, one at a time, beating well between additions. Add a spoonful of the flour if it starts to curdle.

2 Sift over the remaining flour and xanthan, and add the almonds, fudge pieces, and milk. Fold together to form a soft batter and divide between the moulds. Cover each with a square of baking parchment and of foil, pleated in the middle to allow the puddings to rise. Tightly pinch around the edges to form a good seal. Stand the puddings in a roasting tin, pour in enough hot water to come halfway up the outside of the pudding moulds. Bake for 1–1¼ hours or until the sponges are risen and golden. Leave to stand while you make the sauce.

3 In a large jug, mix 6 tablespoons milk with the cornflour, sugar, and vanilla to form a smooth paste. Heat the remaining milk in a non-stick pan until almost boiling, and pour onto the cornflour paste, stirring constantly. Return to the rinsed-out pan and gently bring to the boil, stirring until the mixture thickens. Cook over a low heat for 1 minute, stirring constantly. Pour into a warm jug. To serve, invert the puddings onto serving plates, remove the baking parchment, and hand out the toffee sauce separately.

STATISTICS PER PUDDING

Energy 654kcals/2737kJ

Protein 11g

Fat 37g
Saturated fat 19g

Carbohydrate 69g
Sugar 50g

Fibre 0.8g

Salt 0.7g

● ● ● CALORIES

● ● ● SATURATED FAT

● ● ○ SALT

CARAMELIZED ORANGE PUDDING

SERVES 10   **PREP** 20 MINS   **COOK** 30–40 MINS

Be patient when baking this tangy, orange-topped sponge. Don't open the oven for a peep too early or the pudding won't rise and it may even sink.

GREAT FOR KiDS

275g (9½oz) unsalted butter, plus extra for greasing
3–4 oranges, peeled, pith and pips removed, and thickly sliced
3–4 tbsp demerara sugar
115g (4oz) gluten-free self-raising flour
1 tsp gluten-free baking powder

1 tsp xanthan gum
175g (6oz) golden caster sugar
3 eggs
3 tbsp milk
double cream, crème fraîche, or gluten-free custard (see page 286), to serve

1 Preheat the oven to 180°C (350°F/Gas 4). Grease an 18 x 30cm (7 x 12in) ovenproof dish with a little butter. Melt 100g (3½oz) butter in a large, non-stick frying pan over a medium heat. Add the orange slices and demerara sugar, and cook for 5–6 minutes until the oranges are golden and caramelized. Don't let the sugar burn. Put the oranges and sauce into the ovenproof dish.

2 Sift the flour, baking powder, and xanthan into a large bowl and set aside. Place the remaining butter and caster sugar into a bowl and beat with an electric whisk until light and fluffy. Do this for at least 8 minutes so it is really light. Add the eggs, one at a time, with a spoonful of the flour mixture. Beat until well incorporated, then fold in the remaining flour mix, and stir in the milk.

3 Spoon the mixture over the oranges and bake for 30–40 minutes, or until risen and golden and an inserted skewer comes out clean. Spoon into shallow bowls with the orange slices on top. Serve with double cream, crème fraîche, or gluten-free custard.

STATISTICS PER SERVING

Energy 643kcals/2646kJ

Protein 7g

Fat 42g
Saturated fat 25g

Carbohydrate 57g
Sugar 44g

Fibre 3g

Salt 0.9g

COOK'S TIP

This is a great pudding for children, best when served with gluten-free custard (see page 286).

● ● ● CALORIES

● ● ● SATURATED FAT

● ● ○ SALT

CHOCOLATE AND DATE SPONGE PUDDINGS

MAKES 6   **PREP** 20 MINS   **COOK** 35–40 MINS

A hard-to-beat warming winter pudding served with a creamy chocolate sauce.

250g (9oz) block of dried dates, stoned and chopped
1 tsp gluten-free bicarbonate of soda
145g (5oz) unsalted butter, softened, plus extra for greasing
280g (9½oz) light muscovado sugar
2 tbsp golden syrup
3 eggs
140g (5oz) gluten-free self-raising flour

60g (2oz) cocoa powder
90ml (3fl oz) milk
200ml (7fl oz) double cream
60g (2oz) dark chocolate (70% cocoa solids)

SPECIAL EQUIPMENT 6 x 175ml (6fl oz) dariole moulds or ramekins

1 Preheat the oven to 160°C (325°F/Gas 3). Put the dates in a pan with 175ml (6fl oz) water and bring to the boil. Remove from the heat, add the soda, stir, and set aside to cool. Grease and line the moulds with baking parchment. Place 85g (3oz) butter, 140g (5oz) sugar, and syrup in a large bowl and whisk until creamy. Add the eggs gradually, whisking between additions. Add the flour, cocoa powder, and milk, and whisk again. Stir in date mixture.

2 Divide the mixture between the prepared moulds. Cover each with a square of baking parchment and foil, pleated in the middle to allow the puddings to rise. Tightly pinch around the edges to form a good seal. Stand them in a roasting tin and pour boiling water to halfway up the outside of the moulds. Bake for 35–40 minutes or until the sponges are risen and firm to the touch. Remove from the oven and set aside.

3 For the sauce, place 140g (5oz) sugar, 60g (2oz) butter, and half the cream together in a small pan and bring to the boil, stirring until the sugar dissolves. Bubble for 1 minute. Remove from the heat and add the remaining cream and the chocolate, stirring until the sauce is smooth and runny.

4 Invert the puddings onto serving plates, remove the lining papers, and spoon a little sauce over each.

STATISTICS PER PUDDING

Energy 860kcals/3605kJ

Protein 11g

Fat 48g
Saturated fat 28g

Carbohydrate 99g
Sugar 83g

Fibre 5g

Salt 1.5g

CHRISTMAS PUDDING

MAKES 3   **PREP** 30 MINS   **COOK** 2 HOURS
PLUS SOAKING

GUIDELINES PER SERVING

●●● CALORIES

●●● SATURATED FAT

●○○ SALT

Christmas cakes, puddings, and mincemeat are best made a few weeks in advance to let the flavours mellow and mature.

60g (2oz) each of ready-to-eat dates, dried apricots, and prunes, finely chopped
200g (7oz) each of currants, raisins, and sultanas
115g (4oz) glacé cherries, halved
60g (2oz) mixed peel, chopped
zest and juice of 1 lemon
200ml (7fl oz) dry cider
4 tbsp each of brandy and rum
3 tbsp black treacle
1 tbsp cocoa powder
2 tsp mixed spice

1 tsp ground cinnamon
1 dessert apple, cored and grated
225g (8oz) unsalted butter, softened, plus extra for greasing
225g (8oz) dark muscovado sugar
3 eggs, beaten
85g (3oz) gluten-free self-raising flour
175g (6oz) gluten-free breadcrumbs
60g (2oz) walnut pieces, chopped
60g (2oz) ground almonds

SPECIAL EQUIPMENT 3 x 600ml (1 pint) pudding basins

1 Place the first 12 ingredients, up to and including the grated apple, in a large, non-metallic bowl and mix to combine. Cover with cling film and leave to soak for at least 12 hours or up to 2 days in a cool place.

2 Preheat the oven to 160°C (325°F/Gas 3). Lightly grease the basins and line the base of each one with baking parchment. Cream the butter and sugar in a large bowl until fluffy. Gradually add the eggs, whisking between additions. Fold in the flour. Add the breadcrumbs, walnuts, almonds, and the soaked fruit and juices. Mix well, divide the mixture between the basins, and level the surfaces. Cover each with a square of baking parchment and foil, pleated in the middle to allow the puddings to rise. Tightly pinch around the edges to form a good seal or tie in place with string.

3 Stand the puddings in a roasting tin and pour boiling water to halfway up the outside of the basins. Bake for 2 hours, topping up the water occasionally. Remove and leave to cool before storing. To reheat, follow the same process, but bake at 180°C (350°F/Gas 4) for 35 minutes. Each pudding will serve 6 people.

STATISTICS PER SERVING

Energy 407kcals/1710kJ

Protein 5.6g

Fat 16g
Saturated fat 7.2g

Carbohydrate 55.6g

Sugar 46g

Fibre 2.8g

Salt 0.6g

COFFEE AND WALNUT CAKE

SERVES 12   **PREP** 15 MINS   **COOK** 25-30 MINS

If you don't have an espresso maker, instant coffee works well but make sure it's strong enough for the flavour to come through in the finished cake.

vegetable oil, for greasing
175g (6oz) unsalted butter, softened
175g (6oz) caster sugar
3 eggs
175g (6oz) gluten-free self-raising flour
4 tbsp espresso coffee or 6 tsp strong coffee powder mixed with 4 tbsp boiling water, cooled
1 tsp vanilla extract
60g (2oz) walnut pieces, roughly chopped, plus walnut halves, to decorate

For the buttercream
100g (3½oz) unsalted butter, softened
200g (7oz) icing sugar

SPECIAL EQUIPMENT 2 x 20cm (8in) round springform cake tins

1 Preheat the oven to 180°C (350°F/Gas 4). Lightly oil and line the tins with baking parchment. In a large bowl, mix the butter and sugar with an electric whisk until the mixture is pale, light, and fluffy. Add the eggs one at a time, beating well between additions, until fluffy. Add 1–2 tablespoons flour with the last egg to stop the mixture from curdling.

2 Add the remaining flour, 3 tablespoons of the coffee, and vanilla extract. Whisk again for 1 minute until fluffy. Gently fold in the walnut pieces and divide the mixture equally between the prepared tins. Bake for 25–30 minutes until the sponges look golden and spring back when lightly touched in the centre. Leave to cool in the tins for 5 minutes. Remove, peel away the lining paper, and transfer to a wire rack to cool completely.

3 For the buttercream, beat the butter and icing sugar with a wooden spoon, then beat in the remaining coffee. Spread half the buttercream evenly over the flat side of one of the cakes. Top with the second cake and spread the remaining buttercream over the top. Decorate with the walnuts.

STATISTICS PER SLICE

Energy 399kcals/1672kJ

Protein 4g

Fat 24g

Saturated fat 13g

Carbohydrate 41g

Sugar 31g

Fibre 0.8g

Salt 0.4g

VANILLA CUPCAKES

MAKES 12   PREP 15 MINS   COOK 20 MINS

Ever popular cupcakes don't come much lighter than these!
If you like, add a few drops of yellow food colour to the icing.

115g (4oz) unsalted butter, softened
115g (4oz) caster sugar
2 eggs
115g (4oz) gluten-free self-raising flour
3 tbsp milk
1 tsp vanilla extract
gluten-free cake decorations,
  for sprinkling

For the icing
200g (7oz) icing sugar
½ tsp vanilla extract

SPECIAL EQUIPMENT 12-hole patty tin
  lined with paper cases

1 Preheat the oven to 180°C (350°F/Gas 4). In a large bowl, mix the butter
and sugar with an electric whisk until pale, light, and fluffy. Add the eggs,
one at a time, beating well between additions, until fluffy. Add 1–2
tablespoons flour with the last egg to stop the mixture from curdling.
Add the remaining flour, milk, and vanilla extract and whisk for 1 minute.

2 Divide the mixture between the cases and bake for 20 minutes until the
sponges look golden and spring back when lightly touched in the centre.
Leave to cool in the tin for 5 minutes, then transfer to cool on a wire rack.

3 For the icing, sift the sugar into a bowl, add the vanilla, and gradually
add 2–3 tablespoons water, beating well between additions until smooth.
Spoon the icing over each cake, spreading it to the edges. Sprinkle over the
decorations and leave to set. Store in an airtight container for up to 4 days.

GREAT
FOR KIDS

VARIATIONS
Lemon cupcakes Omit the vanilla extract, beat the finely grated zest of 1 lemon
with the butter and sugar. Replace the water with lemon juice in the icing.
Chocolate cupcakes Replace 60g (2oz) of the flour with cocoa powder. For
the icing, replace 2 tablespoons of the sugar with cocoa powder and sift together.

STATISTICS PER CUPCAKE

Energy 223kcals/940kJ

Protein 2g

Fat 9g
Saturated fat 5.5g

Carbohydrate 33g

Sugar 26g

Fibre 0.5g

Salt 0.3g

● ● ● CALORIES

● ● ● SATURATED FAT

● ○ ○ SALT

CHOCOLATE CAKE

SERVES 12 **PREP** 25-30 MINS **COOK** 25-30 MINS **FREEZE** 3 MONTHS

This light-as-a-feather sponge, smothered in a wickedly delicious chocolate fudge icing, makes for the perfect treat.

GREAT FOR KiDS

butter, for greasing
200g (7oz) dark chocolate, broken
  into pieces
310g (11oz) unsalted butter, softened
225g (8oz) light muscovado sugar
100g (3½oz) gluten-free
  self-raising flour
½ tsp gluten-free bicarbonate of soda
60g (2oz) cocoa powder

60g (2oz) ground almonds
4 tbsp milk
3 eggs, separated
120ml (4fl oz) double cream
200g (7oz) icing sugar, sifted

SPECIAL EQUIPMENT
2 x 20cm (8in) round cake tins

1 Preheat the oven to 180°C (350°F/Gas 4). Grease the tins and line with baking parchment. Melt 60g (2oz) of the chocolate in a heatproof bowl over a pan of simmering water. Cool slightly.

2 In a large bowl, cream together 225g (8oz) of the butter and muscovado sugar with an electric whisk until light and fluffy. Sift in the flour, soda, and cocoa. Add the almonds and milk and gently fold in until well mixed. Whisk the egg whites in a clean bowl to form stiff peaks. Stir a large spoonful into the chocolate mix, then gently fold in the remainder.

3 Divide the mixture between the 2 tins and bake in the centre of the oven for 25–30 minutes or until the sponges bounce back when lightly touched in the centre. Place the tins on a wire rack and cover with a damp tea towel, which will keep them beautifully moist. Leave until cold.

4 For the icing, combine the remaining chocolate and the cream in a large bowl and place over a pan of gently simmering water. Stir occasionally until the chocolate has melted and the mixture is smooth. Remove and cool. In a separate bowl, whisk the remaining butter with the icing sugar until fluffy, add the melted chocolate mixture, and whisk until smooth. Turn out the sponges. Spread a third of the icing over one sponge and top with the second. Spread the remaining icing over the top and sides of the cake.

STATISTICS PER SLICE

Energy 565kcals/2359kJ

Protein 6g

Fat 37g
Saturated fat 21g

Carbohydrate 52g
Sugar 46g

Fibre 2g

Salt 0.8g

● ● ● CALORIES

● ● ● SATURATED FAT

● ○ ○ SALT

GREAT FOR KIDS

DEVIL'S FOOD CAKE

SERVES 12   **PREP** 20 MINS   **COOK** 25–30 MINS   **FREEZE** 3 MONTHS

This cake gets its name from being so tempting and indulgent; you have been warned!

60g (2oz) cocoa powder
115g (4oz) dark muscovado sugar
225g (8oz) gluten-free self-raising flour
1½ tsp gluten-free baking powder
½ tsp gluten-free bicarbonate of soda
140g (5oz) unsalted butter, softened,
  plus extra for greasing
85g (3oz) caster sugar
3 eggs
1 tsp vanilla extract

For the icing
175g (6oz) unsalted butter, cubed
30g (1oz) dark muscovado sugar
225g (8oz) dark chocolate
  (70% cocoa solids)
1 tsp vanilla extract

SPECIAL EQUIPMENT
2 x 20cm (8in) round cake tins

1 Preheat the oven to 180°C (350°F/Gas 4). Lightly grease the tins and line with baking parchment. Put the cocoa and muscovado sugar in a heatproof bowl, pour over 240ml (8fl oz) boiling water, mix well, and leave to cool.

2 In a large bowl, sift together the flour, baking powder, and soda. Cream the butter and caster sugar in another large bowl with an electric whisk until pale and fluffy. Add the eggs, whisking well between additions. Add half the flour mixture, vanilla, and half the cocoa mixture, and whisk for 30 seconds. Scrape down the sides of the bowl and repeat with the remaining flour and cocoa mixtures. Divide the cake mix evenly between the tins. Bake for 25–30 minutes or until the cakes bounce back when lightly touched in the centre. Remove the cakes from the oven. Cool for 5 minutes in the tins before peeling off the parchment and transferring to a wire rack to cool completely.

3 Meanwhile, make the icing. Place the butter and sugar in a pan and gently heat until melted and bubbling. Remove from the heat and stir in the chocolate and vanilla until smooth. Allow to cool, stirring once or twice.

4 When ready to ice the cake, whisk the icing for 30 seconds or until fluffy. Sandwich the cakes with a third of the icing, then spread the remainder over the top and sides. Swirl with the back of a knife for a decorative effect and serve, or store in an airtight container for up to 3 days.

STATISTICS PER SLICE

Energy 463kcals/1949kJ

Protein 6g

Fat 30g
Saturated fat 18g

Carbohydrate 43g
Sugar 30g

Fibre 2g

Salt 0.3g

CHOCOLATE HAZELNUT WHOOPIE PIES

MAKES 10   **PREP** 15 MINS   **COOK** 12–15 MINS   **FREEZE** 3 MONTHS
UNFILLED

Filled with ready-made hazelnut spread, these are very moreish. Whoopie pies are based on cakes made by the Amish community in the United States.

GUIDELINES PER SERVING

CALORIES

SATURATED FAT

SALT

100g (3½oz) gluten-free plain flour
½ tsp xanthan gum
20g (¾oz) cocoa powder
½ tsp gluten-free baking powder
30g (1oz) blanched hazelnuts
60g (2oz) unsalted butter, softened,
  plus extra for greasing

60g (2oz) light muscovado sugar
1 egg
90ml (3fl oz) buttermilk
115g (4oz) gluten-free hazelnut spread

1 Preheat the oven to 180°C (350°F/Gas 4). Lightly grease 2 baking sheets and line with baking parchment. Sift together the flour, xanthan, cocoa, and baking powder. Toast the hazelnuts in the hot oven for 5 minutes and set aside to cool.

2 In a bowl, cream the butter and sugar together using an electric whisk. Add the egg, whisking well. Add half the sifted ingredients and half the buttermilk, then whisk until fluffy. Repeat with the remaining sifted ingredients and buttermilk. Place heaped teaspoons of the mix, 5cm (2in) apart, on the baking sheets to form 20 mounds. Dip a clean spoon in warm water and use the back to smooth the surface of the cake mounds.

3 Bake for 12–15 minutes or until the tops have risen and spring back when lightly touched in the centre. Leave to cool on the baking sheets for 2–3 minutes before transferring to a wire rack to cool completely.

4 Chop the toasted hazelnuts. To finish, spread a little hazelnut spread on the base of half the sponges, sprinkle with some hazelnuts, and then sandwich together with the remaining sponges.

GREAT FOR KIDS

STATISTICS PER PIE

Energy 202kcals/843kJ

Protein 3.5g

Fat 12g
Saturated fat 5g

Carbohydrate 20g
Sugar 13g

Fibre 1g

Salt 0.2g

ROSEMARY AND ORANGE BLOSSOM POLENTA CAKES

MAKES 12 **PREP** 20 MINS **COOK** 35-40 MINS **FREEZE** 3 MONTHS

Infused in a sweet syrup, the aromatic, resinous notes of rosemary combine beautifully with orange and polenta to flavour these moist little cakes.

175g (6oz) ground almonds
85g (3oz) polenta or fine cornmeal
2 tsp gluten-free baking powder
175g (6oz) unsalted butter, softened
175g (6oz) golden caster sugar
3 eggs
zest and juice of 2 oranges

For the rosemary syrup
12 sprigs of rosemary
60g (2oz) caster sugar
4 tsp orange blossom water

SPECIAL EQUIPMENT deep, 12-hole muffin tray lined with paper cases

1 Preheat the oven to 180°C (350°F/Gas 4). In a bowl, mix together the almonds, cornmeal, and baking powder. In another bowl, cream together the butter and sugar with an electric whisk until light and pale. Add the eggs, whisking well between additions. Add half the almond mixture and half the orange juice and whisk together. Stir in the orange zest and remaining juice, then add the remaining almond mixture.

2 Divide the mix between the paper cases and bake in the centre of the oven for 35–40 minutes or until golden on top and the sponge springs back when lightly touched in the centre.

3 When the cakes are nearly ready, make the syrup. Put the rosemary and sugar in a heavy pan with 150ml (5fl oz) water. Bring to the boil, stir until the sugar dissolves, then simmer for 5–8 minutes or until syrupy. Cool slightly, then stir in the orange blossom water. Remove the cakes from the oven, then spoon a little syrup and place a rosemary sprig over each cake. Cool in the tin and store in an airtight container for up to 3 days.

STATISTICS PER CAKE

Energy 324kcals/1360kJ

Protein 6g

Fat 22g
Saturated fat 9g

Carbohydrate 25g
Sugar 20g

Fibre 0.2g

Salt 0.3g

WHITE CHOCOLATE AND RASPBERRY MUFFINS

MAKES 16   **PREP** 15 MINS   **COOK** 25–30 MINS   **FREEZE** 2 MONTHS
PLUS COOLING

GUIDELINES PER SERVING

- ●●○ CALORIES
- ●●● SATURATED FAT
- ●○○ SALT

A perfect balance of sweet white chocolate and tart raspberries makes these muffins hard to resist!

300g (10oz) gluten-free plain flour
1½ tsp gluten-free baking powder
1 tsp xanthan gum
pinch of salt
175g (6oz) caster sugar
2 eggs
100g (3½oz) butter, melted
200ml (7fl oz) milk

175g (6oz) raspberries
140g (5oz) white chocolate, chopped

SPECIAL EQUIPMENT 2 x deep, 12-hole muffin trays lined with 16 paper cases, and a greaseproof paper icing bag

1 Preheat the oven to 200°C (400°F/Gas 6). Sift the flour, baking powder, xanthan, salt, and sugar into a large bowl.

2 In another bowl, mix the eggs, butter, and milk, then pour into the dry ingredients along with the raspberries and 115g (4oz) chocolate. Mix briefly until just combined. Don't over-mix: it should still be a little lumpy.

3 Divide the mixture between the paper cases so they are two-thirds full. Bake in the oven for 25–30 minutes or until the centres spring back when lightly touched. Cool in the trays for 5 minutes before transferring to a wire rack. To finish, melt the remaining chocolate in a small heatproof bowl set over a pan of gently simmering water. Spoon the melted chocolate into the paper icing bag, snip off the tip of the bag, and drizzle the melted chocolate over the cakes in a zigzag pattern. Leave to set.

STATISTICS PER MUFFIN

Energy 296kcals/1246kJ

Protein 5.5g

Fat 12.5g
Saturated fat 7g

Carbohydrate 40g
Sugar 23g

Fibre 1.5g

Salt 0.6g

Vary the fruit »
For a change, mix half raspberries with chopped peaches and nectarines. If fresh raspberries aren't available, try chopped plums or blueberries instead.

RED VELVET CUPCAKES

MAKES 12　　**PREP** 20 MINS　　**COOK** 40-45 MINS　　**FREEZE** 2 MONTHS

These chocolate-flavoured, vanilla-scented cupcakes look stunning with their deep red colour.

175g (6oz) gluten-free self-raising flour
1 tsp xanthan gum
3 tbsp cocoa powder
1 tsp cream of tartar
85g (3oz) unsalted butter, softened
150g (5½oz) caster sugar
2 large eggs
2 tbsp natural red food colouring
2 tsp vanilla extract
1 tsp cider vinegar
200ml (7fl oz) buttermilk

For the cream cheese icing
115g (4oz) full-fat cream cheese
60g (2oz) unsalted butter, softened
½ tsp vanilla extract
350g (12oz) icing sugar, sifted

SPECIAL EQUIPMENT deep 12-hole muffin tray lined with paper cases, piping bag fitted with a 2cm (¾in) star nozzle

1 Preheat the oven to 160°C (325°F/Gas 3). Combine the flour, xanthan, cocoa, and cream of tartar in a large bowl.

2 In another large bowl, beat the butter and sugar with an electric whisk. Add the eggs, one at a time, whisking between additions. Add half the flour mixture, colouring, vanilla, vinegar, and half the buttermilk. Whisk well. Add the remaining flour and buttermilk. Whisk again for 30 seconds. Divide the mixture between the paper cases so they are two-thirds full. Bake for 40–45 minutes or until the centres spring back when lightly touched. Cool for 5 minutes, then transfer to a wire rack to cool completely.

3 For the icing, whisk the cream cheese, butter, and vanilla in a large bowl using an electric whisk. Gradually add the icing sugar, a little at a time, until it is all incorporated. Whisk for 30 seconds until really light and fluffy.

4 Carefully slice and crumble a thin disc from the top of 3 cakes to make crumbs for the topping. Spoon the icing into a piping bag and pipe it in swirls on top of the cakes. Scatter over the cake crumbs to finish.

STATISTICS PER CUPCAKE

Energy 380kcals/1600kJ

Protein 4.5g

Fat 17g
Saturated fat 2g

Carbohydrate 52g
Sugar 42g

Fibre 1g

Salt 0.2g

● ● ● CALORIES

● ● ● SATURATED FAT

● ○ ○ SALT

COCONUT CAKE WITH LIME ICING

SERVES 12   **PREP** 20 MINS   **COOK** 25-30 MINS   **FREEZE** 3 MONTHS

Crunchy desiccated coconut adds texture to this cake, while a zingy lime buttercream cuts through the richness.

175g (6oz) unsalted butter, softened, plus extra for greasing
175g (6oz) golden caster sugar
3 eggs, beaten
175g (6oz) gluten-free self-raising flour
1 tsp gluten-free baking powder
60g (2oz) desiccated coconut
160g can coconut cream

For the icing
85g (3oz) unsalted butter, softened
350g (12oz) icing sugar
finely grated zest and juice of 2 limes
1 tbsp desiccated coconut, toasted

SPECIAL EQUIPMENT 2 x 20cm (8in) round cake tins

1 Preheat the oven to 180°C (350°F/Gas 4). Lightly grease the tins and line with baking parchment. Cream the butter and caster sugar in a large bowl with an electric whisk, until pale and fluffy. Add the eggs, whisking well between additions. Sift over the flour and baking powder, add both kinds of coconut, and whisk briefly. Scrape down the sides of the bowl, then whisk again for 30 seconds.

2 Divide the mixture evenly between the tins and bake for 25–30 minutes or until the cakes bounce back when lightly touched in the centre.

3 For the icing, cream the the butter and icing sugar in a large bowl with an electric whisk until fluffy. Add the lime zest and juice and whisk again for 30 seconds until fluffy and light. Cover and chill until firm.

4 Remove the cakes from the oven and cool in the tins for 5 minutes. Peel off the baking parchment and transfer to a wire rack to cool completely.

5 Sandwich the cakes together with a third of the icing, then spread the remainder over the top and sides. Swirl with the back of a knife for decorative effect. Sprinkle over the toasted coconut to finish.

STATISTICS PER SLICE

Energy 474kcals/1997kJ

Protein 4g

Fat 27g
Saturated fat 18g

Carbohydrate 55g
Sugar 44g

Fibre 1.7g

Salt 0.3g

STICKY GINGER CAKE

SERVES 12   **PREP** 15 MINS   **COOK** 50-55 MINS   **FREEZE** 3 MONTHS

This moist dark ginger cake, flecked with stem ginger,
is best made a day in advance for the flavours to deepen.

2 tbsp ginger syrup, from a jar of
  stem ginger in syrup
140g (5oz) golden syrup
115g (4oz) unsalted butter, plus
  extra for greasing
115g (4oz) dark muscovado sugar
250g (9oz) gluten-free plain flour
2 tsp ground ginger
1½ tsp gluten-free baking powder
1 tsp xanthan gum

1 tsp gluten-free bicarbonate of soda
½ tsp ground cinnamon
pinch of salt
3 balls of stem ginger, from the jar,
  finely chopped
3 eggs
90ml (3fl oz) milk

SPECIAL EQUIPMENT 900g (2lb) loaf tin

1 Preheat the oven to 180°C (350°F/Gas 4). Grease and line the tin with
baking parchment. Place the syrups in a pan, add the butter and sugar,
and heat gently, stirring until the mixture is smooth and melted. Set aside
to cool slightly.

2 Sift the flour, ground ginger, baking powder, xanthan, soda, cinnamon,
and salt into a large bowl. Add the cooled syrup mixture to the dry
ingredients along with the stem ginger, eggs, and milk. Mix well with
a wooden spoon.

3 Pour the mixture into the prepared tin and bake for 50–55 minutes, or
until the sponge springs back when lightly touched in the centre. Leave to
cool in the tin for 10 minutes before turning out to cool completely on a
wire rack. Store in an airtight container for up to 1 week.

COOK'S TIP
If preferred, bake 2 loaves in 450g (1lb) tins and freeze the second loaf.

GUIDELINES PER SERVING

●●○ CALORIES

●●○ SATURATED FAT

●●○ SALT

STATISTICS PER SLICE

Energy 264kcals/1109kJ

Protein 4.25g

Fat 10.5g

Saturated fat 6g

Carbohydrate 38g

Sugar 23.5g

Fibre 1g

Salt 0.8g

VANILLA AND CHESTNUT CAKE

SERVES 12　　**PREP** 15 MINS　　**COOK** 40-45 MINS　　**FREEZE** 3 MONTHS

You could jazz up this cake with a bit of whipped cream: split the cake in two, spread some cream in the middle, and dust the top with icing sugar.

vegetable oil, for greasing
4 eggs, separated
125g (4½oz) light muscovado sugar
200ml (7fl oz) full-fat crème fraîche
2 tsp vanilla extract

140g (5oz) chestnut flour
2 tsp gluten-free baking powder

SPECIAL EQUIPMENT 20cm (8in) round cake tin

1 Preheat the oven to 180°C (350°F/Gas 4). Lightly grease the tin and line the base with baking parchment.

2 Place the egg yolks and sugar in a large bowl and use an electric whisk to mix until light and creamy. Add the crème fraîche and vanilla. Sift in the flour and baking powder and gently fold in.

3 Whisk the egg whites in a clean bowl until they form stiff peaks. Stir 1 heaped tablespoon of the egg whites into the cake mixture, then gently fold through the remainder.

4 Spoon the mixture into the prepared tin and bake for 40–45 minutes or until the sponge springs back when lightly touched in the centre. Cool in the tin for 5 minutes, then turn out and leave to cool completely on a wire rack. Dust with icing sugar and serve.

COOK'S TIP
Chestnut flour is available from good health food shops and Italian delicatessens.

STATISTICS PER SLICE

Energy　141kcals/588kJ

Protein　4g

Fat　9g

Saturated fat　5g

Carbohydrate　19g

Sugar　12g

Fibre　1g

Salt　0.3g

ALMOND CAKE

SERVES 12   **PREP** 20 MINS   **COOK** 1–1¼ HOURS

This moist cake will store for about a week and just seems to get better each day that it lasts.

vegetable oil, for greasing
175g (6oz) unsalted butter, softened
175g (6oz) golden caster sugar
3 eggs, beaten
2 tsp almond extract
250g (9oz) ground almonds
115g (4oz) polenta or fine cornmeal

1½ tsp gluten-free baking powder
150ml (5fl oz) Greek yogurt
30g (1oz) flaked almonds

SPECIAL EQUIPMENT 23cm (9in) round
   springform cake tin

1 Preheat the oven to 160°C (325°F/Gas 3). Grease the tin and line the base with baking parchment.

2 Place the butter and sugar in a large bowl and cream together with an electric whisk until pale and fluffy. Add the eggs, whisking well between additions. Stir in the almond extract.

3 Mix the ground almonds, polenta, and baking powder together, add half to the creamed mixture along with half the yogurt, and whisk well. Whisk in the remaining dry ingredients and the yogurt.

4 Spoon into the prepared tin and level the surface. Scatter over the flaked almonds. Bake in the centre of the oven for 1–1¼ hours or until a skewer inserted in the centre comes out clean. Leave to cool in the tin for 10 minutes before transferring to a wire rack to cool completely. Store in an airtight container for up to 2 weeks.

COOK'S TIP
Golden caster sugar gives the cake a lovely colour, but ordinary white caster sugar can be used too.

STATISTICS PER SLICE

Energy 380kcals/1582kJ

Protein 8.5g

Fat 28g
Saturated fat 9.5g

Carbohydrate 23g
Sugar 16g

Fibre 0.3g

Salt 0.5g

● ● ● CALORIES

● ● ● SATURATED FAT

● ○ ○ SALT

LEMON AND RASPBERRY LAYERED POLENTA CAKE

SERVES 12   **PREP** 20 MINS   **COOK** 25-30 MINS   **FREEZE** 3 MONTHS
UNFILLED SPONGES

Polenta gives this moist sponge a wonderful lemony colour. You can also try strawberries instead of raspberries.

vegetable oil, for greasing
225g (8oz) butter, softened
225g (8oz) caster sugar
3 eggs
115g (4oz) ground almonds
175g (6oz) polenta or fine cornmeal
zest and juice of 2 lemons

300g (10oz) fresh raspberries
200ml (7fl oz) double cream
4 tbsp icing sugar, plus extra
  for dusting

SPECIAL EQUIPMENT
2 x 20cm (8in) round cake tins

1 Preheat the oven to 180°C (350°F/Gas 4). Lightly grease the tins and line with baking parchment.

2 In a large bowl, cream the butter and sugar with an electric whisk until pale and fluffy. Add the eggs, one at a time, beating well between additions. Add 1–2 tablespoons of the ground almonds with the last egg to prevent curdling. Add the remaining almonds, polenta, lemon zest and juice, and a quarter of the raspberries, and gently fold together.

3 Divide the mixture equally between the 2 prepared tins, scattering 15 raspberries over one of them; this will be the top layer. Bake for 25–30 minutes, until the sponges spring back when lightly touched in the centre. Leave to cool for 5 minutes in the tins. Carefully remove from the tins, peel away the paper, and cool completely on a wire rack.

4 With an electric whisk, whip the cream and icing sugar until soft peaks form. Fold in the remaining raspberries. Spoon it over the base sponge, and top with the raspberry-topped sponge. Dust with icing sugar and serve. Once filled, this cake should be served within 4 hours.

STATISTICS PER SLICE

Energy 462kcals/1924kJ

Protein 6g

Fat 32g

Saturated fat 16g

Carbohydrate 36g

Sugar 27g

Fibre 1.3g

Salt 0.36g

⬤⬤◯ CALORIES

⬤⬤◯ SATURATED FAT

⬤◯◯ SALT

SPICED HONEY CAKE

SERVES 12   **PREP** 20 MINS   **COOK** 1 HOUR   **FREEZE** 3 MONTHS

A great cut-and-come-again cake with a wonderfully moist crumb. Sprinkle flaked almonds on top, if preferred.

140g (5oz) clear honey
115g (4oz) unsalted butter,
  plus extra for greasing
115g (4oz) light muscovado sugar
250g (9oz) gluten-free plain flour
1 tsp ground cinnamon
½ tsp ground ginger
1½ tsp gluten-free baking powder
1 tsp xanthan gum
1 tsp gluten-free bicarbonate of soda
pinch of salt

3 eggs
90ml (3fl oz) milk

To decorate
85g (3oz) clear honey
30g (1oz) pistachio nuts, shelled,
  skinned, and chopped

SPECIAL EQUIPMENT 20cm (8in) square
  or 23cm (9in) round cake tin

1 Place the honey, butter, and sugar into a small pan and heat gently, stirring until the mixture is smooth and melted. Set aside to cool slightly.

2 Preheat the oven to 180°C (350°F/Gas 4). Grease and line the tin with baking parchment. In a large bowl, sift together the flour, spices, baking powder, xanthan, soda, and salt. Add the cooled honey mixture to the bowl along with the eggs and milk and mix well with a wooden spoon. Pour the mixture into the prepared tin and bake for 1 hour or until the sponge springs back when lightly touched in the centre.

3 To decorate, place the honey in a small pan, bring to the boil, and bubble for 1–2 minutes or until the honey darkens and thickens. Stir in the pistachios to coat, then pour over the top of the warm sponge. Allow the cake to cool completely before removing from the tin.

« Honey
Honey attracts water, which makes it very good for baking as it keeps cakes moist for longer.

STATISTICS PER SLICE

Energy 276kcals/1161kJ

Protein 4.75g

Fat 11.5g

Saturated fat 6g

Carbohydrate 38g

Sugar 23.5g

Fibre 0.8g

Salt 0.27g

CARROT CAKE

SERVES 12   **PREP** 20 MINS   **COOK** 35-40 MINS   **FREEZE** 3 MONTHS

Everyone loves a carrot cake but if walnuts are not your thing, replace them with the same measure of raisins.

GUIDELINES PER SERVING

● ● ● CALORIES

● ● ○ SATURATED FAT

● ○ ○ SALT

GREAT FOR KIDS

225g (8oz) light muscovado sugar
240ml (8fl oz) sunflower oil,
  plus extra for greasing
1 tsp vanilla extract
3 eggs
225g (8oz) gluten-free plain flour
1 tsp gluten-free baking powder
½ tsp gluten-free bicarbonate of soda
1 tsp xanthan gum
1 tsp ground cinnamon, plus extra
  for dusting
1 tsp ground ginger
225g (8oz) carrots, coarsely grated

60g (2oz) walnuts or raisins,
  finely chopped
a few walnut halves,
  to decorate (optional)

For the icing

30g (1oz) unsalted butter, softened
75g (2½oz) full-fat soft cheese
1 tsp vanilla extract
225g (8oz) icing sugar

SPECIAL EQUIPMENT

2 x 20cm (8in) round cake tins

1 Preheat the oven to 180°C (350°F/Gas 4). Lightly grease the tins and line with baking parchment. Beat the sugar, oil, vanilla, and eggs in a large bowl with an electric whisk until smooth and thick. Sift over the flour, baking powder, soda, xanthan, cinnamon, and ginger, then fold in until well combined. Fold in the carrots and walnuts or raisins.

2 Divide the mixture between the tins. Bake for 35–40 minutes or until golden and risen and the centre bounces back when lightly pressed. Leave to cool in the tin for 5 minutes. Transfer to a wire rack to cool completely.

3 For the icing, place the butter and cheese in a large bowl and cream together using an electric whisk. Add the vanilla and mix. Sift the icing sugar into a large bowl, then add to the cream cheese mix a little at a time, whisking well between additions.

4 Peel away the baking parchment from the cakes. Divide the icing between the 2 cakes, spreading it evenly over the tops. Stack the cakes, decorate with the walnut halves (if using), and dust with cinnamon.

STATISTICS PER SLICE

Energy 464kcals/1943kJ

Protein 5g

Fat 27g
Saturated fat 6g

Carbohydrate 52g
Sugar 38g

Fibre 1.6g

Salt 0.3g

RICH FRUIT CAKE

SERVES 12   **PREP** 20 MINS   **COOK** 2 HOURS   **FREEZE** 3 MONTHS
PLUS SOAKING

This fruit cake matures on storage and it's worth baking it up to 3 months ahead. If you like, make holes with a skewer and spoon over brandy every couple of weeks.

600g (1lb 5oz) mixed dried fruit, such as vine fruits and chopped mixed peel
115g (4oz) glacé cherries, halved
zest and juice of 1 lemon
1 tsp mixed spice
2 tbsp brandy
175g (6oz) unsalted butter, softened, plus extra for greasing
175g (6oz) light muscovado sugar

3 eggs
140g (5oz) gluten-free plain flour
30g (1oz) ground almonds
30g (1oz) chopped walnuts
65 whole blanched almonds, approx. 75g (2½oz) in weight (optional)

SPECIAL EQUIPMENT 20cm (8in) round or 18cm (7in) square cake tin

1 Place the dried fruit, glacé cherries, lemon zest and juice, spice, and brandy in a large bowl. Mix well, cover, and leave to soak for at least 4 hours or preferably overnight.

2 Preheat the oven to 160°C (325°F/Gas 3). Lightly grease and line the tin with baking parchment. In a large bowl, cream the butter and sugar together until pale and fluffy using an electric whisk. Add the eggs, whisking well between additions.

3 Add the flour, ground almonds, walnuts, and soaked fruit, and stir until evenly mixed. Spoon into the prepared tin and level the surface. Top with the whole almonds (if using), arranging them in a pattern of decreasing circles. Alternatively, omit the almonds and decorate after baking with approximately 550g (1¼lb) each of shop-bought gluten-free marzipan and gluten-free icing.

4 Bake in the centre of the oven for 2 hours or until the top is golden and a skewer inserted into the centre comes out clean. Check the cake halfway through and if it's browning too quickly, cover loosely with baking parchment. Cool in the tin, then remove the parchment, re-wrap in clean parchment and foil, and store in an airtight container until ready to use.

STATISTICS PER SLICE

Energy 460kcals/1932kJ

Protein 6.5g

Fat 21g
Saturated fat 9g

Carbohydrate 61g
Sugar 53g

Fibre 2.2g

Salt 0.13g

CRANBERRY AND APPLE CAKE

SERVES 12   **PREP** 20 MINS   **COOK** 1–1¼ HOURS   **FREEZE** 3 MONTHS
PLUS COOLING

GUIDELINES PER SERVING

● ● ● CALORIES

● ● ● SATURATED FAT

● ○ ○ SALT

Choose a red-skinned apple with a little tartness to it for this cake – Jazz apples work well.

GREAT FOR KIDS

200g (7oz) unsalted butter, softened, plus extra for greasing
450g (1lb) red-skinned dessert apples, cored and thinly sliced
85g (3oz) dried cranberries
2 tbsp lemon juice
175g (6oz) light muscovado sugar
3 eggs, beaten

200g (7oz) gluten-free plain flour
2 tsp gluten-free baking powder
½ tsp ground cinnamon
150ml (5fl oz) soured cream
3 tsp demerara sugar

SPECIAL EQUIPMENT 23cm (9in) round springform cake tin

1 Melt 30g (1oz) of the butter in a large frying pan, add the apples, and sauté for 4–5 minutes or until just softened. Stir in the cranberries and lemon juice and set aside to cool. Preheat the oven to 180°C (350°F/Gas 4). Lightly grease and line the tin with baking parchment.

2 Cream the remaining butter and the muscovado sugar until fluffy using an electric whisk. Gradually add the eggs, whisking well between additions. Sift the flour, baking powder, and cinnamon together, add half to the bowl along with the soured cream, and whisk again. Repeat with the remaining flour mix, then fold in two-thirds of the apple and cranberry mixture.

3 Spoon the mixture into the tin, levelling the surface. Arrange the remaining fruit on top and sprinkle with demerara sugar.

4 Bake in the centre of the oven for 1–1¼ hours until golden and springy to the touch and a skewer inserted into the centre comes out clean. Cool in the tin for 10 minutes before transferring to a plate. Serve warm as a dessert with soured cream, or cold in slices.

STATISTICS PER SLICE

Energy 327kcals/1377kJ

Protein 4g

Fat 18g
Saturated fat 11g

Carbohydrate 32g

Sugar 20g

Fibre 2.2g

Salt 0.3g

● ● ● CALORIES

● ● ● SATURATED FAT

● ○ ○ SALT

RHUBARB STREUSEL CAKE

SERVES 12   **PREP** 25 MINS   **COOK** 1¼ HOURS   **FREEZE** 3 MONTHS

Pink forced rhubarb looks pretty in this dessert-style cake, but green rhubarb works just as well.

GREAT FOR KiDS

125g (4½oz) unsalted butter, softened, plus extra for greasing
125g (4½oz) light muscovado sugar
225g (8oz) rhubarb, sliced into 1cm (½in) pieces
115g (4oz) strawberries, chopped
2 eggs
225g (8oz) gluten-free plain flour
1 tsp gluten-free baking powder
½ tsp ground cinnamon
3 tbsp milk
gluten-free custard (see page 286) or crème fraîche, to serve

For the topping
85g (3oz) gluten-free plain flour
85g (3oz) demerara sugar, plus 1 tbsp for sprinkling
½ tsp ground cinnamon
60g (2oz) cold unsalted butter, cubed
30g (1oz) whole blanched hazelnuts, toasted and coarsely chopped

SPECIAL EQUIPMENT
23cm (9in) round cake tin

1 Melt 15g (½oz) each of the butter and muscovado sugar in a frying pan, add the rhubarb and sauté over a medium-low heat for 3–4 minutes or until soft. Remove, stir in the strawberries, and set aside. The fruit should be cold before it's stirred into the cake mix or it will sink to the bottom of the cake.

2 Preheat the oven to 180°C (350°F/Gas 4). Lightly grease the tin and line the base with baking parchment. For the topping, pulse the flour, demerara sugar, cinnamon, and butter in a food processor until it resembles breadcrumbs. Transfer to a bowl, stir in the hazelnuts, and set aside.

3 Cream the remaining butter and muscovado sugar in a large bowl using an electric whisk, until fluffy. Add the eggs, whisking between additions. Sift together the flour, baking powder, and cinnamon. Add half the flour mixture and half the milk to the wet ingredients and whisk; add the remaining flour and milk and whisk. Stir through the rhubarb and strawberries. Spoon the mixture into the tin, scatter over the topping, and sprinkle with demerara sugar. Bake for 1¼ hours or until a skewer inserted into the centre comes out clean. Leave to cool in the tin for 10 minutes. Transfer to a wire rack to cool completely. Serve with gluten-free custard or crème fraîche.

STATISTICS PER SLICE

Energy 310kcals/1306kJ

Protein 4.5g

Fat 16g
Saturated fat 9g

Carbohydrate 38g
Sugar 19g

Fibre 2g

Salt 0.2g

BANANA AND CHESTNUT BREAD

SERVES 12   **PREP** 15 MINS   **COOK** 50-55 MINS   **FREEZE** 3 MONTHS

Loaf-style cakes are easy to prepare, as there is no need to beat in air and retain it with gentle folding – simply mix well, pour into the tin, and bake.

140g (5oz) gluten-free plain flour
140g (5oz) chestnut flour
1½ tsp gluten-free baking powder
1 tsp xanthan gum
1 tsp gluten-free bicarbonate of soda
½ tsp ground cinnamon
½ tsp freshly grated nutmeg
pinch of salt

3 ripe bananas
115g (4oz) unsalted butter, plus
  extra for greasing
115g (4oz) light muscovado sugar
3 eggs
90ml (3fl oz) milk

SPECIAL EQUIPMENT 900g (2lb) loaf tin

1 Preheat the oven to 180°C (350°F/Gas 4). Grease the tin and line with baking parchment. In a large bowl, sift together the flours, baking powder, xanthan, soda, cinnamon, nutmeg, and salt. Mash the bananas.

2 In a small pan, melt the butter, then stir in the sugar. Beat the eggs and milk together. Make a well in the centre of the sifted ingredients, add all the wet ingredients, and mix well with a wooden spoon.

3 Pour the mixture into the prepared tin and bake for 50–55 minutes or until the sponge springs back when lightly touched in the centre. Leave to cool in the tin for 10 minutes before turning out. Cool on a wire rack. Store in an airtight container for up to 1 week.

COOK'S TIP
If preferred, bake 2 loaves in 450g (1lb) tins and freeze the second loaf.

STATISTICS PER SLICE

Energy 219kcals/918kJ

Protein 4.5g

Fat 10.3g
Saturated fat 5.7g

Carbohydrate 34.7g
Sugar 19.7g

Fibre 2.08g

Salt 0.7g

⬤⬤◯ CALORIES

⬤◯◯ SATURATED FAT

⬤◯◯ SALT

APRICOT AND CARDAMOM TEABREAD

SERVES 12 **PREP** 15 MINS **COOK** 1¼–1½ HOURS **FREEZE** 2 MONTHS

Earl Grey tea adds a lovely citrus note to this wonderfully moist teabread, but any other tea will work too.

GREAT FOR KIDS

1 tea bag, such as Earl Grey
225g (8oz) ready-to-eat dried
  apricots, finely chopped
6 cardamom pods, split
175g (6oz) light muscovado sugar
oil, for greasing
225g (8oz) gluten-free plain flour
1 tsp gluten-free baking powder
1 tsp xanthan gum
1 tsp ground cinnamon

pinch of salt
75g (2½oz) cold unslated butter, cubed
2 eggs, beaten
15g (½oz) flaked almonds
2 tbsp demerara sugar
butter, to serve

SPECIAL EQUIPMENT
900g (2lb) loaf tin

STATISTICS PER SLICE

Energy 225kcals/948kJ

Protein 4g

Fat 7g
Saturated fat 3.5g

Carbohydrate 36g
Sugar 23g

Fibre 2.4g

Salt 0.3g

1 Pour 300ml (10fl oz) boiling water over the tea bag and leave to infuse for 5 minutes. Place the apricots in a small pan. Remove the tea bag and add the hot tea, cardamom, and sugar to the pan. Bring to the boil, then simmer, uncovered, for 10 minutes. Leave until cold; the apricot mixture will cool quickly if tipped into a shallow tray. Remove the cardamom pods.

2 Preheat the oven to 180°C (350°F/Gas 4). Lightly oil the tin and line the base with baking parchment. Sift the flour, baking powder, xanthan, cinnamon, and salt into a large bowl. Rub the butter into the flour mixture. Stir the cold apricots and their cooking liquid into the flour, add the eggs, and beat together. Pour into the tin and scatter over the almonds and demerara sugar. Bake in the centre of the oven for 1 hour 20–25 minutes or until well risen and firm to the touch.

3 Cool in the tin for 10 minutes before transferring to a wire rack to cool completely. The tea bread is even better the day after baking and will keep in an airtight container for up to 1 week.

SULTANA SCONES

MAKES 8   **PREP** 10 MINS   **COOK** 15–20 MINS   **FREEZE** 3 MONTHS

A classic teatime treat. Serve split and spread with strawberry jam and clotted cream for extra indulgence.

115g (4oz) gluten-free plain flour
115g (4oz) rice flour
60g (2oz) caster sugar
4 tsp gluten-free baking powder
1½ tsp xanthan gum
pinch of salt
75g (2oz) cold unsalted butter, cubed, plus extra for greasing

200ml (7fl oz) buttermilk, or ½ milk and ½ full-fat natural yogurt
85g (3oz) sultanas
1 egg, beaten, to glaze

SPECIAL EQUIPMENT food processor (optional), 7cm (2¾in) round metal cutter

GREAT FOR KiDS

STATISTICS PER SCONE

Energy 264kcals/1116kJ

Protein 4.5g

Fat 9g

Saturated fat 5.5g

Carbohydrate 40g

Sugar 18.5g

Fibre 1.3g

Salt 0.9g

1 Preheat the oven to 220°C (425°F/Gas 7). Sift the flours, sugar, baking powder, xanthan, and salt into a large bowl. Add the butter and rub it in with your fingertips until the mixture resembles fine breadcrumbs; alternatively, pulse in a food processor.

2 Stir the buttermilk into the crumb mixture, add the sultanas, then gently mix using a round-bladed knife to make a soft dough. Knead briefly. On a lightly floured surface, roll out the dough to a thickness of 2cm (¾in) and press out 8 scones using the cutter, re-rolling the dough as necessary. Dip the cutter in flour before cutting out each round to achieve a clean cut. This will help the scones rise evenly.

3 Place the scones a little apart on a lightly greased baking sheet and brush the tops with egg. Bake near the top of the oven for 15–20 minutes or until risen and golden brown on top. Cool for 5 minutes, then serve warm or cold.

VARIATIONS

Chocolate chip Omit the sultanas and replace with an equal weight of milk chocolate drops.

Cheese scones Omit the sugar and sultanas, add 1 teaspoon mustard powder to the dry ingredients, then stir in 115g (4oz) grated mature Cheddar cheese with the buttermilk. Shape as before, dust the tops with a little paprika and more grated cheese, if desired.

FRESH BERRY SCONES

MAKES 6   **PREP** 15 MINS   **COOK** 15–20 MINS   **FREEZE** 3 MONTHS

A lovely summery twist on the classic scone. Single berries, freshly-picked in season, taste stunning: strawberries in June, raspberries in July, and blackberries in August.

85g (3oz) strawberries, raspberries, or blackberries, or a mix
115g (4oz) gluten-free plain flour
115g (4oz) rice flour
60g (2oz) caster sugar
4 tsp gluten-free baking powder
2 tsp xanthan gum
pinch of salt
60g (2oz) cold unsalted butter, cubed, plus extra for greasing

150ml (5fl oz) buttermilk, or ½ milk and ½ full-fat natural yogurt, plus extra to glaze (see Cook's tip) sprinkle of demerara sugar, to glaze

SPECIAL EQUIPMENT food processor (optional), 7cm (2¾in) round metal cutter

1 Preheat the oven to 220°C (425°F/Gas 7). If using strawberries, cut them into halves or quarters. Sift together the flours, sugar, baking powder, xanthan, and salt into a large bowl. Add the butter and rub it in with your fingertips until fine crumbs form; alternatively, pulse in a food processor. Empty the mixture into a large bowl, stir in the berries, add the buttermilk, and mix using a round-bladed knife to make a soft dough. Knead briefly.

2 On a lightly floured surface, roll out the dough to a thickness of 2cm (¾in) and press out 6 scones using the cutter, re-rolling the dough as necessary. Dip the cutter in flour before cutting out each round to achieve a clean cut. Place the scones a little apart on a lightly greased baking sheet. Brush the tops with buttermilk and sprinkle over the demerara sugar. Bake near the top of the oven for 15–20 minutes or until risen and golden brown on top. Cool for 5 minutes, then serve warm or cold.

COOK'S TIP

Depending on how juicy the berries are, you may need to add a little more or less buttermilk. The dough shouldn't be too soft and wet or the scones won't rise.

STATISTICS PER SCONE

Energy 280kcals/1175kJ

Protein 4g

Fat 9g
Saturated fat 5g

Carbohydrate 44g
Sugar 16g

Fibre 1.5g

Salt 1.1g

● ● ○ CALORIES

● ● ● SATURATED FAT

● ○ ○ SALT

CHOCOLATE AND PECAN BROWNIES

GREAT FOR KIDS

MAKES 20   **PREP** 15 MINS   **COOK** 15–18 MINS   **FREEZE** 3 MONTHS

If you are not keen on nuts, omit the pecans and add 60g (2oz) dried sour cherries instead.

300g (10oz) dark chocolate (at least 60% cocoa solids), broken into pieces
175g (6oz) cold unsalted butter, cubed, plus extra for greasing
300g (10oz) light muscovado sugar
5 eggs
175g (6oz) gluten-free plain flour

30g (1oz) cocoa powder
85g (3oz) pecan nuts

SPECIAL EQUIPMENT
23 x 30cm (9 x 12in) rectangular cake tin

1 Preheat the oven to 200°C (400°F/Gas 6). Lightly grease the tin and line with baking parchment.

2 Put the chocolate in a large heatproof bowl with the butter and place over a pan of gently simmering water, stirring occasionally until melted and smooth. Remove from the heat, stir in the sugar, and allow to cool slightly.

3 Gradually add the eggs, beating well between additions. Sift the flour and cocoa over the mixture, add the pecans, and then fold together. The mixture should be thick and glossy.

4 Spoon the mixture into the prepared tin and bake for 15–18 minutes or until the top is firm to the touch, but the centre is still slightly sticky when tested with the tip of a knife. Leave to cool in the tin. Once cold, remove from the tin and cut the brownies into about 20 squares.

COOK'S TIP
If you overcook the brownies, you'll end up with chocolate cake. You want them to be crusty on the top but gooey in the centre. They firm up as they cool.

STATISTICS PER BROWNIE

Energy 282kcals/1178kJ

Protein 4g

Fat 16.5g
Saturated fat 8g

Carbohydrate 30g
Sugar 24g

Fibre 1.5g

Salt 0.25g

SHORTBREAD BISCUITS

GREAT FOR KiDS

MAKES 16   **PREP** 10 MINS   **COOK** 25-30 MINS   **FREEZE** 3 MONTHS

These biscuits have a wonderfully buttery flavour and short, crumbly texture.

GUIDELINES PER SERVING

● ● ○ CALORIES

● ● ○ SATURATED FAT

● ○ ○ SALT

175g (6oz) unsalted butter, softened, plus extra for greasing
85g (3oz) golden caster sugar, plus extra for sprinkling
175g (6oz) gluten-free plain flour
85g (3oz) rice flour

30g (1oz) cornflour
1 tsp xanthan gum

SPECIAL EQUIPMENT
25 x 16cm (10 x 6in) rectangular tin
  or 18cm (7in) round tin

1 Preheat the oven to 180°C (350°F/Gas 4) and lightly grease the tin. Use an electric whisk to cream together the butter and sugar in a large bowl until light and fluffy. Sift over the flours and xanthan, then mix well with a wooden spoon to form a smooth, stiff dough; stop as soon as the flours are mixed through. Bring the dough together with your hands.

2 Press the dough into the bottom of the tin. Level and smooth it with the back of a metal spoon, then prick all over with a fork. Bake for 25–30 minutes or until pale golden. Remove from the oven and, using a sharp knife, cut it into 16 fingers and sprinkle generously with sugar. Cool in the tin. Use a spatula to remove the squares and store in an airtight container.

VARIATIONS
Lemon Add the finely grated zest of 1 lemon to the butter and sugar when creaming it.
Lavender Instead of ordinary sugar, use lavender sugar. You can make your own by mixing whole dried lavender flowers with sugar and leaving to infuse for 2 days; you need about 1 teaspoon flowers per 500g (1lb 2oz) sugar.

COOK'S TIPS
Choose good-quality butter for this recipe; margarine just won't do. It's also very important to let the shortbread cool in the tin, otherwise it will crumble and break easily. If freezing, leave to cool completely and wrap the biscuits in foil.

STATISTICS PER BISCUIT

Energy 166kcals/699kJ

Protein 1.5g

Fat 9g
Saturated fat 6g

Carbohydrate 19g
Sugar 5.5g

Fibre 0.6g

Salt trace

CHOCOLATE CHIP COOKIES

MAKES 14   **PREP** 10 MINS   **COOK** 15 MINS   **FREEZE** 3 MONTHS

For an even more chocolatey treat, replace 30g (1oz) of the flour with cocoa powder.

115g (4oz) unsalted butter, softened, plus extra for greasing
175g (6oz) caster sugar
1 egg
1 tsp vanilla extract

175g (6oz) gluten-free self-raising flour
60g (2oz) rice flour
85g (3oz) chocolate chips, or chocolate broken into small chunks (see below)

1 Preheat the oven to 190°C (375°F/Gas 5). Lightly grease 2 baking sheets and line with baking parchment. Cream together the butter and sugar until fluffy, using an electric whisk. Add the egg and vanilla and whisk again.

2 Sift the flours into the mixture, add the chocolate chips, and mix well with a wooden spoon. Heap 14 dessertspoonfuls of the mixture onto the prepared baking sheets; place them well apart since they will spread as they bake. Flatten them slightly with your fingertips.

3 Bake for 15 minutes or until golden. Leave to cool for 2 minutes on the sheet, then use a palette knife to transfer the cookies to a wire rack. Leave to cool completely. Don't worry if the cookies seem a bit soft when you first take them out of the oven; they crisp up as they cool.

STATISTICS PER COOKIE

Energy 204kcals/858kJ

Protein 2.3g

Fat 9g

Saturated fat 5.5g

Carbohydrate 28g

Sugar 16g

Fibre 0.8g

Salt 0.2g

« Chocolate
You could use dark, milk, or white chocolate chips or chunks in these cookies. If making for children, avoid dark chocolate, which doesn't seem to appeal to younger palates.

OAT AND RAISIN COOKIES

MAKES 18   **PREP** 10 MINS   **COOK** 15 MINS   **FREEZE** 3 MONTHS

Crunchy on the outside and lightly chewy in the middle, the whole family will love these easy-to-make cookies. Omit the raisins if you prefer.

GREAT FOR KIDS

115g (4oz) unsalted butter, softened, plus extra for greasing
225g (8oz) demerara sugar
1 egg
1 tsp vanilla extract
75g (2½oz) gluten-free plain flour

1 tsp ground cinnamon
½ tsp gluten-free bicarbonate of soda
pinch of salt
175g (6oz) rolled oats
60g (2oz) raisins (optional)

1 Preheat the oven to 190°C (375°F/Gas 5). Lightly grease the baking sheet and line with baking parchment.

2 Cream together the butter and sugar until fluffy, using an electric whisk. Add the egg and vanilla and whisk again.

3 Sift the flour, cinnamon, soda, and salt into the mixture, add the oats and the raisins (if using), and mix well with a wooden spoon.

4 Roll the mixture into 18 walnut-sized balls and place them well apart on the baking sheet. Flatten them with your fingertips and bake for 15 minutes or until the cookies are golden brown. Leave to cool on the baking sheet for 2 minutes, then use a palette knife to transfer the cookies to a wire rack to cool completely.

STATISTICS PER COOKIE

Energy 160kcals/677kJ

Protein 2g

Fat 7g
Saturated fat 3.5g

Carbohydrate 24g
Sugar 14g

Fibre 1g

Salt 0.2g

VIENNESE BISCUITS

MAKES 9   **PREP** 10 MINS   **COOK** 15–20 MINS   **FREEZE** 3 MONTHS

These swirly, chocolate-dipped biscuits look as good as they taste.

125g (4½oz) unsalted butter, softened, plus extra for greasing
60g (2oz) icing sugar
115g (4oz) gluten-free plain flour
30g (1oz) cornflour
2 tsp xanthan gum
¼ tsp gluten-free baking powder

½ tsp vanilla extract
115g (4oz) dark chocolate (70% cocoa solids), broken into even pieces

SPECIAL EQUIPMENT piping bag fitted with a 2cm (¾in) plain or star nozzle

1 Preheat the oven to 190°C (375°F/Gas 5) and lightly grease 2 large baking sheets. Place the butter and icing sugar in a large bowl and use an electric whisk to beat until pale and fluffy.

2 Sift over the flours, xanthan, and baking powder. Add the vanilla, then beat again with the whisk until a soft dough forms.

3 Spoon the dough into a piping bag and, holding the nozzle with one hand while squeezing with the other, pipe 9 biscuits in a zigzag fashion onto the baking sheets. Space them well apart as they will spread during baking.

4 Bake for 15–20 minutes or until pale golden brown. Leave to cool slightly before transferring to a wire rack to cool completely.

5 Place the chocolate in a heatproof bowl set over a pan of simmering water. Heat gently until the chocolate melts, stirring occasionally. Dip one half of each biscuit in melted chocolate and leave to set on baking parchment.

COOK'S TIPS

To fill a piping bag easily, stand it in a tall drinking glass and pull the sides of the bag over the glass to open it up. You can store the biscuits in an airtight container for up to 5 days.

STATISTICS PER BISCUIT

Energy 254kcals/1063kJ

Protein 2g

Fat 16g

Saturated fat 10g

Carbohydrate 26g

Sugar 14.5g

Fibre 1g

Salt 0.2g

● ○ ○   CALORIES

● ● ○   SATURATED FAT

● ○ ○   SALT

STEM GINGER BISCUITS

MAKES 24   **PREP** 10 MINS   **COOK** 15 MINS   **FREEZE** 3 MONTHS

With little chunks of stem ginger baked into them, these spicy biscuits are very moreish!

3 balls of preserved stem ginger, finely chopped, and 1 tbsp syrup from the jar
115g (4oz) unsalted butter, softened, plus extra for greasing
85g (3oz) light muscovado sugar

1 egg
175g (6oz) gluten-free self-raising flour
60g (2oz) rice flour, plus extra for dusting
1 tsp ground ginger
pinch of salt

1 Preheat the oven to 190°C (375°F/Gas 5). Lightly grease 2 baking sheets and line with baking parchment.

2 Place the butter, sugar, and ginger syrup in a large bowl and cream together using an electric whisk, until light and fluffy. Thoroughly whisk in the eggs. Sift over the flours, ground ginger, and salt, then fold into the mixture along with the chopped stem ginger.

3 Heap 24 dessertspoonfuls of the mixture onto the prepared baking sheets. Place the dollops well apart as they will spread during baking. Flatten the dollops with your fingertips; if the mixture is too sticky, then dust your fingers with rice flour before flattening.

4 Bake for 15 minutes until golden. Cool for 5 minutes on the baking sheets and, using a palette knife, transfer to a wire rack and leave to cool completely. You can store them in an airtight container for up to 3 days.

STATISTICS PER BISCUIT

Energy 93kcals/391kJ

Protein 1g

Fat 4g
Saturated fat 2.5g

Carbohydrate 12g
Sugar 5g

Fibre 0.4g

Salt trace

VARIATION
For a citrus tang, add the finely grated zest of 1 lemon to the mixture.

AMARETTI BISCUITS

MAKES 20   **PREP** 10 MINS   **COOK** 15-20 MINS   **FREEZE** 3 MONTHS

These crunchy Italian-style macaroons are highly versatile.
Use them for a cheesecake base, in a trifle, with ice cream
or mousse, or on their own with coffee or dessert wine.

vegetable oil, for greasing
2 egg whites
200g (7oz) caster sugar

200g (7oz) ground almonds
1 tbsp amaretto liqueur
(see Cook's tips)

GREAT FOR KIDS

1 Preheat the oven to 180°C (350°F/Gas 4). Lightly grease 2 baking sheets
and line with baking parchment.

2 In a bowl, whisk the egg whites using an electric whisk until they form
stiff peaks. Add the sugar and whisk again until glossy. Sprinkle over the
ground almonds and liqueur and gently fold in, using a large metal spoon,
until well mixed.

3 Divide the mixture into 20 portions and roll each into a ball. Place them
on the baking sheets, well apart as they will spread during baking. Bake for
15–20 minutes or until golden brown. Use a palette knife to transfer the
biscuits to a wire rack and leave to cool completely.

COOK'S TIPS
If you prefer, omit the amaretto liqueur and add 1 teaspoon almond extract with
2 teaspoons water. The biscuits will store in an airtight container for up to 3 days.

STATISTICS PER BISCUIT

Energy 104kcals/436kJ

Protein 2.5g

Fat 6g
Saturated fat 0.4g

Carbohydrate 11g
Sugar 11g

Fibre 0.2g

Salt trace

INDEX

Page numbers in *italics* refer to nuggets of information about individual ingredients (e.g. their nutrient content). Variations on the main recipe on a page are indicated by *(V)*.

ABOUT THE AUTHORS

Heather Whinney is an experienced food writer and home economist. She has worked as a food editor and freelance food writer for several magazines including *BBC Good Food, Family Circle, Good Housekeeping, Prima,* and *Woman and Home.* She is the author of DK's *Cook Express* and co-author of *The Diabetes Cooking Book.* Her food philosophy has always been to write simple recipes for the everyday cook.

Jane Lawrie has been baking ever since she could stand on a chair. As an experienced food stylist and cookery writer, she has worked for numerous food and women's magazines, including *BBC Good Food, Bella, Best,* and *Good Housekeeping.* Jane also works as a consultant for the British Egg Information Service. She has worked on several DK books including *The Preserving Book* and *The Allotment Cookbook Through the Year,* as well as several *Mary Berry* and *Masterchef* cookery books.

Fiona Hunter is a food writer and nutritionist of over 25 years' experience. With a degree in Nutrition and a postgraduate diploma in Dietetics, she began her career as a dietitian in the NHS before going on to write for magazines including *BBC Good Food, Good Housekeeping,* and *Health and Fitness,* as well as making many appearances on television and radio. She is the co-author of several books, including DK's *The Diabetes Cooking Book.*

ACKNOWLEDGEMENTS

Dorling Kindersley would like to thank:

Recipe Editors Jane Bamforth, Holly Kyte
Recipe testers Rebecca Blackstone, Anna Burges-Lumsden, Amy Carter, Jan Fullwood, Laura Fyfe, Katy Greenwood, Anne Harnan, Catherine Rose, Rachel Wood
Proofreader Sue Morony
Indexer Sue Bosanko

Photography art direction and props styling Luis Peral-Aranda, Katherine Raj
Food stylists Marie-Ange Lapierre, Emily Jonzen

Charis Bhagianathan and David Fentiman for editorial assistance. Mahua Mandal for design assistance. Danaya Bunnag for hand modelling.